The Blue Monk

CONTAINING

A PERSONAL ACCOUNT OF ADVENTURES AT SEA, INCLUDING DESCRIPTIONS OF MIAMI'S DINNER KEY ANCHORAGE, PASSAGES TO THE ABACO AND EXUMA CAYS OF THE BAHAMA ISLANDS, AND A JOURNEY VIA THE AZORES TO GIBRALTAR

BY

DAVID E. BRICKER

Illustrated

WITH NAUTICAL CHARTS AND
DIAGRAMS OF SAILING EQUIPMENT

INCLUDING ALL NECESSARY
DEFINITIONS OF NAUTICAL TERMS

ESSENTIAL ABSURDITIES PRESS

The Blue Monk
By David E Bricker
All Rights Reserved.
Copyright ©2014

Cover and book design by Dave Bricker.
ISBN: 978-0-9843009-6-9
Library of Congress Control Number: 2014932029

ESSENTIAL ABSURDITIES PRESS

http://www.theworldsgreatestbook.com
http://www.thebluemonkbook.com
http://www.pubml.com

This book is dedicated to the extraordinary people of Dinner Key Anchorage, to my daughter Eva, to those on their journeys, and to those preparing to take their first step.

The philosopher asks, "If a tree falls and nobody is there to hear, does it make a sound?"

The empiricist answers, "Sound is intrinsically related to hearing, which implies the presence of an ear. Without an ear to perceive it, there can be no sound."

The Blue Monk disregards the question altogether, knowing there is no tree and there is no somebody.

Table of Contents

voyage the first

Table of Contents

Table of Contents

Table of Illustrations

The Blue Monk

Goddamned Derelicts

1980

GENE AND MARCOS AND I have the same study periods at Ransom Everglades High School, though we prefer to call them "free" periods. Instead of studying, we meet down at the football field to climb on the limestone boulders that separate the end zone from Biscayne Bay, shooting at fish in the shallows with our slingshots or trying to knock small rocks into the water.

A line of dense foliage separates the rocky seawall from the field. Behind the trees, we enjoy our own private world on the water. We're not supposed to be here but no one can see us.

A mangrove[1] swamp borders the north side of the field. We've contrived a walkway over the roots and mud from old boards and plywood drifted in from Biscayne Bay. An ever-fascinating array of marine junk gets entangled here, stranded by the falling tide: fishing floats, driftwood, plastic bottles, countless Styrofoam beads, the occasional sacrificed Haitian voodoo chicken. We've grown

---

1 - *Mangroves*—are tropical trees that begin life as drifting seedlings about the size of a carrot. After stranding in shallow water, the plant sends out a network of roots that arch over and down into the water. These roots trap sediment, debris and more mangrove seedlings, forming swamps and islands, and adding to shorelines.

accustomed to the unique stink of rotting seagrass at low water; the smell is natural, nautical. The pungent scent of the mangrove forest is jarring at first and then oddly fragrant.[2]

"Hey, check this out." Marcos points to a grubby powerboat stranded in the shallows at the edge of the mangroves.

"Just one of those damned derelicts," says Gene. "It probably broke loose from the anchorage and drifted in."

We gaze out across Biscayne Bay, past neat rows of tidy vessels lined up in the Coconut Grove Sailing Club's mooring field to the other side of South Mole Island where shanty boats squat atop their reflections in the calm water. A few list forlornly. Some are sunk, protruding from the shallow sea. One old hull is stacked high with dinghies, sailboat rigging, and trash. A boxy, plywood-patched houseboat beats lightly against a barren, mastless sailboat tied alongside. Two dinghies sit overturned on makeshift sawhorses on a raft lashed behind them. The anchorage is a floating Tortilla Flat.

"Do people live out there?" I ask. I've seen the anchorage boats before but they never penetrated the periphery of my consciousness. Now I'm looking at one of the hulks up close. Like a beached whale decomposing on a beach, it's unpleasant but begs inspection.

---

2 *StyroFoam*® - Dow Chemical Corporation's scourge of the oceans. Used in the manufacture of thousands of cheap coolers and throwaway packaging inserts, StyroFoam® is comprised of a mass of polystyrene beads. Once discarded, the foam breaks up and inevitably finds its way to the ocean where the tiny beads inflict environmental damage for tens of thousands of years.

"You don't think anyone lives on that thing?" I rephrase my question, eyeing the stranded vessel, not directing my query at either of my companions in particular. Both of them grew up around boats. I am only beginning to learn from them the simple joys of being on the water.

"Wouldn't surprise me at all," says Gene derisively as he loads a rock into his slingshot. "That anchorage," he proclaims, "is nothing but a collection of derelicts, bums, winos, drug addicts, illegal aliens, fugitives, hippies, wackos and thieves hanging out on a bunch of rotting, decrepit, shitty old boats, getting wasted and dumping crap in the bay."

Marcos and I smile at Gene's extemporaneous list of undesirable people and aberrant behaviors.

We aim and fire.

"Derelicts," affirms Marcos. "Just a bunch of derelicts."

This poverty is disturbing. I'm hardly affluent but I've never wanted for food or shelter. I have my own room. I live in a safe neighborhood. Next year, when I get my driver's license, my father will give me his old Dodge.

I try to imagine living aboard a small deteriorating powerboat.

I have it pretty good.

Two ragged men row up in a battered plywood dinghy to recover their boat. They glare at us standing on the rocks in our khaki slacks and polo shirts. "You kids know who busted the windshield on our boat?"

We shake our heads. Our slingshots are already buried deep in our bookbags.

"When I find out, I'm gonna kick somebody's butt. All I got in this world is this piece o' shit boat and somebody's gotta go and mess with it. What the hell's the matter with people?"

"We'll ask around," we assure them, as if our worlds might cross again and we'll be able to tell them the result of some investigation performed on their behalf.

I feel bad about shooting up their boat; I thought it was abandoned. My nature is to confess my crime and offer restitution but who knows what these 'derelict' men are capable of?

Gene shoots me a stern glance.

I swallow my impulse. "Sorry about your windshield, man. That really stinks."

"Whatever," grumbles the sandy-haired man clothed in a ripped tee shirt and grimy cutoff jeans. Deliberately, he turns away to his shirtless companion with the faded blue tattoos. Ignoring us, they clean the broken glass from their foredeck.

Our free period is over; time for class.

We turn and walk across the football field, up the hill, past the tennis courts toward our classrooms.

"Goddamned derelicts," mutters Marcos.

The World As You Know It

Fall, 1991

I'M RETURNING to my sailboat *Blue Monk*, moored in the northern-most islands of the Bahamas. I look down from the small twin-engine aircraft at the rippling cobalt waters of the Gulf Stream dotted sparsely with cruise ships and freighters, a vast sheet of textured blue I sailed across only a few months ago. Seated next to me on the small plane is a newlywed couple off on a romantic island honeymoon.

We pass the time talking while moody waters roll thousands of feet below us. When I tell them I'm going home to a small sailboat, they're incredulous.

"Do you ever get seasick?" the young bride asks.

"And what about storms? Does it get rough?" adds the new groom.

"I could never live on a boat," she says, shaking her head.

Words come to me. "Sailing," I say with an added pause for effect, "is like being in love. Hidden obstacles lie just beneath the surface. You never know if you're going to land at your intended destination. You can sink or be dashed on the rocks. You can get marooned in a lonely place. The ocean can make you so sick you wish you could die. But, when everything is going right, when the sun is shining and the waves are sparkling, when the water is clear and the wind is blowing, no feeling in the world is more beautiful and powerful."

The newlyweds nod politely and return to their magazines.

I close my eyes and smile to myself. I know I'm from another planet—I've made different choices. I'm twenty-four-years old. I walked away from a budding technology career to live aboard a twenty-six-foot boat in a third-world country on a monthly budget most people would spend on dinner for two. I'm lonely, scared out of my wits, happy as can be, and having the adventure of my life.

I can hear Trimaran John laughing.

July, 1983

After a year at the University of Florida, I come home to Miami disillusioned. The transition from small classes in high school to huge auditoriums packed with hundreds of students taught by dispassionate grad assistants was jarring. *Maybe I'm not ready for college. What am I ready for?* I need time to think. The morning after I arrive home, I begin working on the "Surrounded Islands" project for Christo, a famous artist who is installing a 200-foot wide border of pink fabric around each of fourteen islands in Biscayne Bay.

My summer job involves sitting in an inflatable boat guarding the art project. This afternoon, I am paired on my shift with a scruffy, red-bearded character who introduces himself in a W.C. Fields-ish voice, as if he's speaking through the odd-shaped hole in the middle of the letter R.

"Hey, mate. I'm John—John Bennett. My friends call me 'Trimaran John.'"

"Isn't that a kind of boat?"

"Got that right, mate. I live on a thirty-foot trimaran[3] at Dinner Key in Coconut Grove. Sailed here from Hawaii with a friend through the Panama Canal on a big fifty foot tri and then bought my own when I got here."

"You sailed here from *Hawaii?*" I'm astonished. John may just as well have sailed here from the moon.

"Never been sailin', have you, mate?" John reaches into his backpack for an Old Milwaukee from the twelve-pack he's smuggled onto the job with him.

"A time or two," I reply, "but I can't say I know the first thing about it."

---

3 *Trimaran* - a vessel with three connected hulls. Catamarans have two hulls. Traditional monohull vessels have one.

Trimaran John sinks his empty beer can and reaches for a full one. "No problem, mate," he assures me, catching the expression on my face. "That aluminum can will disintegrate soon enough in the salt water."

Home base calls on the walkie-talkie. Do we want to work a second shift tonight? We tell them we'll stay until morning. Hell, we're getting paid to sit in an inflatable boat and bullshit. As far as John is concerned, he's being paid to sit in an inflatable boat and *get drunk* and bullshit.

Midnight. Biscayne Bay is deserted except for an occasional barge moving down the Intracoastal Waterway. We're supposed to constantly circle the island on patrol but we're the only boat around; there's no need. We tie off to one of the buoys that keep the pink fabric spread out around the islands. John regales me with stories of adventure: storms at sea, the girl who was knocked overboard and never found, a friend who got busted running dope and lost his boat, the beauty of the South Pacific and the Bahamas.

"That's where I'm headed, mate. I'm getting my boat together and then *boom*—I'm going cruisin'—off to the Bahamas and then south to the Virgins."

John pauses to roll a cigarette. "You ought to come out some time. Sailing will blow your mind. The people and the lifestyle are a different world, mate, and the anchorage—you won't believe you're still in Miami."

"I'd love to," I tell him, intrigued.

Other characters work on the project, attracted by the prospects of working with Christo and being a part of his art, or by the simple opportunity to get paid to sit in a boat; I share watches with a number of them. Chris, a high school friend, joins me. Enrique, a Cuban with blond New Wave hair, wears military fatigues, carries a plastic machine gun, and looks like a B-movie revolutionary. But that's just his getup; I wouldn't want to watch him try to survive on a battlefield. June, a Miami painter, enjoys the project as a way to have some summer fun while staying focused on artistic pursuits. Clem and Becky, also from the anchorage, are a gentle, soft-spoken couple who live on a houseboat. Hamilton Fields lives at Dinner Key on a trimaran much like John Bennett's. He's new to boating—new to Miami—and using the anchorage as a cheap place to live while he starts a business in Coconut Grove.

Summer marches slowly, unnoticeably by. Cheerfully afloat, I work double shifts with an array of storybook characters, studying the waves and talking about life with the confidence and naïveté of youth.

I am eighteen—immortal.

Sunscreen? That's for wimps.

On the "Surrounded Islands" project's final night, I radio in to report a herd of caribou on the fabric. What can they do? Fire me?

The Project ends. I was skeptical at first of Christo's plan to install a veneer of man-made plastic on this natural setting, but I'll miss the odd and diverse community of people, the opinions it catalyzed, and even its impact on the landscape. Certainly, I'll miss my days on Biscayne Bay.

We dismantle the pink bloom around the islands.

Friends disperse.

Artists, anchorage dwellers, would-be topplers of Fidel Castro's regime, students on summer break, and small time entrepreneurs are reabsorbed into the vast anonymity of the City of Miami.

The next Saturday, I accept Trimaran John's invitation to meet on the dock in Coconut Grove. Old beer cans, green algae, and an inch of soupy water slosh around in the bottom of his aluminum dinghy. "Good to see you, mate. Thanks for comin' early to help get the boat ready."

I'm excited and happy to be back on the water. I toss my gear bag onto the front seat where it will stay dry and climb in.

"Do you know how t' row, mate?"

"Well, I..."

"No time like the present to learn, I say." Bennett laughs, releasing a short burst of Rs. He shifts to the back seat of the dinghy. "You row. I'll bail."

I tried rowing once at summer camp years ago, but never in anything other than a placid lake. Oar blades splash when I don't lower them deep enough into the water. When I dig too deep, we roll precariously. Much course correction is required as I slowly acclimate to this strange mode of backward locomotion.

Bennett smiles. "You're doin' fine, mate. Just relax and let the oars do the work." He pops the top on another beer.

I've heard more practical advice but I give John's method a try.

It works!

We're moving now, not quickly, but steadily away from the dinghy dock out toward the channel.

I guide the motion of the oars, swiveling them forward, dropping them into the water, letting them arc gracefully toward the stern and then raising them just off the surface to swing them back into position for another stroke, measuring the distance between the handles in front of me to gauge how far they should extend past the oarlocks. I can go faster if I pull harder but I'm moving right along, hardly pulling at all; rowing is all about rhythm.

"Now you got it, mate. See what I mean about letting the oars do the work? You can row for miles if you don't strain on the oars.

"And before we pick up the others," John continues, "on the way back in, let's drag the dinghy over to the island and scrape the barnacles off her. You'll be amazed at the difference a clean bottom makes."

At this point, I don't even care about sailing. Rowing is a revelation unto itself. We're moving, gliding across the water in a little aluminum tub as easily as we might ride a bicycle. The oar is as simple and profound a discovery as the wheel.

Past the prim white fleet of sailboats and motor yachts tied up in the marina, we cross the channel between the ends of the piers and the barrier island that shelters them, approaching a red marker at the point of the island.

"Just head out past the marker," says Bennett, "but leave a little distance. If you pass too close, you'll go aground in the shallows." A cormorant perched atop the channel marker stares down at us nervously, opening its wings in preparation for flight as we row by.

"We're going *outside* past the island?" I ask, surprised. "Isn't that where all the derelicts live?"

"Mate, there's a whole universe out there most people don't know the first fucking thing about. Welcome to Dinner Key Anchorage. The world as you know it ends here."

Song of the Sea

August, 1983

WE APPROACH Trimaran John's boat in the dinghy. She's cream-colored with an orange sheer[4] stripe on each hull, and almost as wide as she is long. A smoked Plexiglas "windshield" admits sunlight into the front of her low cabin. I park the tender under the bridge between the main hull and one of the outer hulls. "The outer hulls are called 'amas,'" John explains. On the transom, in hand-painted script worn by countless dinghy impacts, is her name, *Chanson de Mer*—Song of the Sea.

After recovering in the cockpit from the long row, I don my dive mask and jump overboard. I land hard, feet first in the seagrass, not realizing the water is only four feet deep. Trimaran John hands me down a short, rusty garden hoe. "This'll knock the little sons o' bitches right off, mate," he assures. "Start with the deeper spots and save the waterline for when you're tired out."

---

4 *Sheer* - The sheer line of a boat is the curve where her deck meets the sides of her hull. On a traditional, wood-planked vessel, the sheer strake is the topmost and longest plank of the hull. A decorative "sheer stripe" is often painted or carved just below the deck line.

I expected sailing to involve more sailing, but I'm not raking leaves or mowing grass. Rowing dinghies and scraping barnacles are jobs associated with a different, unfamiliar, and exciting world. If this is what mariners do, I'm eager to learn.

"Trimarans have a few advantages over traditional monohull sail-boats," John explains to me when I come up for air. "They're much roomier on deck for a given length and they don't heel[5] much under sail." But when you're scraping barnacles long after the bottom paint[6] loses its potency, there's three times the work to be done." Somehow, hull scraping doesn't offer as many stylistic inroads to elegance as rowing, no matter how much imagination one applies to "letting the scraper do the work."

A shower of barnacle shells and marine life rains to the bottom: sponges, soft corals, weeds, algae, tiny crabs, a lobster the size of the last two segments of my little finger, small pieces of fiberglass cloth, and annoying shrimp the size of ants that make me itch all over. After an hour of labor, I climb on deck exhausted. John pours fresh warm water from a blue five-gallon jug over my head. I stopped bleeding a while ago, but a sharp barnacle shell claimed a chunk of my knuckle flesh. "Welcome to the wonderful world of

5 *Heel* - Sailboats are designed to *heel* or lean over while sailing at certain angles relative to the wind.

6 *Bottom paint* - special paint used below a boat's waterline to deter the growth of barnacles and other marine life on the hull. Also called "antifouling paint."

boating, mate," my host announces. I sit in the cockpit, catching my breath and drying in the sun.

"I straightened out down below while you were cleaning the bottom," he proclaims proudly. "Dry off and take a look. Catch your breath. Then we'll haul the anchors up and get this boat moving; we don't want to keep our friends waiting on the dock."

I descend the companionway steps. On the port[7] side, a rusty soot-covered propane stove, laced together with fishing wire, lies in hospice beneath a set of locker doors I presume open on a food pantry. The starboard side is identical except the small counter top is free of deteriorating cooking appliances. Forward, narrow settees on each side of the cabin run the length of a central walkway. Low-ceilinged double bunks extend out beyond them. The main cabin is smaller inside than I imagined; it doesn't communicate with the interiors of the outer hulls. John explains that the floor is called the "cabin-sole," the walls are the "ceilings," and the ceiling is the "overhead." The cabin top joins the deck at chest-height; the double bunks are at deck level. A sail bag packed with dirty laundry squats inelegantly on the starboard bunk. A few other sail bags—these packed with sails—lie on the port side on top of a stack of old *Playboy* magazines.

---

7 *Port and Starboard* - The port side of the boat is left and starboard is right *when you're aboard the vessel and facing the bow.* Left and right change relative to the orientation of a viewer, but port and starboard do not. Mnemonic devices: "Port" and "left" both have four letters, and port wine is red like the navigation lights on the port side.

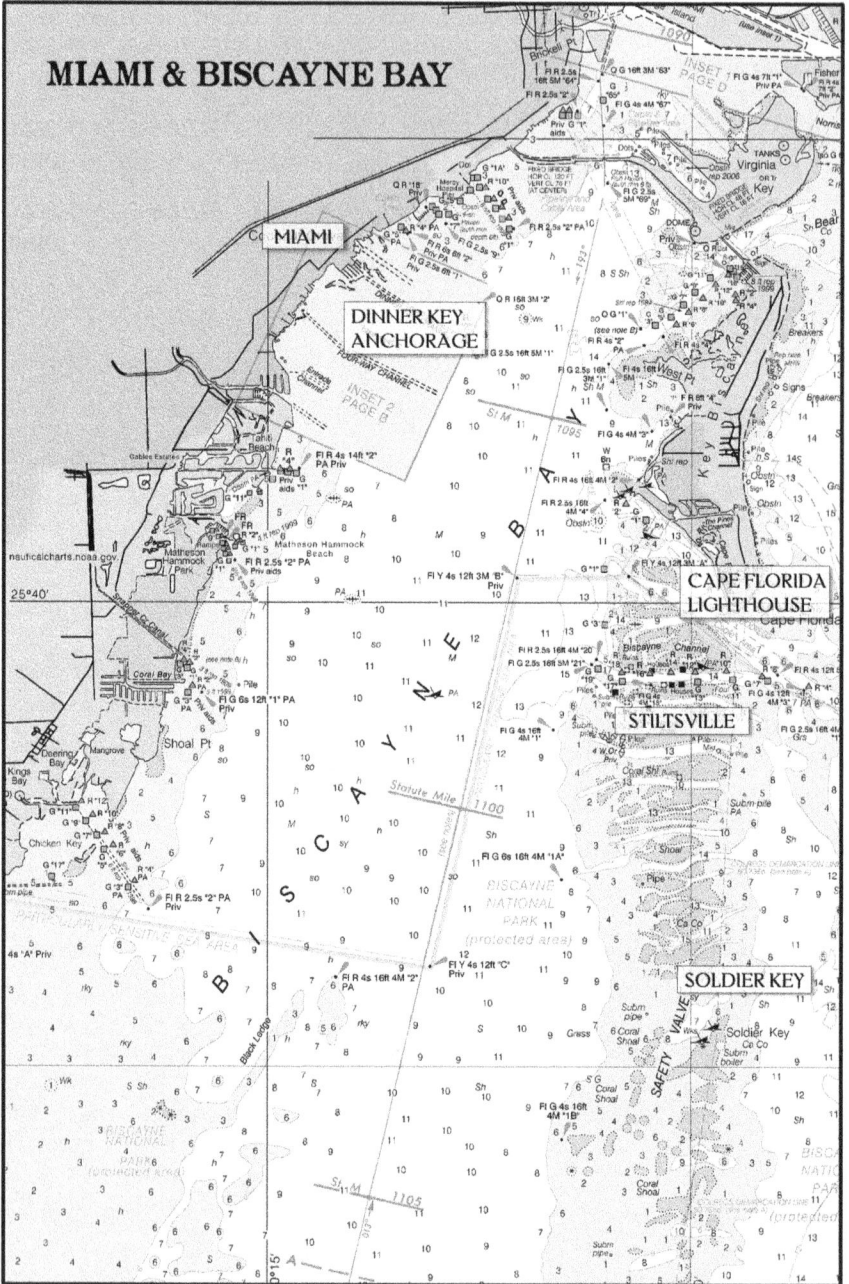

Miami, Florida and North Part of Biscayne Bay

Dinner Key Marina and Free Anchorage (detail)

"You can trade those for just about anything you want in the islands," says John. Tiny cockroaches scatter as I walk forward. A low doorway with a nautically arched top passes beneath a heavy crossmember that structurally connects the three hulls. Beyond the door, a set of cubbyhole lockers on either side leads to a triangle-shaped "vee-berth" bunk and a chain locker in the very tip of the bow.

But to balance the squalor, a refreshing breeze pours through the open hatches. A playful sound of waves reverberates between the hulls. Certainly, John's boat could use some cleaning up, but in this appealing new environment I sense a connection to something bold, traditional, primal. The machine I stand within offers as much potential as any conceived by H.G. Wells. "With a little TLC," John assures me, "a boat like this can sail around the world."

After no small number of pulls on the starter cord and squeezes of the fuel line's siphon bulb, the outboard starts. A rainbow sheen of oil blossoms on the water. The old Mercury idles roughly at first and gradually warms up. "Okay, mate, we're gonna start with the port anchor. Let the line on the starboard hook run out as I steer toward the port one. Haul in the line on the other side as we approach. Once the first hook's up, we'll fall back and pick up the other one."

I have absolutely no idea what he's talking about but I haul in on the anchor line as directed. The rope, covered with seagrass, is rough on my hands. The rode gets rougher where the nylon line is spliced to a length of rusty chain.[8]

I can't hear John over the sound of the outboard but I finally figure out he's making hand signals for me to make hand signals. I point in the direction of the anchor as indicated by the angle of the chain. He alters course. I motion for him to slow down as we get close and then I pull up hard, straining to free the flukes from the bottom.

"Cleat her off! Cleat her off!" calls John.

"What?"

John lets the engine idle in neutral while he runs forward from the cockpit to wrap the chain around a foredeck cleat. "We'll use the motor and the weight of the boat to break 'er loose, mate" he explains, "and these things we tie the lines to on the foredeck are called 'cleats.'"

Returning to the cockpit, he puts the engine in gear again and accelerates over the anchor. The chain goes taut, arresting our progress for a moment until an explosion of cloudy silt on the sea bottom announces the anchor's release. I signal John with a hitchhiker's thumb and haul the heavy anchor to the foredeck, laying the muddy hook on top of the pile of weed-covered chain.

I clutch the forestay and catch my breath.

"Tell you what, mate," John says, joining me on the foredeck while *Chanson de Mer* drifts back down to hang on her one remaining anchor.

---

8 *Rode* - an anchor line, usually a combination of line and chain. And how often does one get a chance to use a phrase like "the rode gets rougher?"

"That hook was in pretty deep. I'll tie a float on the other one; we'll leave the second anchor here. When we come back, we'll just pick up the float and have one less anchor to deal with."

"Won't someone...?"

"Nah...it'll be fine. Nobody'll mess with it. Nobody locks their doors or worries about stuff like that here, mate. Dinner Key is the safest neighborhood in Miami."

I'm fine with this arrangement. After rowing and bottom scraping and anchor hauling, I silently pray I won't be asked to work a bellows or a treadmill to supplement what energy we can derive from the engine and the wind.

But we're moving now.

The outboard hums.

John steers us through the anchorage, passing behind rather than in front of the other boats to avoid their mooring lines. Neighbors wave and laugh at us encouragingly. "Go, John! You finally got that tub unstuck from the bottom!"

Somehow, I pictured John sailing every day. I envisioned anchoring as a thing anchorage people do when it's time to sleep. If you're going to be "free" and not have a regular job, it only makes sense that, as a sailor, you spend your days...well...sailing. There are ropes to pull and anchors to haul and courses to plot. A real sextant is aboard for navigating with the stars. A compass is mounted in the cockpit. A VHF radio hangs inside the companionway. Surely, someone must have the job of going adventuring while the rest of us sit in school, work in offices, raise families, and hassle with the bank?

Chanson de Mer hovers in the turning basin in the marina near the boat ramp while I ferry dinghy-loads of friends out to the boat. June, the artist, brings her daughter, Dana. Christo project refugees clamber from the dinghy onto the trimaran. Coolers and grocery bags are passed aboard. We total eight people but once we scatter around the capacious deck, we have plenty of room.

For the third time today, I pass the channel marker at the end of Middle Island. We cruise between the anchored boats once again, heading out into the open waters of Biscayne Bay.

Michael Burtt rows by. He jumps aboard at John's invitation and hands me up a homemade, coffin-shaped guitar case. I stow the instrument on the starboard bunk next to my own while he cleats his dory[9] to the aft deck and lets it fall behind to ride in our wake.

Michael is a balding, dark-bearded man with thick glasses. Thin, wiry, and shirted only with a prodigious quantity of body hair, he conveys a peaceful, almost mystical demeanor and shares a confident smile. He built his own boat of concrete and sailed her across the Atlantic and back; he's no stranger to the nomenclatural tar pit of sheets, halyards, hanks, stays, shrouds, cleats, and thingamajigs I find myself entangled in. He takes the helm[10] while John instructs me which lines to connect to what parts of the sails, how to use the

---

9 *Dory* - a rowing craft with a narrow, flat bottom, high bow and flaring sides.

halyard winches, and how to attach the jib to the forestay with the little brass clips (oh, those are the "hanks") that must all be put on facing the same direction.

John motions to Michael to turn the boat into the wind.

With a mast winch, I tighten the halyard—a rope that goes up the mast to haul the mainsail aloft. Rising canvas flaps chaotically. The aluminum boom rattles over the cockpit as the wind shakes the sail.

"Fall off," calls John to Michael who, to my relief, does not fall off the boat but rather, steers the boat off the wind.

The sail fills.

Michael hauls in on the mainsheet tackle to tighten the sail.

The boom stops shaking.

Chanson de Mer heels slightly.

An invisible hand pushes us forward.

I raise the jib—the forward sail—with a winch and halyard on the other side of the mast. The canvas flaps violently. Lines jump around on the deck like scalded snakes.

"Tight, mate, tight. Crank that jib up as tight as you can," John shouts. I pull hard on the winch handle and watch the scalloped areas between the sail hanks flatten. "That's it, mate. Good. Now cleat 'er off." A grinding sound issues from one of the cockpit winches as Michael tightens the jib[11] sheet.

---

10 *Helm* - a boat's steering station, a steering wheel in the case of *Chanson de Mer.* Some boats have a tiller which functions as a lever attached directly to the rudder.

The sail calms, filling like a balloon.

A second invisible hand joins the first.

John silences the engine's lawnmower whine and, with some effort, hauls the outboard up out of the water on its pivoting mount. The silence is monumental, the sound of waves splashing against our bows, echoing between the hulls, effervescent. I shouldn't be, but I'm surprised we're still moving. Michael is amused; he reads the confusion on my face as I try to reconcile our velocity with the apparent lack of motive power.

We snack on sandwiches and chips. Michael and I trade tunes on our guitars. He explains to me how his concrete boat displaces a volume of water that weighs more than the boat does and can therefore float as well as any other vessel.

I take a stint at the helm. "You're pointin' too high, mate," urges John. "Fall off." I'm unaware of any reference points against which to judge "high" or "off," but I spin the wheel, the odds being 50:50 I'll turn in the right direction.

"That's it, mate. Now hold her steady."

Though I'm insufficiently oriented to confidently direct the boat relative to the wind, I find I can rely on the compass mounted next to the helm. Steering the compass instead of the boat feels like cheating, but the needle responds to the wheel. With practice, I'm able to stay closer and closer to my chosen heading. I'm puzzled, though, over

---

11 *Jib* – the forward sail. The *sheet* is the line that tensions it.

how we can be sailing with the wind blowing over our forward quarter.

"Steering a straight compass course is one mark of a good helmsman," Michael explains, spacing his words unhurriedly and deliberately, "and I see you're getting the hang of it. But let me explain how the wind works with the sails and the hull. It's simple. Once you understand it, you'll learn to *feel* the boat; keeping on course becomes second nature. The boat becomes a living, breathing thing through which you sense the wind and the waves. I'll get a piece of paper and draw you a diagram."

With some direction from John, Michael procures a pencil and notepad from the cabin and then returns to the cockpit. I hand the helm over to Trimaran John while Michael draws a faint circle in the center of the page and a dark arrow pointing down from the top. "Imagine a little car with wheels and a mast and a sail on it," he begins. Seen from above, it looks like this: He draws a small rectangle at the bottom of the circle and adds little dashes for tires. "Now this car is headed out of the circle away from the wind. Which way does the sail go?"

"All the way out on one side or the other?"

"Exactly. Sailing downwind is called 'running.'"

He draws two more cars at three and nine o'clock. "Now the wind is abeam. This is called 'reaching.'"

"The sails would have to be at a forty-five degree angle to the wind," I suggest, "...and the tires prevent the car from slipping sideways, right? It might lean over some, but if it can't move sideways, the wind energy gets transferred into forward motion."

"Yes" says Michael encouragingly, "and on a sailboat, the keel, or in our case, the three hulls, keep the boat from slipping sideways. It's not like tires on pavement—there's some slippage—but not as

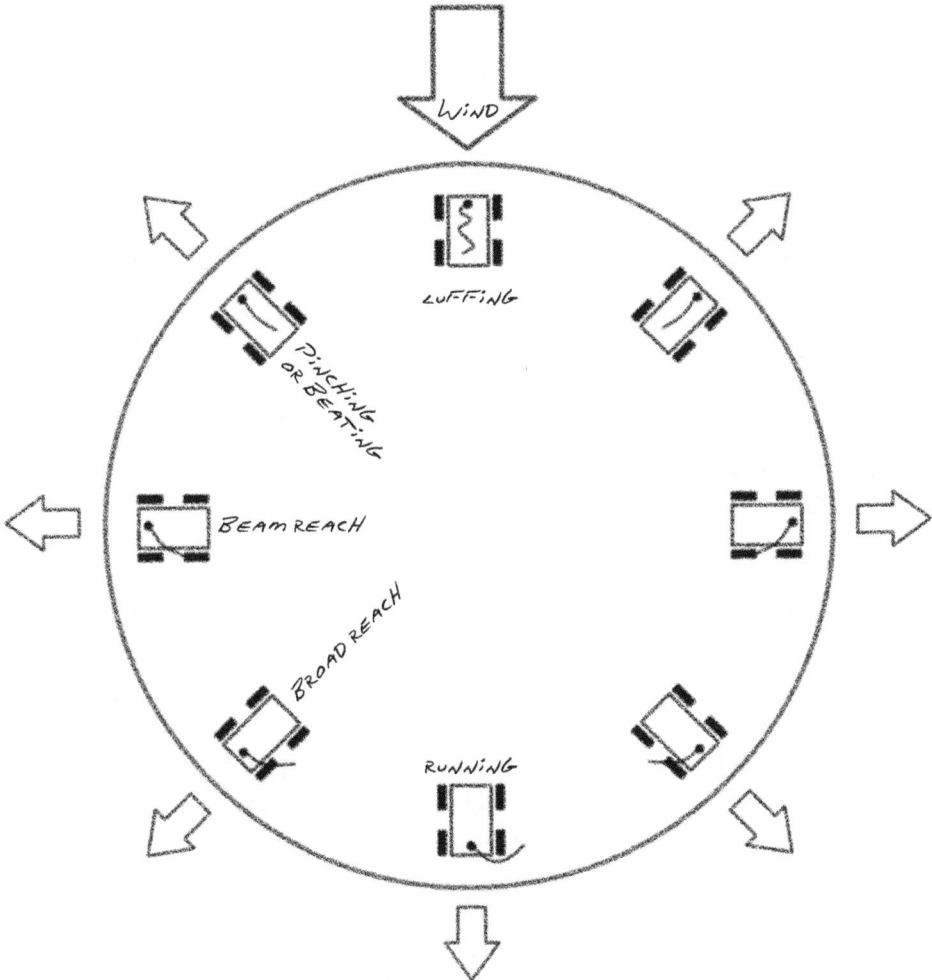

much as you might think. And on a multihull—on a trimaran or a catamaran—the outer hulls keep the boat from heeling and that force gets converted back into kinetic energy."

He draws a sailcar heading straight up at twelve o'clock. "Here, the sail will 'luff' or flap around. You can't sail directly into the wind..."

"But, I'll bet you can fall off the wind and sail here," I suggest, taking the pencil, drawing sailcars at ten and two o'clock, feeling proud of myself.

Michael smiles. "If you sheet the sails in tight, you can sail about forty-five degrees off the wind. The sails act like an airfoil—like an airplane wing. They create lift that sucks the boat forward. Sail too high into the wind and the boat will lose power. Sail too far off the wind and you'll just heel more as the wind pushes you over. There's a 'slot'—a sweet spot—where everything balances."

John pops the top on another beer and relinquishes the helm to me.

"You're pointin' too high again, mate."

Michael silently puts a hand on his shoulder, gently urging him to give me time to explore. "See those pieces of yarn on the shrouds? They're called 'telltales.' Watch them; you'll see where the wind is blowing from. Then play with the heading. *Feel it.*"

I steer off the wind. We speed up, then slow down. "I'm too far off, aren't I?"

Michael nods. I steer back toward the wind until the jib begins to luff and then fall off a tiny bit. "Yes. Here's the 'slot' you were talking about."

I pass in and out of the "sweet spot" a few times, but now I understand what it means to be "in the groove."

"That was a pretty good bit of teaching, mate," John says to Michael.

Michael accepts the compliment with humility, nodding his head.

At the helm where the wind's melody meets the water's counterpoint, I am the conduit for an elemental duet. Through the ship's wheel, I conduct the song of the sea.

The Blue Monk

Choices

A One-Week Cruise to Key West

September, 1983

ANA, the daughter of June, the artist I worked with on Christo's "Surrounded Islands," walks with me on the dock. We've been living aboard *Chanson de Mer* with Trimaran John for a month now. This arrangement has something to do with the most recent disaster in her life, some overblown minor disagreement that caused June to kick her out of the house. Again. I'm eighteen, loyal, idealistic and now living in Dinner Key Anchorage with an attractive blond girlfriend. We're in love. Like much youthful folly, this was never meant to last, but it's full of important lessons that lie just beyond the jagged horizon of adolescent perspectives.

Having moved out to the anchorage, we're on our own. We have to earn money to buy groceries and gas. Life afloat is blissful but we're low on supplies. We redouble our efforts to find work on the docks, varnishing teak and waxing sun-faded hulls.

Shortly after sundown, we're walking behind Miami City Hall by the marina. We're about to row home when Strider intercepts us. In tow is Murphy, a husky Alaskan oil-worker, a friend of his who's enjoying a few weeks in South Florida. Both are laughing and a bit drunk.

Strider is Murphy's physical opposite. Small of build and skeletally wiry, he's long-haired with a scraggly beard—in his mid-thirties, I guess. His face is simultaneously aged by his lifestyle and made youthful by his passion for it. "Check this out," he says with a grin, pulling a pistol crossbow from his backpack and firing a bolt into a nearby coconut palm. "We picked this up at the sporting goods store. Cool toy, eh?"

We don't know Strider well but he isn't planning to shoot anyone. I remember climbing around on the rocks by the high school football field with my slingshot only a few years before. The way a weapon is handled reveals insights into a man's character. Strider is not interested in power, predation, or pain; he's strictly into fun. The crossbow is a tool that increases the range of his mischief.

I decline a turn with the crossbow, concerned I might miss the coconut palm and damage a parked car. Strider extends a wavering arm, squints through the sights and places a second bolt into the center of the tree trunk a few inches from his first shot.

He sniffs the air, surveys the clouds, and snaps his fingers. "Y'all wanna take a sail tonight?"

"Whatever you say, boss," barks Murphy. "I'm on vacation and ain't gonna do a goddamned thing got to do with no schedule."

"How about you guys?" Strider grins. "Want to go to Soldier Key with us tonight? We're gonna have us a beautiful moon."

I look at Dana and shake my head. "Thanks, Strider, but we're broke. We've got to be on the docks tomorrow morning looking for work. Can we go another time?"

Strider cocks his head to one side as if sizing us up. "Down to stems and seeds, huh? Tell you what—I'll pay you guys twenty bucks each to help me sail my boat to Soldier Key tonight. Would that make a difference?"

"Thanks, Strider, but we can't. Tomorrow ..."

"How 'bout forty each?"

Dana and I look at each other. If we hadn't met Strider before, we'd be suspicious, but he's been a friendly anchorage neighbor for a month now. We need the money—and we're naïve teenagers who haven't built up any measure of that urban paranoia traditionally considered necessary to protect oneself from scammers, pushers, thieves, politicians, and bankers.

I shrug my shoulders, smile at Dana, and look at Strider. "We're in. We need a few minutes to row out to the boat so we can tell John where we're going and pack some clothes and stuff."

"I'll come by John's boat and pick you up in the *General Delivery*," offers Strider, gesturing over the seawall to where his dory floats with the other dinghies.

A half-hour later, we pass a duffel bag up to Murphy and climb aboard *Mother Ocean*, Strider's 32-foot Bristol sloop.

The moment we're aboard, Strider hauls up the mainsail and sheets it in hard. The boat tacks off to one side and then stops when she reaches the end of the anchor chain. As the hull falls back across the wind and tacks in the other direction, he hauls in anchor rode until he meets resistance, then cleats the line off and waits for the boat to tack again.

"How come you don't just motor up to the anchor?" I ask, sitting on the cabin top, staying close in case I'm asked to help with something.

"Ain't got one and don't want one," laughs Strider. "Don't want no fuel or no fumes or mechanical shit to break down. I got everything I need on board to go sailin' and that's all."

After a few tacks back and forth, we break the anchor loose. Strider hauls it to the deck. "Just gotta let the wind do the work," explains Strider. "That's what sailin's all about."

Murphy laughs heartily. He does this frequently, though what he's laughing about is not always clear.

The jib rises up the forestay.[12] We're under weigh,[13] tacking through the anchored boats in a light wind out into Biscayne Bay.

---

12 *Stays* - wire cables that support the mast fore and aft. The jib (forward sail) is hanked (clipped) to the forestay (the forward stay that runs from the tip of the bow to the top of the mast).

"Can you steer a compass course?" asks Strider, gesturing toward the helm.

"Sure," I say with confidence, having done so two or three times before on *Chanson de Mer*. I sit on the port side of the cockpit and hang onto the tiller. The moon, as Strider predicted, rises large, full and bright, illuminating the bay like a floodlight. I turn away from its blinding glare to focus on the red glow of the compass, feeling how the ship responds to the wind, the waves, and the touch of my hand.

Strider lights the first of many joints he'll consume on our voyage, interspersed with hand-rolled cigarettes from a light blue Bugler tobacco pouch and occasional slugs from a bottle of the sailor's traditional favorite libation, rum. Chemical recreation appeals little to me, especially given the naturally intoxicating effects of waves and moonlight. I decline his offer to share the smoke and the bottle and shoot a cautionary eyebrow at Dana.

Marijuana has a pacifying, stupefying effect that is far less egregious than the obnoxious and often dangerous effects of alcohol. Though I prefer the company of lucid conversationalists, nobody ever got high on cannabis and beat up his girlfriend. Apparently satisfied with my ability to keep *Mother Ocean* on course, Strider allows himself to drift peacefully in the moonlight.

---

13 *Under weigh* – on old ships, the crew would "weigh" the heavy anchors and chain when they hauled them up with a huge winch (windlass). Though contemporary usage considers a boat to be "making way" through the water, I prefer the color of the traditional form.

An hour or so into our voyage, he's dissatisfied with the quality of what remains in his stash bag. He tips the remaining seeds and twigs overboard and asks Murphy to move to the other side of the cockpit so he can access a five-gallon olive jug stored inside the locker under his seat.

I've never seen so much marijuana in my life.

At two in the morning, Strider staggers to the bow. "We're comin' up on the Safety Valve. Ain't nothin' but shoals and finger channels between here and Soldier Key so keep a lookout for shallow water."

At the eastern edge of Biscayne Bay lies a chain of islands and shallows; the northernmost end of the Florida Keys. South of Key Biscayne lies the "Safety Valve," an area of shallows cut by natural channels through which a vigorous tidal current flows. At low tide, many of the shoals are high and dry meadows of brown seagrass and gray mud. I've sailed in here with John on *Chanson de Mer* once or twice during daylight; it's hard enough to find a way through when you can see.

Soldier Key, our destination, is a tiny, privately owned island. Brad and Lynne, the caretakers, are always willing to share their paradise. A treehouse in the mangroves on the south side conceals a comfortable hammock. A lookout tower on the north side offers an inspiring view. A small cookhouse stands near a charming Robinson Crusoe-style cottage with screen doors on both sides of a short entrance corridor designed to keep mosquitoes out. Brad dropped out of a burnout broadcasting business after a heart attack almost killed him. Now, he's content to live a less harried existence disconnected from the mainland and the mainstream, surrounded by seagrass flats and mangrove trees.

While snorkeling around those mangroves at the perimeter of the island, I once encountered two seahorses as big as my hand— a green one and an orange one. Unafraid, they curled their tails around my fingers and allowed me to hold them gently before I released them. Brad and Lynn's dogs romped and played on the barely submerged grass at low tide a quarter mile from the island, appearing from shore to be running across the water's surface.

Brad told me of a night when a black Cigarette boat[14] came blasting in from the ocean only to run aground on the shoals north of the island. He watched through binoculars while silhouetted figures unloaded bales of marijuana, stacking them on the grass flats, hoping to lighten their boat enough to push it off into deeper water. The tide eventually rose and floated their boat free, but the current carried off their cargo. Brad's is not the first story I've heard of Florida's "square grouper." Local fishermen who encounter floating bales describe their "catch" this way. The smile that follows its telling suggests there might be more to it—but I don't ask questions about things that aren't my business.

---

14 The Cigarette Company manufactured long, fast speedboats that became a favorite of drug smugglers during the 1980s.

Strider extends a pointing finger off the bow. "A bit to starboard...that's it...hold 'er...good. Now fall back off a few degrees... a little more...good...good." Engineless, we pick our way through the channels between the shoals. Strider—stoned and drunk on the foredeck[15]—calls directions to me—inexperienced and sleepy at the helm. The shallow flats are clearly visible beneath the clear water in the silver moonlight. "That's it. Okay...we're gonna make a little dogleg to port here...ready...fall off...now pull her back up...Good...Murphy, keep an eye on that mainsail; just watch the tension on that mainsheet and keep her so she barely fills without luffin' up."

Ten very long minutes later, we pass through the shoals into deeper water.

Strider uncleats the halyards.

Sails drop to the deck.

The sound of anchor chain flying over the bow roller rattles through the hull.

The captain returns to the cockpit, laughing triumphantly.

"Goddamn," says Murphy. "Came a point where I figgered you knew what the hell you was doin' or you didn't, but either way there weren't no sense in me worrying about it. I damn sure don't know

---

15 The *foredeck* is not actually a separate deck on most vessels; it's simply the part of the deck at the front of the boat. Usually surrounded by a rail or "pulpit," the foredeck is the place from which anchors are deployed and retrieved and sails are "bent" to the forestay.

what the hell *I'm* doin', but I think that was a hell of a thing we just did."

In spite of the enormous quantity of depressants surging through their brains, Strider and Murphy are just getting warmed up. I'm exhausted. The hour is late and manning the helm of a boat requires concentration. I take Dana's hand. We bid our hosts good night, descend the companionway steps, clamber into the forward bunk, and quickly fall asleep, glowing from our sailing adventure, excited about our planned visit to Soldier Key in the morning.

I'm not sure how many hours later it is when I'm awakened by the clatter of anchor chain falling from the foredeck into the locker forward of my bunk, but it can't be more than four. Dana, who can sleep through anything, snores away beside me, but the early morning's light makes the translucent cover of the forward hatch glow. *How can those guys still be functioning? It's not possible.*

The motion of the boat is different now.

The water rushes by us instead of lapping at the hull as it would at anchor.

The bunk heels a few degrees to starboard.

We're sailing—somewhere.

I consider climbing out of bed to ask what's going on, but a few hours of sleep is worse than none at all; I'm still tired and disoriented. Are we heading south? Back to Dinner Key? East to the Bahamas? I'm worried…and then it dawns on me; I don't have to work today. I don't have to go to school today. My beautiful girlfriend and I have been kidnapped and forced to enjoy ourselves on no particular schedule. We're *sailing*. In life, we're told we have to do so many things; but we don't really *have* to do any of them— at least not today.

Life is choices, not sluices.

If you *want*, you can sail at night through moonlit shoals without an engine.

If you *want*, you can change course and go someplace other than your original destination.

If you *want*, you can toss a few bucks at a couple of teenagers, show them a little adventure, and see if they *get* it.

I take a deep breath and close my eyes.

This morning, I choose to sleep in.

Homecoming

1985

SIX MONTHS after moving aboard, Dana leaves.

I move home to my mother's house.

Trimaran John sails off to the Bahamas.

I take a job at a record store and then return to college as a jazz guitar major. I hack away at earning a degree, jumping from school to school trying to find my place. I can't say I want to be in school but it feels like what I'm supposed to be doing.

Two years pass.

I find myself in Coconut Grove one day. On a lark, I drive down to Dinner Key Marina.

Memories flood back. I didn't realize how much I missed this place.

I encounter a familiar face on the shrimp docks. "Any word from Trimaran John?" I ask. "Did anyone ever hear from him?"

"John got back a while ago," Shrimper Jim tells me, looking over his shoulder out the channel. "He's back out in the anchorage in his old spot."

"Can you tell him I'm looking for him when you run across him? Here's my phone number." I scribble a note on a scrap of paper.

"Sure, Dave. No problem."

"What else is going on around here?"

"Well, the City's been raising hell with us, as always. The cops are hassling people, slapping stickers on boats, threatening to 'run all us hippies out of here.' You know; the usual bullshit."

It's the same old story; the desperate nastiness of the Miami City Administration has always been a dark cloud on the anchorage's western horizon. To the City, the anchorage residents are "those people"—freeloaders, alcoholics, the ones responsible for local crime. Living as they do, they must surely be hiding something.

I pin a second scrawled note to the bulletin board at the dinghy dock. Two years have passed since I stood on this weatherbeaten old raft. The ragtag collection of dinghies is still here; I even recognize some of them.

Three days later, a familiar voice springs from my answering machine. Over the next few days I drive down to the marina whenever I can. I eventually catch up with Trimaran John limping along the dock.

"Hey, mate. Good to see you. When are you comin' sailing?"

"Soon, I hope. I've missed it."

I hand John a small roll of bills. "I still owe you rent. You showed me some fantastic adventures and gave me my first chance to sail and live on the water. I'm sorry I wasn't able to put the money together back when..."

"No problem, mate." John smiles. His rotten teeth have gotten worse. "I can always use a little cash. I appreciate you tracking me down to give it to me; that's mighty good of you. Have you heard from Dana?"

"Not a word. I ran into her mother at school, though. She told me Dana had a baby...not mine. She has a different life now. Dana taught me a lot but sometimes things just don't work out. I took it hard for a while, but life goes on. I'm glad the whole thing happened, but..."

I'm rambling. Trimaran John changes the subject. His face turns serious. "Well, let me tell you what's been goin' on with *me*, mate. I got back from Georgetown completely broke. I got a job working up in the Grove at Zayre's in the shipping department. The forklift was broken and they had me unloading heavy stuff off a truck. Made me keep working even after I told them my back was acting up. I've been in and out of surgery, rehab, physical therapy, all sorts of shit you wouldn't believe. The surgeons screwed up my back even more. I have a big lawsuit going; we're talking *beaucoup* bucks here. One of these days soon—*boom*—my boat's gonna get completely redone and I'll be out of here." John pulls another Old Milwaukee from the fast-dwindling twenty-four-pack in his bag. "My lawyer says they'll settle any day now and then

I'm goin' cruisin'. Gonna stay gone this time; gonna head down to the Virgins."

I focus on school during the week. On weekends, I enjoy a secret life on the far side of the moon.

Trimaran John rows me out to *The Music Man*. Actually, I do the rowing, but together in the dinghy, we make our way past the channel markers out into the anchorage just past the south spoil island. Donated by an anchorage benefactor, *The Music Man* is a gigantic seventy-four-foot engineless, ferrocement[16] houseboat with a piano, a book-trading library, a fractured Lucite torso of a nude woman on a stand, and a big galley—the perfect anchorage community center. On top is an expansive deck accessed by a spiral stairway on the back porch.

I buy a cheap plywood dinghy—one of the ever-circulating anchorage beaters—and make my way out to the anchorage when I can. Some days I visit Trimaran John. Other times I row out to *The Music Man* to experience the water on my own. I'll get my own sailboat someday but this isn't a bad compromise. With my own dinghy, I can come here any time I want.

Sunday mornings, I teach music classes on *The Music Man*. A crew of shrimpers and dock bums arrives each weekend to beat drums, strum guitars, and hammer on the piano. They're hungry for this—hungry for something. They leave smiling and openly

---

16 *Ferrocement* vessels are made from cement formed over a metal structure.

grateful. Playing simple music offers them a chance to touch a part of themselves that would otherwise lie dormant. They're proud and delighted as they master each simple chord or scale. I sometimes question my choice to major in jazz guitar at school. How strange to find that path validated on a giant houseboat in the middle of Biscayne Bay.

"You haven't been sailing with Trimaran John much lately," observes Michael Burtt after one of my Sunday morning music gatherings.

"John's a good friend," I explain, "but he's making it his business to be sick for a living. If he lets his back get better, his disability checks will stop and the company he's suing will gain an advantage. He's drinking himself to death while his boat falls apart; he's living off his own decline. The alcohol and the shipworms are working faster than the lawyers. I can only spend so much time watching."

Michael looks down, processing my perspective. He nods and shrugs.

A few months later, Trimaran John runs *Chanson de Mer* aground in the shallows off the north spoil island to keep her from sinking. With her outer hulls propped up on cinder blocks, she at least provides a level place to live.

I make new friends in the anchorage. Some are cruising sailors. Some are dock bums. All are part of the tapestry of the secret floating village. So am I. Even without my own sailboat, I've become part of this; Dinner Key Anchorage is part of me.

One Friday afternoon after school, I arrive at the dinghy dock to find a sign bolted to one of the pilings:

By city ordinance, vessels moored illegally to this dock will be towed at owner's expense.

I've heard stories about police harassment from anchorage residents but this is the first time I've encountered the City of Miami's Gestapo tactics in action. The strategy is naïve: make it illegal for anchorage people to come ashore and they'll be forced to leave. Like many of the Evil Empire's "By City Ordinance" signs, this one fails to reference an actual, numbered ordinance, but that won't keep the police from seizing dinghies.

I draft a response letter on behalf of the anchorage.

A meeting is held on *The Music Man* that night. People are panicked, scared, indignant. "How can I go to work if I don't have a place to tie my dinghy?" "What right does the City have to deny us access to shore? I'm a goddamned U.S. citizen!" "Nice o' those bastards to give us some notice; they can't just make somethin' illegal without no public hearin' or nothin'."

"I have a phone and a computer," I offer. "Get a temporary dinghy dock set up somewhere. I'll set up a meeting with the City." I read my letter aloud at the meeting and am roundly cheered.

"How many here, besides me, have Captain's licenses?" asks Richard Heydemann. "We can put a launch service together; the City can't say anything about it. I can run a few shifts."

"I have a boat you can use as a tender, long as you don't beat 'er up," volunteers a shrimper. "She don' got no engine, but if someone..."

"I got a fifteen-horse outboard that'll run if someone'll spring for some new spark plugs," offers a gray-bearded, shirtless man in jeans.

"I got a buttload of good life jackets," says another. "Took 'em off *The Golden Mean* 'fore she sunk a few months back."

"You can use my float as a dinghy dock; just anchor it right out there on the shoal behind *The Music Man*," says Buddy. "A couple pieces of plywood nailed on top and she'll be good as new."

"*Sundowner* Jack's got a Captain's license, too, Richard. I'm sure he'd be game to run the launch some just to poke the City in the eye."

The plan comes together. A collection jar fills with quarters and dollar bills. By early the next morning, a twenty-four-hour launch service is organized. The boat has a dozen life preservers, a new emergency flare gun, and a first-aid kit. A U.S. Coast Guard-licensed captain pilots her. Every twenty minutes, the launch runs from the improvised floating dinghy dock in the anchorage to the pier at the public boat ramp and back. The cost is twenty cents per-person per-trip to cover fuel expenses. The City Manager is mad as hell. Our impromptu operation is completely legitimate. He's underestimated "those damned anchorage people" again.

I call The Miami *Herald* and explain the situation, hoping to get them to cover the story. They're not interested.

Meanwhile, the City has real problems. They tow away several dinghies left at the dock. None of them have titles, Florida license numbers, or hull numbers—and they're not required to. The City's private towing contractor has no way to verify whether they're releasing the dinghies to their true owners when people show up at the impound lot to reluctantly pay the towing fees and reclaim their boats. "Liability" is one of the secret words the Evil Wizard cannot stand to hear.

Cesar Odio, the City Manager, is the man in charge. In the anchorage, they call him "Odious." I ring his office. To my surprise, his secretary grants me an appointment without interrogating or stonewalling me. A diplomatic crew of six anchorites accompanies me to read him our letter. The missive is eloquent, sophisticated, righteous—a twenty-year-old college student's grassroots Anchorage Declaration of Independence. I speak of the fundamental right of man to access the shores of his own country, of the willingness of anchorage residents to pay a fair price for services, of the hypocrisy of accusing a man of polluting the bay while denying him simple, civilized access to a toilet. Halfway through the reading of the letter, Odious gets up to pace around the room. He opens windows and noisily jostles chairs.

I pause.

"It's okay; I am listening," he assures me in a thick Cuban accent.

"Thank you. I'll wait for you to get comfortable," I reply.

Annoyed, he sighs and returns to his chair.

Naïvely, I believe this man is a public servant. I believe his job is to hear the voice of the citizenry and to administer the hand of government with fairness and reason. I'm certain he never expected such a well-stated and articulate response from our simple band of drunks, bums, hippies and ne'er-do-wells. Surely, he's impressed by our polite, professional request to pay our fair share, to act as responsible citizens, to cooperate with the city to solve problems.

He suffers visibly through the rest of my letter.

Years later, Odious will become the target of a Federal criminal investigation. He's as much a public servant as any other fox sworn to protect a henhouse. But today, I unwittingly engineered the back-firing of his plan. Our band of drunks, bums, hippies and ne'er-do-wells is now sitting at his conference table discussing basic human dignity and the Constitutionally guaranteed freedom to navigate in federal waters. If we'd appeared with wings, halos, and golden robes, his opinion of us wouldn't have changed. What he wants more than anything is for us to *go away.*

To end his torment, the manager offers us a deal. In exchange for a fee, he'll issue shower keys, parking decals, access to fresh water, a dumpster, and garbage pickup. The cost, he declares, will be based on the length of a boater's dinghy. The fee might as well be based on a yachtsman's astrological sign or the number of hairs in his left nostril. I begin to speak but Kerry, next to me at the table, puts a gentle elbow in my ribs. The deal is a stupid deal, but it's a deal—more than the anchorage has ever had before. This time, lack of public process works in our favor. The dictator has made his decree.

I thank Mr. Odious for his fairness and generosity. Then we give him what he really wants; we leave.

The sign disappears from the dinghy dock.

A flatbed truck returns a small collection of battered dinghies and leaves them as they were when they were hauled away—tied unlocked to the dinghy dock.

The anchorage launch service is discontinued. Most of the anchorage folk buy dinghy decals. The arrangement is a win for everybody, even the City. All dinghies are reported at the marina office to be eight feet long—close enough; they don't care. Nobody from the dock office comes to the dinghy dock with a tape measure to check.

It's a victory for the world as we know it.

Weekends on *The Music Man* continue with music lessons on Sunday mornings. Parties occur spontaneously on the upper deck. Potluck dinners are prepared in the capacious galley. I've gotten good enough at the helm by now to make a few extra dollars on Saturday mornings teaching for Easy Sailing, the local sailboat rental company.

Trimaran John is found face down next to his boat one morning, drowned in a foot of water. I'm sad to see him go but not surprised. I wish I was more moved, but his passing marks an end to my mourning, not a beginning. For too long, I watched his decline helplessly. As a prayer for his final voyage I can offer only a sigh.

"Just you wait and—*boom*—I'm outta here."

Wind in your sails, John.

Ray Newgarden rows up, ties off to the wooden float behind *The Music Man* and steps aboard. He's mad as can be—fuming. "You know the big banyan tree next to the dinghy dock? The City's cutting it down because the bums hang out under it and drink in the shade. They're cutting down a huge, ancient, beautiful tree to get rid of people who aren't doing anything but trying to get out of the sun. It's the craziest damned thing I've ever..."

The City is at it again, waging war on common sense and the drunks, bums, hippies, and losers of the secret floating village.

A squall is approaching; it's going to rain and blow like hell any minute. I help close windows and the sliding glass doors that divide the galley from the foredeck of *The Music Man*.

A bright flash accompanies an explosion of thunder.

The air cools.

The wind shifts.

The Music Man is caught broadside by the first blast of the storm as the wind suddenly changes direction. She spins awkwardly, dragging dinghies along as she's blown back on her mooring lines. The atmosphere glows with unearthly green light. The air pulses with energy.

The Music Man's upper deck extends from behind her foredeck all the way to her stern, providing a solid awning over her aft deck. I look at Ray. "Watch the show?"

He smiles warmly and sits down next to me on a folding chair. "Thanks, Dave. I wouldn't miss it."

"Sorry about that tree, man. That's a shame."

"Yeah…sure is."

I close my eyes and breathe slowly, inhaling the electric air. School and work are my "other" life now. I have arrived here in this place for people who have no place, a place populated by misfits where only misfits fit in. What this says about me is uncertain, but Dinner Key feels like home.

The rain begins.

Optimism and Spontaneity

1987

"I have heard there are troubles of more than one kind.
Some come from ahead and some come from behind.
But I've bought a big boat. I'm all ready you see.
Now my troubles are going to have troubles with me!"

—*Theodor Geisel (Dr. Seuss)*

PEARL CANVAS with its lighthearted atmosphere is as good a place as any to pass time. Colorful people come in to drop off sails for repair or to talk to Bill about having a new Bimini top made. A shaggy yellow Labrador retriever sleeps under the sewing table. Suzy's busy stitching a sun cover on a furling jib.[17] A crib stands next to Debbie's desk. Everyone here lives in the anchorage. Everyone laughs while they work. Kathy's almost finished at her sewing machine. Soon, we will head out to the bay.

---

17 *Furling jib* - a sail that rolls up on the forestay like a window shade. Because the sail is never taken down, its outer edge has a sun-resistant canvas strip sewn to it. After years in the sun, the sacrificial cover must be replaced by a sailmaker.

Kathy lives on a thirty-two-foot center-cockpit[18] sloop left to her by an ex-husband. Her boat is engineless, though she does have a mast—even if that mast is sitting in a boatyard somewhere up the Miami River. Her husband isn't *officially* an *ex*-husband. The boat isn't *officially* hers. It's complicated—but not this weekend. Twenty-three is an age for optimism and spontaneity. I'm ready to spend a romantic weekend on the water. What could be less complicated?

Maybe we'll fix Kathy's boat up and go sailing?

Maybe we'll go to the Bahamas to explore the mysterious islands my sailor friends talk so much about?

Maybe this is *it?*

Maybe it's not, but it will do for now.

Sarah walks into the shop just before closing time. She no longer lives aboard but she's tied to that world; she's a boat broker. Her makeup can't hide her fifties, but we're fine with what's beneath her cosmetics, even if she isn't.

"I just got a listing for a neat little sailboat," Sarah announces. "She's a dynamite starter boat—a Whitby 26—a Continental Folkboat. She needs some TLC, but she's a good full-keeled[19] sea boat."

---

18 *Center cockpit* - Some vessels are designed with an aft cockpit in the back; others offer a center cockpit located between aft and forward cabins.

19 *Keel* - the "blade" that extends down into the water from the hull. *Keels* come in a variety of sizes, shapes, and weights to accommodate different combinations of stability, maneuverability, and shallow-water sailing capability. *Full-keeled* vessels have larger, heavier keels for greater stability and sail-carrying capacity.

She smiles at me. "Might be perfect for you, Dave."

"How much?"

"Five thousand. She comes with a good outboard motor and decent sails."

I recall how Kathy reacted when I first took a job to finance fixing up her boat. The cruising dream made for romantic conversation but the reality of planning a voyage evoked noticeable hesitation.

I don't want to *talk* about going sailing; I want to *do* it.

Words tumble from my mouth. "I suppose taking a look can't hurt."

I arrange to meet Sarah at King's Bay Marina the next day. Kathy wears a hurt expression but she's impulsive; she succumbs easily to the excitement of a new idea.

I'm not planning to buy a boat—at least not yet. I'm still in school. I have an apartment close to the University of Miami and a room-mate. I think I'd prefer something bigger than twenty-six feet when I do buy a boat.

I meet Sarah on the dock the next afternoon.

The sloop hasn't sailed for years. She's stuffy inside. The overhead is darkened with mildew. Built in '63, her interior is typical for her time—plywood bulkheads[20] covered with mahogany veneer, trimmed with weathered teak. Under the forward berth is a marine

---

20 *Bulkheads* - walls of a boat oriented across the hull. Often, they are structural, helping the hull hold its shape.

toilet. Curved shelves conform to the insides of the bow under the deck on either side. A chain locker lies forward of the bunk. In the main cabin, burnt-orange vinyl cushions cover a pair of settees. An area next to the companionway[21] serves as a chart table and counter top, housing a small sink and a stove. Under the steps, an empty compartment gapes where a long-gone inboard engine once sat. A blue milk crate full of spray bottles and cleaning supplies squats in its place. On deck, the varnish is deteriorated; peeling yellow flakes cling to sun-grayed wood. The galvanized fastening bolts have rusted and exploded inside the weathered mahogany cockpit coamings.[22] The grab rails[23] on the cabin top aren't safe to grab. Plexiglas ports are fogged with a latticework of tiny sun cracks. The outboard engine appears to be a recent addition, but the rusting mount it sits on is precarious. Faded blue paint covers her fiberglass hull.

But she's a heavy, full-keeled boat, which makes her safer in a big sea—not that I've ever been in a big sea. The rudder is transom-hung;[24] that eliminates steering cables, rudder bearings, and other mechanical complexities. If I tilt my head, I can stand upright in her cabin, at least under the main hatch. An early fiberglass[25]

---

21 *Companionway* - a boat's "front door," leading from the main cabin to the cockpit.

22 *Coamings* - boards bolted edgewise around the cockpit to form a low "fence." They help keep water from running off the deck into the helmsman's seat.

23 *Grab rails* are, as their name implies, designed to be grabbed onto for safer maneuvering around the deck.

boat, she's thickly built with quality resin and reinforced with heavy wooden stringers glassed into her hull. Her cabin top is strong, too, built to support the pressure of a deck-stepped mast. She's twenty-five years old; if something was going to fail structurally, the problem would likely have already shown itself.

My personal wealth amounts to two thousand dollars. I offer this as a down payment plus another thousand within a month. The boat is a project, one that's costing its owner a monthly dock fee.

Sarah makes the call.

My offer is accepted without negotiation.

I write a check and empty my bank account.

I'm excited and a little scared. I'm still trying to finish school. My job takes up a lot of time. What am I going to do with a boat? I suppose I'll keep her as a place to escape to on weekends. This boat isn't big enough to live on, but she will give me Biscayne Bay.

The next evening after work, I arrive at the marina with a friend to sail the boat up to Dinner Key. The night is dark and moonless. From the dock, we stare out the channel into inky blackness.

I open up the boat.

---

24 *Transom* - the very back part of the hull facing aft. On some sailboats, the rudder (the part of a boat that steers it through the water) is mounted directly on the transom. On others, a rudder post extends through the bottom of the hull.

25 *Fiberglass* boats are made with petroleum products. When the 1973 oil embargo drove oil prices up, the formulas for polyester resins were changed to keep down the costs of manufacturing boats. Many sailors believe the pre-1973 resins offer better water resistance.

The battery is dead. Navigation lights won't be an option tonight.

My friend has no sailing experience.

We abort the mission and go to dinner.

The next Saturday, Kathy and I point the bow of my little sloop seaward. The channel cuts a long, narrow path across a very shallow shoal. I'm grateful that I waited to make my first sail in daylight. Only the markers at the far end of the channel have lights on them. I could easily have wandered outside the channel and gone aground in the dark.

The engine runs. We are under weigh. I hank a jib onto the forestay and run the sheets through their turning blocks to the cockpit. I pull off the mainsail cover and discover halyard winches on either side of the mast—good equipment to have on a small boat.[26]

The wind is easterly, in our faces as we exit the channel. We keep the sails furled while we motor east toward deeper water, out into the middle of Biscayne Bay.

Nothing but open water ahead.

I haul sails to the masthead.

We turn north and trim the canvas.

I turn off the engine.

Silence.

"Kathy, can you tighten up that jib sheet for me?"

---

26 *Winches* offer mechanical advantage for safely adjusting the tension of lines under tremendous pressure. Mast winches provide leverage for cranking sails up tight.

She inserts the winch handle not-quite-all-the-way into the port winch, starts to crank in the line, and immediately flips the bronze lever over the side.

That didn't last long.

I smile and hand her the remaining winch handle. She shrugs, and with a more careful second attempt, pulls the jib in tight. I'm disappointed but not about to let my moment get sucked under by a piece of lost hardware.

We're purring along. The little blue sloop heels comfortably. I lean over the transom to fumble with the engine bracket; the long-neglected mechanism is stiff—a potential finger-biter. With a groan, I manage to haul the engine up and tilt the propeller forward out of the water.

I pull my portable stereo from the cabin. The essential piece of gear fits perfectly in the forward edge of the cockpit, just in front of the companionway dropboards.[27] The cockpit is no place for electronics in a big sea or a rain squall but for a light sail on Biscayne Bay, the risk is minimal. I put on a cassette tape—*Thelonious Monk in Action.*

"What's this?" asks Kathy. She's no culture hound but she's willing to try something new. She's certainly not stuck in the cultural ruts worn across the societal landscape by the treadless tires of Top 40

---

27 *Dropboards* - In lieu of a door that could possibly be crushed inward by a heavy sea, many vessels use *dropboards*—a series of sturdy planks that are dropped into grooves on either side of the companionway.

radio. I suppose that comes naturally with living closer to the Gulf Stream than the mainstream.

"Thelonious Monk—he's profound and amusing at the same time. Listen to those chords; they're 'wrong' but they work anyway. His compositions are strange and angular, but they're beautiful. He can take the most tired jazz standard and make the tune his own. There's something meditative and personal and deep about him and at the same time, his playing is lighthearted—almost mischievous. Sometimes, his improvisations sound like you're listening to the hundred billionth random monkey accidentally stumbling across a great jazz arrangement by pure chance. He faded away after the early seventies and died a few years ago in '82."

Kathy grins at my pedantry. "You sure know a lot about him."

"I could blame that on being a jazz student but mostly, I like his music; I did a little reading. Other music fans know all about The Beatles or Mozart. I'm no different except in my tastes. When music touches me, I like to learn about who's playing."

I experiment with the mainsheet, easing the line slightly, then pulling it in, feeling the pressure change on the tiller. The boat balances well. I study the glass bubble of the compass as I develop a sense for the way she drifts and pulls.

"Listen to what Monk does with this tune; it's just a little blues melody, almost like a children's song but he takes it to…"

"Yeah, Dave; I like it."

It's always gratifying to share something esoteric and have it appreciated. Anyone who likes Monk surely has a heart and a brain.

The strange houses of Stiltsville draw abeam to starboard, followed by the lighthouse at Key Biscayne. We adjust course to port and begin our approach to Dinner Key Anchorage.

Monk's piano accompanies our dance across the bay.

The waves sparkle.

Late in the afternoon, we pass through the anchored boats into the marina behind the spoil islands. The islands block the wind, making it easier to take sails down and get the engine lowered and started.

After putting the ship in order, we motor out to the anchorage.

Now I will choose an anchoring spot—*my* spot.

"I'd rather go farther out," I explain to Kathy. "I don't mind a longer row. Better to park where the anchorage is less crowded."

Serious cruisers prefer the outer anchorage while 'floaters' stay closer to shore where they're better protected from northerly winds. I trust the cruisers' anchoring skills; when the next squall comes, there's less chance that some unattended boat will drag into mine while I'm not here…"and of course, Kathy, I'll rest easier knowing she's where you can keep an eye on her."

Kathy nods and smiles.

The ground tackle[28] aboard is not quite to my standards; the anchors are small, but they'll hold until I can get bigger ones and

---

28 *Ground tackle* - anchors

some new chain. Big, heavy anchors are the best insurance you can buy for a boat. They're the *only* insurance I can afford for this one. We drop the first hook a quarter-mile off the spoil islands in the middle of a loosely spaced cluster of sailboats a few hundred feet from Kathy's boat. A second anchor goes out to the southwest.

"We're neighbors."

"Welcome to Dinner Key," says Kathy. "You're official, now."

She's excited for me. Now that I've chosen a spot, the boat somehow feels a little more mine.

"So, Dave, what are you going to name her?"

"Remember the little blues tune we were listening to?"

"Yeah..."

"*Blue Monk.* The name of the tune is the name of the boat."

I stand on deck and gaze at Biscayne Bay, at the anchored boats around me, at the sky and the lighthouse on Key Biscayne, at the houses of Stiltsville on the horizon and the seagrass under my keel. My little sloop doesn't offer much living space, but my view is inspiring; my back yard is boundless. I can't know yet of the adventures *Blue Monk* will carry me through, but my world is an ocean sparkling with sunlight and spontaneity, and emboldened with optimism. With my anchors secure in the Dinner Key bottom, I am home on my tiny ship.

Souls and Stories

1987

INANIMATE OBJECTS capable of sustaining a soul merit elevation in status from "it" to "he" or "she," and are often given proper names. Musical instruments, vehicles, and boats, especially wooden boats fabricated from living things, are traditionally named. Gear that works well long after its expected lifetime may earn a familiar title. Any machine betraying the presence of an interior ghost may thus join the ranks of the animata.

Now that I own a sailboat moored in the Dinner Key Anchorage, I need a way to get out to her. My boss's girlfriend is willing to part with an eight-foot fiberglass dinghy with a two-piece mast, a pair of oars, and a good sail for $100. Small black vinyl letters on her transom declare her name, *Artemisia Gentileschi*—after the 17th century painter. I lash the boat to the roof of *Little Red Riding Hood,* my 1969 Dodge Dart—white with a red hood. The oars barely fit, lying diagonally from the passenger side dashboard to the deck behind the back seat. The front seat will still accommodate a passenger as long as she doesn't mind a pair of oars crossing her left shoulder.

At the dinghy dock, I lift *Artemisia Gentileschi* from the roof of *Little Red Riding Hood* and drop her in the bay so I can row myself to *Blue Monk.* Maybe this is Dinner Key's secret source of color. My modes of transportation sound like a children's story about baroque art on acid jazz.

The weekend is over. My new, old boat is clean. The mildew has been scrubbed away. The rotten teak grab rails are gone; I bought replacements from Shell Lumber and put the first few coats of varnish on them. After five more coats, I'll bolt them to the cabin top on either side of the teak main hatch I've likewise begun to restore.

I still can't believe I have my own sailboat, my own private apartment in the secret floating village, my own key to a hidden doorway leading to an alternate dimension. I row back through the anchored boats toward the channel to the dinghy dock. My guitar lies in its case on the back seat.

While rowing past the channel marker at the edge of the world as you know it, I narrowly miss colliding with another dinghy. Black, wooden, and tubby with firehose rub rails, the craft is piloted by a tall, lanky, fortyish man with short sandy hair and a friendly smile. Propped up in his stern is an instrument case.

"Hey banjo man, can you play that thing?"

"Yes, sir," he responds. "Can you play a good rhythm guitar?"

"I like to think so. I'm Dave. I just put my boat out in the middle anchorage."

"We're neighbors, then. I'm John—John Nation. Come on out and visit me on *Zebra Dun*. She's the only boat in the anchorage with no spreaders on her masts. Know what a schooner is?"

"Not exactly."

I'm embarrassed; I should know these things. I silently guess spreaders are the crosspieces seen on most sailboat masts. I know the difference between a sloop and a ketch, but I wasn't in class the day they covered schooners, cutters, and yawls. John perceives the inexperience on my twenty-three year old face and enlightens me. "A schooner and a ketch both have two or more masts. A ketch has the taller mast in front. On a schooner, the taller mast is in back. The *Zebra Dun* is white with black bulwarks and tanbark sails; you can't miss her. When are you coming out again?"

"Next weekend; I have to go back to school tomorrow."

"School? Nuts. Whatcha studying?"

"Jazz guitar."

"Well, I guess you *can* play that thing. Tell you what—I have a hand-cranked cedar bucket ice-cream maker on board. Round up a bag of rock salt and we'll put us a party together next Sunday."

Dinner Key has a way of assimilating you into its great patchwork quilt. Yesterday, I stood on the periphery—a jazz guitar student working at a software company—looking in on a strange collection of eccentric storybook characters. Today, I lead a secret life on weekends with homemade ice cream parties on Biscayne Bay. Whatever draws people to Dinner Key is powerful enough to break the gravitational pull of traditional, terrestrial life. Therein lies a story—your story. I can't say mine amounts to much yet, but having found its way into a marvelous anthology, I sense it will only get better.

John smiles, nods his head warmly, then slips around the channel marker to disappear into the anchorage.

The week goes by slowly.

I'm no longer me.

I'm a tiny alien sitting in somebody's head, peering out through somebody's eyes, saying the things he's supposed to say. The classrooms and the office and the apartment are not of my home planet.

During the week, I do some research. Bulwarks are tall wooden rails that extend the height of a ship's sides above the deck line. Tanbark sails are reddish brown.[29]

Sunday afternoon, I tie a float to *Blue Monk's* mooring line and cast off, motoring over to the white schooner with the tall black bulwarks and the raked-back main mast. I tie fenders[30] alongside my hull and raft up to John's forty-foot pirate ship. Built in a Texas back yard of mahogany planks, she's a replica of a 1911 Nova Scotia Tancook

29 *Tanbark* - In the days of cottons sails, some sailcloth was tanned—dipped in tannins derived from tree bark—to protect them from rot, mold and mildew. The process turned the sails a red-brown color.

30 *Fenders* - Durable, inflatable *fenders* are hung between two boats or between a boat and the dock to keep them from banging together. Fenders also make convenient buoys for anchor lines.

Whaler fishing schooner. If my little fiberglass sloop is the moon, this is Saturn—a good distance farther away from the straight and level, clock-punching, rent-paying world I find myself estranged from.

John gives me a tour of his ship. A long tiller extends from her rudder to a standing well in the stern that serves as a cockpit. Forward of that is a low aft cabin with a roof raised a few short inches above the deck. Down below, John's sleeping quarters are only high enough to sit up in. On the port side, a double bunk complements shelves and lockers to starboard. Steps descend between them. Light scatters from glass deck prisms overhead. Growing up, I spent much of my free time in a treehouse I cobbled together in my back yard; this is the nautical equivalent.

The main mast comes up through the deck just forward of the aft cabin. A bridge deck of mahogany boards introduces the raised, main cabin trunk. John slides the hatch forward. We descend into a charming wooden saloon[31] tall enough to stand up in only if I hunch over. Bronze ports[32] and brass lanterns add a traditional touch. Varnished mahogany beams accentuate the neat, white planks of the overhead. A varnished shear plank glows where her white cabin sides meet the deck. *Zebra Dun's* small but comfortable interior reflects her builder's skill as a shipwright and his respect for nautical tradition.

---

31 *Saloon* - (pronounced *"salon"*) is a vessel's main cabin.

32 *Ports* - Windows on a boat

The *Zebra Dun's* kitchen is in her bow, between the main cabin and the chain locker all the way forward. Though cooking is an endeavor traditionally practiced standing up, John Nation's sensible design for his ship's galley places the stove, oven, counter top and pantry within arms' reach, enabling the chef to sit comfortably while preparing a meal.

I take in the *Zebra Dun's* interior with my hands on my knees, feeling like Gulliver in Lilliput. "Sit down and get comfortable," John urges.

"You could have built the cabin trunk six inches higher, no? I'm sure you..."

"Of course I thought of it; I'm six-foot-two—and I had a wife back when I built the boat. She *definitely* thought of it, but next time you're coming or going, visualize a tall cabin while you're looking at the lines of the boat. Tancook Whalers were originally designed as open fishing boats. You can get away with a small cabin trunk, but if you build the houses too tall, the boat will look like she's got two refrigerators lying on deck. Headroom is like love; it's nice to have, but a lot of crimes have been committed in its name."

Aside from being an able boat carpenter, John is an ex-planetarium director, a talented writer, a former administrator of the Oklahoma City Ballet, and an authority on classical music. His quick mind stores endless obscure facts and details. On his galley countertop is a small toy. "My titanothere," John explains. "A plastic, prehistoric rhinoceros I found on the street in Coconut Grove. *Brontotheriidae* are more closely related to horses than rhinos, if you care to get technical about the taxonomy, but I figured I'd give it a home on the *Zebra Dun*; everything else is a relic or a reissue. If you haven't figured it out yet, I was born a century or two later than I should have been."

A small Siamese cat crawls onto John's lap and purrs under his chin. "This is Kipling," he explains, "ship's cat."

"And the name of the boat?"

"Zebra Dun was the name of a wild bucking horse in an old cowboy poem. As the story goes, the cowboys are sitting around the fire when a stranger comes along who speaks just a little too fancy and educated for their liking. He needs a horse, so they play a trick on him and give him the Zebra Dun."

My host closes his eyes and recites:

We could see the tops of mountains under Dunny's every jump,
But the stranger he was growed there just like the camel's hump.
The stranger sat upon him and twirled his black mustache
Just like a summer boarder waiting for his hash.
He thumped him in the shoulders and spurred him when he whirled
And hollered to them punchers, "I'm the wolf of the world!"
When the stranger had dismounted and was once more upon the ground,
We knew he was a thoroughbred and not a dude from town.

"I grew up on a farm in Oklahoma, but my mother was a poet and I've always been fascinated by just about everything. I'm an astronomer and a writer but I'm still a cowboy at heart. I figure the name connects me to the boat."

We hear a commotion outside and go topside to investigate.

"John Nation!" calls a cheerful voice from an approaching sailboat. "Prepare to be boarded."

"I'll be hot-dipped," exclaims John. "It's Bob Treat."

We fasten dock lines to deck cleats. Soon, three vessels are rafted together on the bay a half-mile from shore.

Social awkwardness is absent out here; you can safely assume everyone is an eccentric worth talking to. Meeting new people in Dinner Key Anchorage is like going to a potluck book exchange. A great deal usually gets said before the conversation ever meanders around to "What do you do in *real life?*" The sarcasm inherent in the question is lost on no one. Bob works as a pilot for dubiously named Midway Airlines. He sails and plays guitar when he's not flying. In his forties, he's jocular, thin-haired, and stocky with a boyish and sharply intelligent gleam in his eye. Today, he successfully absconded with a group of bluegrass musicians after their performance at a local festival. Afloat at Dinner Key, they're lost in an alternate universe.

They hand instrument cases carefully over the rope rails. I stack them on top of John's aft cabin before assisting their owners aboard.

Pam's here with her banjo. Two girls play fiddles. There's a mandolin. Bob plays guitar. I have mine and, of course, John's got his banjo. Before long, we're arranged on deck on chairs improvised from sail bags, singing, playing, and taking turns cranking the ice-cream maker.

The ice cream is delicious, the music transporting.

We swap songs, jokes, and stories as a red sun sets the clouds on fire.

"I'm reminded," says John, in between *Hot Corn Cold Corn* and *The Wabash Cannonball,* "of a time years ago when the Oklahoma City Ballet did a *Nutcracker* tour at Christmas. I was driving the bus and it broke down. We pulled over by a little park in a small town at two in the morning to try to find the problem and get back on the road. With the engine out, things got pretty cold pretty fast. Before long, we had twenty costumed dancers stomping their feet and rubbing their hands trying to keep warm. With nothing else to do, they put on a complete performance of *The Nutcracker* right there in the park. Not a soul was around to see, hear, or know about it. Anyone walking in the park the next morning had no idea that something spontaneous, extraordinary, and beautiful had happened there during the night."

Three hours later, after returning *Blue Monk* to her anchors, I row *Artemisia Gentileschi* past the red channel marker at the edge of the world as you know it to the dinghy dock. I slide my oars through the passenger door of *Little Red Riding Hood* and return to my apartment that has no name.

The Blue Monk

Dog Patch

"Keep, ancient lands, your storied pomp!
Cries she with silent lips.
Give me your tired, your poor,
Your huddled masses yearning to breathe free,
The wretched refuse of your teeming shore.
Send these, the homeless, tempest-tossed, to me;
I lift my lamp beside the golden door."
—Emma Lazarus

MANY IN DINNER KEY ANCHORAGE are known by nicknames. Metal Burt, Shrimper Dave, English John, and a score of others are called only by their informal handles. Everyone has a story, though not all are telling; anonymity is part of the culture.

Dog Patch is a three-foot-deep-at-low-tide anchorage south of the southernmost spoil island, named for its ragtag collection of derelicts, sunken wrecks, and other boats headed generally toward artificial reefdom. To the noncognoscenti, Dog Patch is a community of the homeless, though it's really anything but. The south anchorage does harbor plenty of desperadoes: fugitives, illegal aliens, a dope dealer or two, Vietnam veterans who made it home but never quite made it back, a few poor families, and a collection of hard drinkers. Many eke out a living working the shrimp boats—dragging nets and trawls across the bay bottom all night to supply bait shops across the South. That and a book of government food stamps can keep a man in beans, rice, and beer if he's not paying rent or making car payments. But humble living is not homelessness; homelessness means giving up on having even a tiny piece of *mine*. Every man here goes home to his own boat and his own bunk. Even the dope dealers work hard.

Johnny Frau has lived on a small boat in Dog Patch since the 1960s. A descendant of original Coconut Grove settlers, he claims to have his family's deed to the submerged land beneath the anchorage—though nobody has ever seen it.

Small powerboats are abandoned with regularity in Miami, most often by people who can't afford to replace blown-up engines. The broken boats deteriorate, take up space, cost money to store, and are finally given away, sold cheap, or discarded. Many wind up in the anchorage.

Wilbur is one of Dinner Key Anchorage's powerless powerboaters. During his service in Vietnam, he was tripping on LSD when the Vietcong attacked his unit. He had a beautiful time of it until he came down and found twelve of his buddies dead. Today, his face is rotten with skin cancer. The doctors at the veterans' hospital say that Agent Orange has nothing to do with his condition. He works the shrimp boats at night while the sun is hiding, and lives with his burden in Dog Patch. He's a good man—helpful, friendly, and always ready if you need something.

He shows me his collection of antique post cards from old Florida and Cuba. Wrapped in plastic garbage bags to keep out the moisture, his album dates back to the early twentieth century.

Jack and Fay depart from their own humble powerboat in a boxy plywood dinghy driven by short, jerky strokes of the oars. Jack is old and thin with a wisp of white beard. Fay is heavyset, riding in the stern with three dogs. Jack wears a pacemaker but he's a tough old codger. They possess little in the way of either money or teeth, but Fay still manages to smile the way she must have those many years ago back in Ireland when Jack won her hand in a fistfight. Jack loves to tell people he's living on *Borrowed Time;* it's the name of his boat.

Rumored to be a crack cocaine addict, Coast Guard is a young blond kid with glassy eyes and bad teeth. He breaks the all-time record for skirting homelessness by sleeping on a Styrofoam surfboard.

Eventually, he moves in with Peter Rabbit, a red-bearded Coconut Grove hippy on a rotten, mastless sailboat. *Jupiter* was once a beautiful sloop—a strip-planked sharpie[33] built for these shallow waters—but she's been neglected long past the point of no return. She's not *officially* Peter's boat, but the whereabouts of titles to boats like this are long lost mysteries. Regardless, the legal owners aren't likely to come looking for that kind of liability; the hull is as good as Peter's.

Over the years, shipworms and dry rot compromise *Jupiter's* hull; she begins to take on water. Peter beaches her off the point of the south island and continues to live aboard as before. Decomposition below the waterline is no longer a matter of concern. Flat-bottomed and hard aground, *Jupiter* sits stable and still in the roughest of weather, offering all the advantages of life at sea with few of the liabilities.

Inebriated in Coconut Grove one night, Coast Guard is questioned by a police officer. He answers truthfully. "My name is Coast Guard. I live on *Jupiter* with Peter Rabbit."

Ray Newgarden lives in Dog Patch on another castaway power-boat. He works the shrimp boats for a while, but feels compassion for the tropical fish and other creatures killed or stunned by the shrimping trawls. Tossed back into the sea, they are immediately eaten by the seagulls flocking behind the boat. Motivated by guilt and a general lack of passion for working, he gives up the job.

Up in Coconut Grove at the Taurus restaurant, the cook loses his temper.

Words are exchanged.

---

33 *Sharpie* - a type of sailboat with a flat bottom, extremely shallow draft, and straight, flaring sides.

The cook fires his gun.

A block away, Ray is hit in the head by the stray bullet. (This misfortune is worse than the time he was drunk and thirsty on the shrimp docks and chugged down a jar of battery acid, thinking it was water.) They rush him to the hospital where he survives again, as always. Nothing has managed to kill him yet. Damned near everything has tried.

During the criminal proceedings surrounding the shooting, Ray is deposed by a lawyer. It's not as if the bullet struck anyone important, and it would be a travesty to pay damages to a ne'er-do-well like Ray. "Are you having any trouble focusing or understanding since the incident?" asks the defendant's counsel.

"Yes, sir, I am," Ray answers respectfully.

The attorney sneers. "I suppose you're having trouble understanding Einstein's theories, then?"

Newgarden reaches into his jacket pocket and, by sheer happenstance, pulls out a worn paperback that explains Albert Einstein's theory of relativity.

"Yes sir," he repeats. "I'm having trouble understanding this book."

The attorney has no further questions.

Though our terrestrial neighbors think of us as a community of alcoholics and derelicts, things aren't always what they seem. Most of the hardest drinkers don't even live in the anchorage, but their constant presence on the dinghy dock is a setback for anchorage public relations. Local police arrest the drunks or tell them to drink on the dinghy dock where they won't *technically* be drinking on the City's public land. Every vagrant in Coconut Grove pretends to anchorage residency; the water is subject to federal, rather than municipal regulation. For the police, enforcement is a simple matter of pushing the problem beyond their jurisdiction.

Instead of arresting the dinghy dock bums, the cops try throwing them in the back of a squad car. They're dropped off at some distant part of town to dissuade them from repeatedly becoming an unruly nuisance. This happens to Newgarden a time or two until he relieves his bladder of a 12-pack of Old Milwaukee in the back seat.

The road-tripping stops.

The cops give up.

The drunks return to the dinghy dock.

I'm not sure how Robert Hermann came by the name "Captain Midnight." Rumor says that's his amateur radio operator's handle. Someone told me he used to work for NASA. Someone else told me he's retired from a government job and has special immunity from prosecution. Nobody even knew Midnight's real name was Hermann until the article about the other shooting came out in The Miami *Herald* the next morning.

Captain Midnight is a surly, gray old man, anchored on a small, faded, red and white powerboat with no engine. A half-dozen dogs live aboard with him. A dog will suffer his master's folly without question or complaint and will naturally defend his home. Any time a dinghy goes near Midnight's nameless hulk, the dogs bark cacophonously.

One afternoon, I row over to Dog Patch to visit Ham, a neighbor about my age who lives with his wife aboard a two-story, shallow-draft houseboat. Anchored in three feet of water, he suffers the faded colors of the local landscape to enjoy the comfort of calmer seas in the lee of the south island.

I pass by Captain Midnight's boat. His ratty sailing canoe is tied behind.

The dogs go berserk.

A scowling gray-haired head with yellow teeth appears. "Hey dummy..."

I look back but offer no response.

"If you get too close to the boat, the dogs start barking."

He hasn't the slightest notion his problem is brought on by his own choice to establish a floating kennel in a free right of way, but it's always easier to humor a fool than it is to argue with him. I continue rowing slowly, deliberately, and silently.

"Stay away from my goddamned boat!" Midnight shakes his fist and disappears.

Apparently, I got off easy. It's rumored he sometimes throws dog shit at people who get within range.

"I heard Midnight shouting at you," says Ham as I tie up to the floating deck behind his houseboat. "He's pissed off because someone poured epoxy in the carburetor of his generator."

"Any idea who?" I inquire.

"I know who did it but I'd prefer not to say." Ham smiles. "In any case, he won't be running the damned noisy thing all hours of the night."

On the way home, I take a less direct route back out to the far anchorage. I'd rather not deal with Midnight's vitriol.

One evening, Shrimper Tom is over on South Island working on his dinghy. Tom, a wiry man in his late twenties with sandy blond hair, is down on his luck. He works the shrimp boats at night but he's no dinghy dock drunk.

Captain Midnight lands on the island to walk his dogs.

Words are exchanged.

Midnight fires a gun.

Ray Newgarden hears the shot and rows ashore to investigate. He finds Tom on the island bleeding, shot in the chest with a huge exit wound in his shoulder.

Tom dies in the hospital later that night.

The next afternoon, a meeting takes place on *The Music Man*. Everyone is there. People are concerned and upset. They're angry. Some are crying. *How could this happen?*

Two police officers come aboard to talk to us but only Midnight's side of the story can be told; nobody knows what really transpired. Tom apparently has a criminal record. Maybe he threatened Midnight or one of the dogs? Maybe Midnight claimed the island as his own?

Captain Midnight is never prosecuted. He becomes more paranoid and reclusive, sailing his dogs back and forth in his disintegrating aluminum canoe and driving around Coconut Grove in a rusting green 1959 Cadillac limousine which he parks on the circle in front of Miami City Hall—a strange, sinister mechanical broom with tailfins for the anchorage's own wicked witch.

Nothing much comes of the whole affair. Shrimper Tom fades into anchorage memory. People give Midnight's boat an even wider berth when they row through Dog Patch.

Through some twist of fate, Ray Newgarden is given a small sailboat. He discovers the pleasures of navigating Biscayne Bay. He quits drinking and becomes part of the joyful fabric of the anchorage community, learning the ways of the sea, discovering a vibrant new life on the doorstep of desperation. When Ray sails—which is almost every waking moment—he makes it his mission to recover plastic bags he finds floating in Biscayne Bay; he doesn't want the bags to be consumed by sea turtles that are known to mistake them for jellyfish. On *The Music Man*, he's always present for potluck dinners and parties, engaging everyone with warmth and curiosity.

The Blue Monk

Ham and Richard Crook are interested in magnet motors, perpetual motion machines driven by magnetic fields. A perfect alternative to fossil fuels, they run quietly and cleanly. Scientists say they're impossible but Crook and Ham design and build one. They test it in the marina parking lot. It runs for almost a minute before spinning out of control and destroying itself.

This afternoon, Crook holds court on the shrimp dock. He's drunk at least a case of beer. His monologue is brilliant—a rambling summary of the history of ancient civilization. Moors and Visigoths and Saxons dance spastically on his rhetorical tightrope but somehow manage to stumble successfully across the raging rapids of the Old Milwaukee River. I resolve to buy a case of beer for Crook one day in exchange for a chance to record his lecture but regrettably never do before his liver gives out.

The sun is setting. It's time for the changing of the guard at Dinner Key. A strange assembly of shadow men row in from Dog Patch to tie their dinghies to the shrimp dock seawall and prepare nets and trawls for another night on Biscayne Bay. Engines idle. A psychedelic sheen of spilled diesel fuel spreads across the water. At the dinghy dock, the city gives up an unusual group of usual-looking people— teachers, construction workers, nurses, mechanics. They greet each other amicably as they untie their dinghies, row past the spoil islands and head out the channel to the anchorage.

Everyone in Dinner Key Anchorage has a story, though you'd never know it. To the casual observer, the floating village is just a bunch of derelict boats and bums and winos.

Some people need shorter, simpler stories.

We're fine with that.

It keeps out the riffraff.

The Blue Monk

David E. Bricker

voyage the first

The Blue Monk

A Better Place to Go

June, 1989

AFTER SEVEN YEARS OF EXPLORING Biscayne Bay and dreaming about faraway places, my time to cross the Gulf Stream to the Bahamas has come. The project boat I bought a year ago is now a comfortable pocket cruiser. College is behind me.

Boat upgrades empty my pockets but *Blue Monk* comes together smartly. I furnish John Nation with a sketch. While I work at a graphics company, he builds me a clever, compact interior trimmed with varnished, knotty pine wainscoting. The main saloon sports a mahogany chart table, a tile counter top, two drawers for clothes, plenty of storage space under the galley, and a stainless steel oven with a two-burner gas stove. Above the galley on the port side is a locker for plates and cups. Pots and pans have a space under the oven. To starboard, the original low bunk is raised up to accommodate stored food and supplies—and this makes my bed six inches wider. Above my bunk, a food hammock holds vegetables and fruit. I'm no master carpenter but I'm proud of the newly varnished teak cockpit coamings I built myself under John's tutelage. My new bronze winch pads are still shiny. *Blue Monk* is ready to go to sea.

So is John Nation. "I'm off," he declares. "I'm sick of Miami. I'm going back to the Bahamas."

"I need to stay a while longer," I explain. "I want to make a little more money and fix a few more things on the boat before I go."

John looks at me resolutely. "When it's time to go, it's time to go. All you need is a tank of fresh water, food in the lockers, and a better place to go."

Brown sails rise to the schooner's mastheads.

Zebra Dun heads east to the Abacos.

I give two months' notice at my job. My boss has been good to me and I won't walk out on her without ample warning; I offer to train my replacement. Three weeks later, Eastern Airlines, one of Miami's biggest employers, goes on strike. A huge battle rages between the union and the management. As the standoff continues, the local economy freefalls. The flow of customers into the studio dwindles.

Work becomes hell. Alan, a co-worker, is promoted to manager. His own sailboat is gathering barnacles in an overpriced slip; he doesn't like the idea of some twenty-three year old kid running off and living his dream. With no work to do for customers, he directs me to sit quietly at my desk, stare at my screen, and do nothing. I suffer his management style for ten minutes before walking out.

When it's time to go, it's time to go.

I've accumulated a collection of keys over the years—house keys, old apartment keys, car keys—I can't remember what half of them are for. I remove two or three I want to save and then, as I row out the channel toward *Blue Monk,* I stand up in the dinghy and throw the others as far as I can. The bay swallows them with a satisfying *"urp."*

My friend and anchorage neighbor Ron offers to accompany me to the Bahamas. The voyage will have to be a fast-paced one—his daughter is due to give birth any day—but Ron loves sailing; he has always encouraged me. I've known him for years but I can't say I know him well. He's older than me, but how much older is anyone's guess; there's a certain agelessness about him. He holds an advanced engineering degree, but at some point he opted for a simpler life afloat. Ron is quiet, reserved, and free from pretense. Ron is here. Ron is now. Ron is Ron. An experienced sailor, he's a good teacher. His emotional operating temperature is cool and steady, making him an ideal shipmate.

We lash *Artemisia Gentileschi* and my oars to the cabin top of *Blue Monk,* haul up the anchors, and sail off across Biscayne Bay toward Key Biscayne and the Gulf Stream flowing beyond it.

The masts of boats in Dinner Key Anchorage recede into the Coconut Grove shoreline behind us.

An orange sun kisses the land and sinks beneath it.

We pass Cape Florida lighthouse and head east into deep water. Ron goes over the chart with me, explaining how we'll be carried north thirty-five miles by the two-and-a-half knot current during our fourteen-hour trip. We aim that far south of West End, Grand Bahama Island. By sailing forty-five miles due east, we'll make a ninety mile passage northeast and arrive in the morning. "We don't want to arrive too early," Ron explains. "The other side is shallow but the water's clear. After the sun comes up, you can read the water to avoid shoals and coral heads."

The wind is light but I'm unaccustomed to the ocean swells; the motion is different from the chop I'm used to on Biscayne Bay. After a few hours, I'm seasick. Ron takes the helm for most of the crossing but doesn't complain. He only asks me to take a turn at the tiller just before dawn when he's too tired to steer a straight course any longer.

Navigating is easy from here. The tall radio tower at West End with its flashing red light rises above the waves ahead of us.

The stars fade.

The sky turns purple-gray.

The face of the Gulf Stream changes from black to gray to deepest blue.

Flying fish flee from our bow, skipping across the wave tops.

Trees appear on the horizon ahead of us.

At the edge of the Little Bahama Bank, the water changes abruptly. The ocean is deep but clear; the bottom is visible over a hundred feet below us.

Suddenly, we're in shallow water.

We're here, on the other side of the Gulf Stream.

We make our way around Indian Cay[34] and sail across the shallow Bahama Banks into West End anchorage.

I run my yellow quarantine flag up to the mast spreaders.[35]

The sketch chart in the cruising guidebook[36] shows an airstrip and a building clearly marked CUSTOMS. We dinghy ashore with our passports, tie up to a mangrove branch, and clamber through the woods in the general direction of the structure indicated on the chart. A short hike takes us to the runway. From the pavement, we find our way to the office.

The Customs man on duty is less than pleased to see a pair of soggy, sleep-deprived sailors emerge from the jungle. We're ordered tersely back to the dinghy to bring our boat into the marina. One would think the marina office—not the airport office—would be indicated on the sketch chart as the place for yachts to clear Customs, but our excursion is not a wasted trip; a few steps ashore greatly settle my stomach.

---

34 *Cay*, derived from the Spanish *'Cayo,'* is pronounced "Key." It refers to an island.

35 When arriving in foreign ports, a yellow *quarantine flag* is displayed until a vessel is cleared to enter by the port authorities. After clearance is granted, an ensign depicting the country's flag is flown.

36 *Cruising Guidebooks* - (I used *The Yachtsman's Guide to the Bahamas*) provide sketch charts along with descriptions of passages, landmarks, harbor entrances and approaches, navigational hazards, and other indispensible information. Cruising guides are updated annually to reflect changes in politics and topography.

ॐ The Blue Monk

In the marina, the Customs man stamps our passports. I purchase cruising and fishing permits and place a collect call on the payphone to alert friends and family we survived the crossing while Ron cooks eggs on the stove. I'm down to $30. He springs for a night's stay in a slip so we can rest and put the boat back together for our journey across the Bahama Banks the next morning.

We leave at first light, making our way northeast to tiny Mangrove Cay, anchoring overnight and proceeding on to Great Sale Cay in the morning. The anchorage is well-protected. The beach on the north side of the island is spectacular and deserted. No human footprints disturb the pure white sand. At night, a shimmering river of stars appears overhead.

We are two men on a tiny boat in an endless, quiet wilderness, untainted by power lines, bright lights, noisy trucks, or honking horns. If I were to injure myself or get sick, I'd have no way to call for help in this world without policemen or firefighters or ambulances. The sense of separation is disconcerting at first, but as much as I'm grateful to come from a place where such services are available, I like the "natural authenticity" of this world without guard rails and safety nets.

When you wear shoes, the whole earth is covered with leather.[37]

I settle into this new feeling.

---

37 Baba Hari Dass

I like this.

The experience is natural, primitive, authentic, *meaningful.*

How many people, I wonder, live out their entire lives without ever encountering this? At what cost do we live in a straight and level world where sharp corners are padded and survival depends on staying close to a telephone?

In the morning, we sail around the northern end of Great Sale Cay and turn the corner, heading southeast into the wind, tacking back and forth across the Sea of Abaco to call at Foxtown in the late afternoon. A small fishing village on Little Abaco Island, Foxtown is just a row of shacks painted in blues, pinks, and beiges inspired by the Caribbean landscape. After anchoring behind a line of large rocks, we dinghy to shore. A simple cinderblock church and a small grocery store stand unpretentiously by the roadside. Back in Miami, two whites walking in a black neighborhood would be in danger—or at least, they'd feel that way—but the locals wish us a cheerful "good evenin'" as we stroll through town. We buy a loaf of bread and a few other supplies, then return to *Blue Monk* to retire early.

Funny—I can't imagine living in a wooden shanty in the squalor of a Bahamian fishing village, but I'm happy as can be living in a fraction of the space on my little sloop.

We spend the next day tacking again, making slow progress to windward, passing within fifty feet of Center of the World Rock, an unspectacular piece of coral protruding from the middle of the Sea of Abaco. I don't know the story behind its name but I'm tickled to encounter the center of the world in the middle of nowhere.

The night's anchorage at Powell Cay is spectacular. Dramatic coral cliffs rise over a white sand bottom in sparkling clear water. A grove of coconut palms lends an exotic, tropical air to the beach east of the bluff, like a postcard from the South Pacific.

We're in the Abacos proper now, in the out-islands, following the chain of green beads. On the other side of the islands lies a channel of clear, shallow water dotted with coral heads, extending north to the edge of the Little Bahama Bank. Beyond these shallows, the world's third largest barrier reef breaks the surface, marking the subcontinent's steep drop-off into the deep North Atlantic.

We press on at first light, racing Ron's unborn grandson, making Green Turtle Cay by nightfall. Green Turtle is a large settlement with hotels and restaurants and shops, but it retains a provincial flavor. Whitewashed colonial-style houses rimmed with conch shells and festooned with fishing floats are the authentic article, relics from the days of the American Revolution when loyalist holdouts were granted land here by King George. The island offers a Customs office and a boatyard, groceries, and other supplies. I top off my water and fuel tanks at the marina.

How easy it is to take simple things for granted. Fresh water costs a nickel a gallon—not much—but in these islands, "sweet water" must either be collected in cisterns during the summer monsoons or extracted from seawater. Thirty gallons of fresh water in a tank under my forward bunk and another twelve stored in a cockpit locker in blue plastic jugs become a form of wealth.

In the morning, we sail gently into the rising sun.

To avoid a gigantic shoal between Whale Cay and the mainland[38] of Great Abaco, we exit the Banks, round Whale Cay on the Atlantic side and come back through the cut north of Great Guana Cay. Whale Cay is impassable in windy weather, but the breeze is light this morning. We motor through big, gentle, rolling swells. Trolling a lure behind us, we catch a small painted mackerel—lunch.

In the afternoon, we anchor at Marsh Harbour,[39] the third-largest settlement in the Bahamas and Ron's point of departure. We had a grand adventure but his new grandson is due any moment. Shortly after we anchor, he calls for a taxi on the VHF radio.

I row him to the dock.

He embraces me warmly and climbs into the cab.

I return to *Blue Monk*, tie my dinghy astern, sit in my cockpit, and look around me. I'm twenty-three years old, just about penniless, and alone in a foreign land. Where do I go? What do I do next? I've

---

38 The connected islands of Great Abaco and Little Abaco are 95 miles long. Though technically islands, they dwarf the tiny out-islands and are spoken of as "the mainland."

39 *Harbour* ~ The Bahamas was a British colony until July 10, 1973. The English spelling, "harbour," is used in this book for proper names and for *harbours* in general in the Bahamas and Europe. In American ports, the American spelling, "harbor" is used.

wanted to experience this for so long but, suddenly, I realize I have no idea what *this* really is. I've sailed hard for a week—two hundred fifty miles to windward—to get here. I'm ready to stop and rest but Marsh Harbour is not the destination I envisioned. The harbour offers facilities and a protected anchorage, but it's unremarkable— too much like where I came from, not worth a long haul.

I don't feel like doing more sailing at the moment, either...though I suppose that will change; it always does. Sailing is just that way. No matter how tired of it I may get, no matter how unpleasant the last passage may have been, the madness always returns—like a lover I somehow can't find the strength to leave—even when there are times I know I should. *She's no good for you. Why do you bring this unhappiness upon yourself?* I laugh aloud, alone on my tiny boat in this faraway place. *There are these moments, these times when it works so well.*

I switch on my radio and press the button on the microphone. "Does anyone know the whereabouts of the schooner *Zebra Dun?* Sailing vessel *Blue Monk*. Over."[40]

After some bursts of static and a few oddly accented, unrelated exchanges in Bahamian English, someone answers.

"Blue Monk, Blue Monk: John's over here at Man-O-War Cay. I don't think he keeps his radio on. Stand by. I'll go get him. Over."

---

40 *"Over"* ~ When talking on the VHF radio (the mariner's telephone) one person talks while the other listens. When you're finished speaking, you say "over" to indicate you're releasing your microphone's "talk" button and are ready to listen to the response.

"Thank you. *Blue Monk* standing by. Over."

A familiar voice pops out of the radio chatter. "Dave! You're here! You made it! Leave now and you'll get to Man-O-War before dark. I'll put dinner on. I'm an hour's sail across the Sea of Abaco. Once you get inside the harbour, turn to starboard. You'll see me down near the end of the lagoon. Over."

When it's time to go, it's time to go.

It takes only a few minutes to get anchors and sails back up. I can see what must be Man-O-War Cay as soon as I round the point.

For the first time this trip, the wind blows across my beam. *Blue Monk* heels lightly on a comfortable reach across the Sea of Abaco. *This* is sailing. The helm is balanced. The water is clear and blue. I've got a tank full of fresh water, food in the lockers, and a better place to go.

This is this.

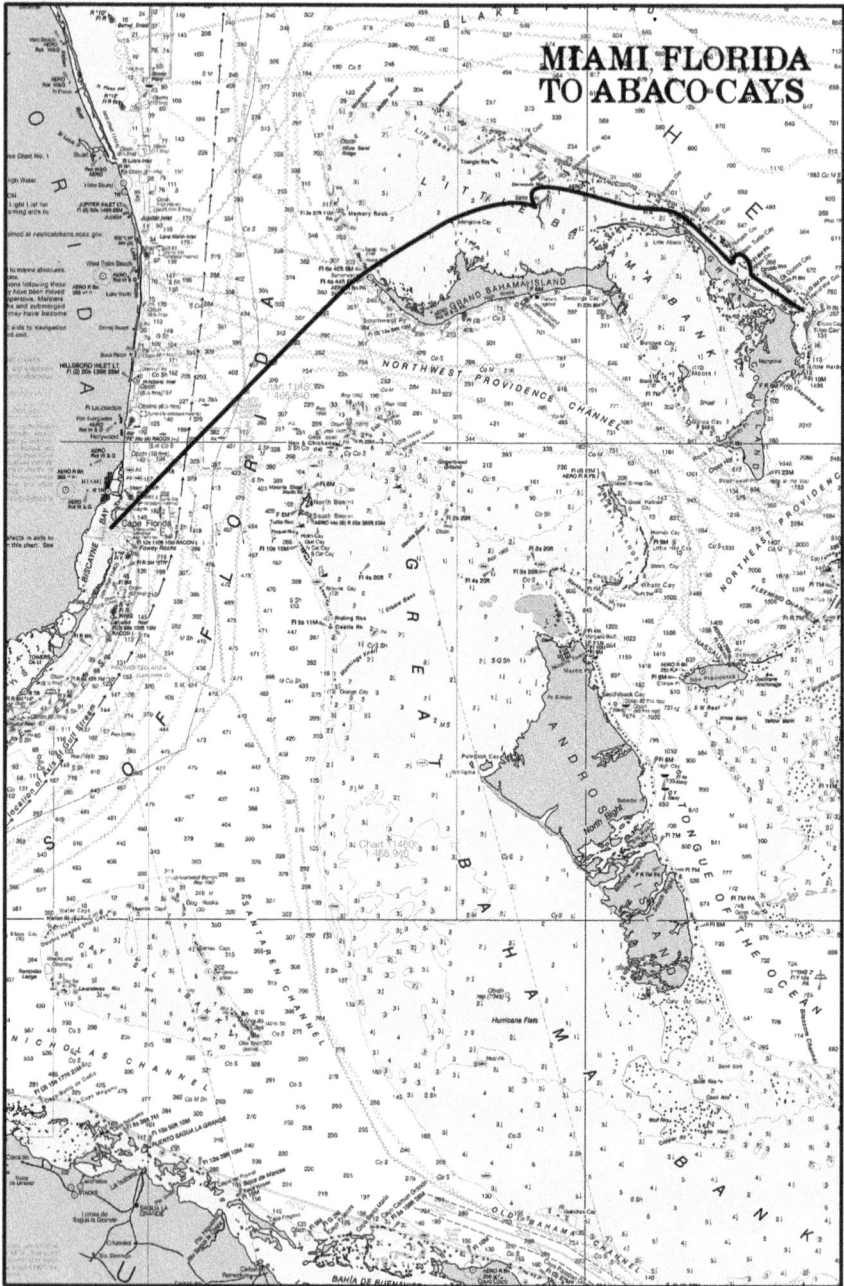

Breathing Underwater
July, 1989

DIVING EVERY DAY, I grow accustomed to holding my breath. I don't know exactly how long I can stay down but the anxious feeling of running out of air simply disappears one day. I swim along the bottom of the reef, hunting under rocks and ledges. *Haven't I been down a while?* I swim some more, looking for the telltale antennae of spiny lobster protruding from hollows in the coral. *I really should go back up and take a breath.* I'm more nervous about being this comfortable staying down this long. I swim around some more and then, because it seems like a wise idea, I ascend, take a breath and return to the bottom.

"How ya comin' along, Dave?" John's voice crackles over the radio.
"Coming up on Man-O-War, but I can't see the entrance. Over."
"Keep on sailing. You can't miss it. Over."

I round Sandy Cay and Garden Cay, two small islets guarding Man-O-War's entrance channel. Man-O-War still looks like nothing but trees and coral. "I'll take your word for it. Over."

Over millennia, the waves have deeply undercut Man-O-War's rocky shoreline. The island sings strangely as the sea slaps metallically under the coral shelf.

It's calm in the lee of the island, a good place to take my sails down. I start my engine and continue on.

I still can't see a harbour entrance.

The bow of a boat emerges from the coral and scrub jungle shoreline. It's the Man-O-War ferry bound for Marsh Harbour. Good thing I wasn't in the channel—I'd have been run down—but now I know the way.

Inside is a different world. High hills rise before me. Prim white houses poke through the hardwood trees. Wooden docks line the shore of a secret lagoon, sheltered from high winds and surf. A fleet of tidy sailboats sleeps on moorings.

Just inside the entrance lies *Journeyman*, a classic double-ender.[41] Looking like the featured exhibit in a wooden boat museum, her hull is a symphony of varnish. A traditional, lapstraked[42] dinghy sits capsized on her cabin top under a sun awning. She's the most beautiful boat I've ever seen. *Now here's a boat I'd love to sail!*

---

41 *Double-ended* - A double-ended vessel has a pointed bow and also a pointed stern.

42 *Lapstraked* planks (a *strake* is a board) are arranged like shingles where the bottom of one plank overlaps the top of the plank below it.

Motoring east through the moored boats, I leave the shoal inside the entrance to starboard. There are no Dinner Key derelicts here. All these boats are solid enough to have made it across the Gulf Stream and on across the Bahama Banks against the trade winds. Today, I join them.

The unmistakable white-tipped masts of *Zebra Dun* appear. John stands shirtless on deck wearing zebra-striped sweat pants, hanging on to the shrouds. "Grab yourself that empty spot right over there," he calls, pointing to a place with some swinging room a hundred feet from his schooner.

I set my first anchor from the foredeck, fall back downwind and row a second hook out in the dinghy. After adjusting the rodes to position *Blue Monk* at a comfortable proximity to her new neighbors, I paddle over to the schooner.

True to his word, John has dinner simmering on the stove. Kipling, the ship's cat, comes out of hiding to rub her head against my hand. John smiles, then fixes me with his gaze, suggesting the importance of what he is about to impart. "You have arrived at a very special time in a very special place. I can't explain it but there's some sort of energy vortex here. Be careful what you ask for; you really *will* get it. This is a magic place." He doesn't elaborate further. "You'll see for yourself soon enough," he says after a reflective pause. "Here's your plate. Welcome to the Vortex."

After years of dreaming, months of preparation, a queasy passage across the Gulf Stream, and a hard week of sailing to windward, I'm here—*somewhere.* I have time on my hands—lots of time. I practice guitar. I read a book every day. Coral heads lie just off the beach on the other side of the island. A short hike through the hardwood hammock[43] takes me to where I can swim out to them to hunt for fish and lobster. Sometimes, friends with motor dinghies offer a ride to the big barrier reef a mile offshore to stalk hogfish and grouper and lobster among the corals.

I dive on the wreck of the *Adirondack,* a Civil War ship sunk on the reef in 1862. Old boilers, engine parts, and cannon lie strewn among the corals. A shimmering paisley peacock flounder undulates over a brain coral. Thousands of tiny, silvery fish flash in the sun, moving in unison as if controlled by a single will.

In the cut between the west side of Man-O-War Cay and the Fowl Cays, I don my dive mask, lean over and poke my head under-water. Conch[44] amble slowly across the shallow bottom. They're small but hopefully big enough to make dinner of. By the time I kick my way to the sea floor, I'm completely out of breath. The water is at least fifty feet deep, but so clear I would never have guessed. The conch aren't small—they're *huge.* Many who have been here longer than me can make this dive easily, but I'm barely able. With one of the head-sized, weed-covered shells in each hand, I kick off

---

43 *Hammock* - a hardwood hammock is a tropical forest, not something you sleep in

44 *Conch* - (pronounced *konk*) are large sea snails with attractive spiral shells. Conch meat is a staple of the Bahamian diet and one of the country's major exports.

the bottom, struggling to the surface, barely mastering my body's overpowering urge to inhale.

Hunting for my supper is new to me. I don't like killing things, even fish, but I learn to do it with conviction. It's worse to wound a fish and have it swim away to die slowly. I wait for a clean shot, pull back as far as I can on the rubber tubing that launches the pole spear through my hands, and aim carefully. Once I skewer enough food for dinner, I often linger on the reef to enjoy the scenery, but the hunt is over; I'm a guest here. Fish and other sea creatures brought home to the galley are always thanked and apologized to. I've never been fond of superstition or ritual but there are predators in the ocean who would just as happily have *me* for dinner. I feel spontaneously grateful every time I am privileged to be the eater, and not the eatee.

Pizza with lobster on it emerges from John's oven.

I cook lobster omelets for breakfast.

I confess to John I'm growing tired of the stuff. He feels the same way but we can only laugh at ourselves—two penniless boat bums growing weary of the food of the rich.

"Be careful what you wish for," John repeats with a laugh.

I usually take to my bunk not long after sundown. I rise at first light, in sync with the rhythm of the earth. Tonight, before retiring, I put a piece of fish on a hook and drop it in the water beside *Blue Monk*, wrapping the fishing line around the starboard cockpit winch. In the middle of the night, the clicking of the winch pall awakens me. A mutton snapper fights at the end my line—a big one—more than John and I could ever eat before it would spoil in our unrefrigerated galleys, but wasting a bounty like this would be an unacceptable affront. In the morning, I clean the snapper and then row around Man-O-War anchorage distributing baggies of fresh fish to my neighbors.

In the afternoons, I row into town to the tiny Man-O-War post office to ask pretty young Charmaine Albury if there's any mail for me. When I'm not inclined to row, I tie my dinghy at the Lee's private dock—they don't mind me landing there—to hike the Queen's Highway through the hardwood hammock up the spine of the island into the settlement. Near the far end of the southeastern harbour where we're anchored, the Queen's Highway is nothing more than a simple, unpaved footpath through the jungle. Terrestrial scents of gumelemi, seagrape, and poisonwood trees blend with sea smells as the breeze filters through the tropical woods. Ambient, crashing surf on the rocks beyond the trees accompanies the rhythm of my feet. I carry my shoes until my feet grow uncomfortable; they aren't tough enough yet to handle the entire journey.

A paved road joins the coral path at the edge of town. Tidy pastel houses of wood or cinderblock sit in yards lined with conch shells. Some are festooned with fishing floats. A row of whale vertebrae lines a front fence. The hardware store sits near the boatyard where the Albury family still builds boats by hand, the way they have for generations. A few small grocery stores stand among Man-O-War's colonial houses, churches, marinas, and the schoolhouse. Down a short side street, overlooking the ocean, stands the world's most exquisite baseball field. In view of third base, past a strip of sandy beach, the surf explodes into spray against the rocks. I rest on a log bench here at the edge of the field before turning back. To the north, the Atlantic is turquoise, dappled with coral heads and cloud shadows out to a white strip where breakers collide with the reef. Beyond the breakers, the bottom drops off into a band of deep blue beneath the horizon.

The beach is deserted. Today I'll walk back along the shoreline and cut back to the Queen's highway through the woods farther down.

I'm offered a small varnishing job—strictly under the table—foreigners aren't allowed to work here—but it puts a hundred dollars in my pocket. That should cover fresh vegetables and laundry expenses for another six weeks.

In spite of living on so little, I have never lived so well, but a lingering restlessness follows me. Old habits of arranging my day to confront a list of obligations don't fade easily. My life has been work, work, work, schedule, schedule, schedule. Now, I can do anything I want, any time I want—in spite of the nagging feeling I'm neglecting something. I'm used to laboring all week for a paycheck that barely keeps up with expenses. Here, three days of work carries me for months.

Is it *acceptable* to live like this?

Can life be *this* easy?

"The human being," declares John Nation, "is the only animal on planet earth not in captivity that doesn't do exactly what it wants to do."

I have some money in my pocket. John's earned some, too. I suggest a change of pace, a run to Marsh Harbour to restock our pantries at a big grocery store. It's time for a supply run and maybe even a splurge at a local restaurant. Late Saturday afternoon, we hoist sails and haul anchors. Our two boats reach together across the Sea of Abaco into the falling sun.

Sunday morning is filled with island sounds.

A rooster crows.

Somewhere in town, a big diesel generator sputters and begins to drone.

A few dinghies and some larger speedboats zoom about the harbour.

A big ketch arrives and drops anchor.

Two other cruising yachts leave with a rattle of anchor chains.

A short walk up the hill, across the main road, past the telephone company and the liquor store takes us to the Saint Frances de Sales Catholic Mission, a small concrete building next to which a tent has been erected over a cement foundation—a temporary substitute for the wooden sanctuary that burned the year before.

Beneath the canopy, Marsh Harbour's Haitian community gathers for Sunday mass.

"Don't worry," John encourages. "I'm not a Catholic either, but you don't want to miss this. Catholics don't really care if you're Catholic or not; that's one of the things I like about 'em."

The morning is hot, still, and humid. Mosquitoes stalk unprotected ankles above the wet grass. People sweat, wipe dripping foreheads, fan themselves, and shuffle on their feet. These humble refugees have come in their finest clothing to offer gratitude for deliverance into a land of new hope. No strangers to the tropical heat, the spirited worshipers refuse to acknowledge it. Higher priorities are in play. The air is festive.

An electric guitar squawks through a tinny amplifier as its player makes a futile attempt to tune it. Random beats sound on a drum. The priest steps up to the lectern at the front of the tent. The chatter of the crowd quickly dies away.

After a few words in Creole, the guitar and drums begin. The congregation rises to sing *Papa Nou* (Our Father). We are among the few light-skinned attendees, but we are welcomed. We join hands with the worshipers in the back of the open-sided tent and sing along as best we can.

After the crowd disperses, John introduces me to a thin, fiftyish woman. "Meet Sister Eleanor, an old friend from my last Abaco trip. She's in charge of the mission school."

Sister Eleanor is nothing like what I expect a nun to be. After working with inner city kids in New York, she's tough but also kind and humorous and witty. We're welcomed and invited to have lunch with the current crop of recent college graduates who have volunteered to teach at the mission school. They seek experience to enhance their résumés—to help them find jobs when they return to their faraway homes on the other side of the Gulf Stream.

I raise an eyebrow at John and question him telepathically. *You mean this place even comes with a house full of twenty-two-year old girls?*

My friend nods discreetly and smiles.

Gathering around a wooden table before a plate full of peanut butter sandwiches and a pitcher of 'bug juice,' we link our little fingers together and close our eyes.

"Terry, you say grace," says Sister Eleanor.

"Rub-a-dub-dub. Thanks for the grub," chants Terry. After a brief pause, she opens her eyes and continues, "Amen. Everybody dig in."

Man-O-War is only an hour's sail away.

I'm in no rush to sail back.

John strings a hammock between his two masts under a large canvas awning.

The breeze fills in.

"Do you mind if I...?"

"Not at all," says John. "I want to do some writing. Crawl in there and take a nap. Enjoy yourself."

I recall nothing of the next three days. I remain ensconced in a cotton chrysalis, suspended between two spruce masts. If I ate, used the toilet, or got out of the hammock even once during that time, I have no recollection of it.

The restlessness disappears.

Is it *acceptable* to live any way else?

I am happy here.

Now.

"I'm ready to sail back over to Man-O-War," I announce to John.

I want to hike barefoot down the Queen's Highway.

The soles of my feet are tough as leather.

I want to dive for conch in Man-O-War cut.

I can stay down forever.

The Blue Monk

Wave of Beauty

August, 1989

MAN IS NATURALLY INCLINED to prefer his environment straight and level. At sea, the sailor cooks on a gimbaled stove and may even eat from a gimbaled table, hinged at the top and weighted at the bottom so its surface swings perpendicular to Earth's gravitational pull. His vessel is similarly endowed with a heavy keel, relying like the mariner himself on the captivating influence of *terra firma* to compensate for the most violent efforts of the ocean to turn him over.

Water is but a layer of atmosphere that covers the earth. A sailboat is but a vehicle conceived to fly over and through that medium. It relies on earth's attraction for steady flight as much as it relies on water's buoyancy for altitude. A boat is designed to remain waterborne, often floating thousands of feet above the land that invisibly steadies it. It has no landing gear; a ship cannot stand upright if taken from the sea. Like the pelican, so graceful in the sky who hobbles like a drunken clown ashore, or a streamlined fish who flops about when laid on the dock, a sailboat deprived of its watery support can only heel gracelessly, awaiting the return of the tide.

⑤ The Blue Monk

On a trip across the Sea of Abaco, in the company of the *Zebra Dun* and an assemblage of sunburned teachers from the Abaco Mission, *Blue Monk* bounces twice on the bottom and staggers to a stop. John Nation, seeing my predicament from the cockpit of his schooner, adjusts his course to starboard of the shoal. After anchoring a few hundred yards away, he arrives in his rowing dory to deliver the passengers from my stranded vessel to the dock at Marsh Harbour.

Relieved of their weight, *Blue Monk* floats an inch or two higher. The tide, being not quite at full flood, rises ever so slightly. My keel bounces on the sand, imparting a hopeful suggestion that I might be released from Neptune's grip. With the engine straining, I move my vessel a yard or two, but only to an even shallower spot. This is full moon high tide—one of the worst times to run aground.[45]

John returns in his dory. "You're welcome to bunk on my boat tonight. Things are going to become rather off-level for *Blue Monk* out here on the shoal when the tide goes out. I'll help you try to get her off in the morning."

"Thanks, but I'll stay here." I shrug with resignation. "I'm not worried much about anyone bothering with the boat, but what if she's got a leak I don't know about at the deck-hull joint? Or what if we get a wind that drives waves into the cockpit? I want to be

---

45 Full moon and new moon high tides bring the highest and lowest tidal depths in the 28-day cycle. Get stuck on a full moon high tide and you may have to wait weeks for another tide sufficiently high to get free.

here with one hand on the caulking gun and the other on the bilge pump handle."

Standing beside me in his dory, John looks down at his large feet tucked into home-made leather sandals soled with pieces of old tire tread. He knows my plan is a prudent one. "Come on over to the *Zebra Dun* in the morning, early. I'll make us up a batch of corn cakes and coffee. High tide is about seven thirty; she's not moving anywhere before then. After breakfast, we'll row over and see what we can do."

Before long, the ebbing tide stops bouncing my keel against the bottom. *Blue Monk* begins to heel over. I prepare a quick meal and secure anything in the cabin likely to fly, fall, or flop when inevitable horizontality comes. Locker doors are dogged shut. With a piece of sail twine, I lace closed a food hammock full of vegetables hanging from the overhead. On deck, I lash my anchors to the bow pulpit so they can't slide off. I check and tighten the clamps securing the outboard motor to its adjustable mount.

A bold orange sun falls behind the pine forests of Great Abaco, slipping below the western horizon in advance of a full moon that holds its breath, waiting to begin its own ascent into the Bahamian sky. The day's startling sonata of effervescent blues, greens, and beiges fades into a quiet nocturne of silvers and blacks, bleached of color by starlight from the Milky Way. Green traces of phosphorescence dance beneath the water's surface—luminescent messages exchanged by microscopic sea creatures transparent and mysterious.

I lay my bunk cushion between the cabin sole and the edge of the settee, hoping to set up a marginally satisfactory bed, but find myself wedged uncomfortably in the fold. I return to the cockpit to lose myself in the stars, but no arrangement of cushions softens the effects of my vessel's awkward floundering motion.

When the tide is at its lowest ebb, the motion stops. *Blue Monk* lies at a severe angle. Wavelets come over the cap rail to lap at the ports on the starboard side. I find little comfort in a world so far off-kilter—but at least my windows don't leak.

The moon rises, calling to the water. The sea, gravity's captive, begins to slowly flood. From leagues away, waves and salt-laden currents pour over reefs, between islands, across glistening sand banks—a wind of water flows stealthily yet steadily from all directions, creeping up docks and beaches, filling tidal pools on rocky shores, blanketing grassy shoals laid bare to the moonlight.

Faraway lovers, poets, dreamers, criminals, and werewolves, composed mostly of water themselves, succumb to the influence of the full moon. Eggs escape fallopian tubes. Embryos kick, swimming toward the unseen light. Sea turtle hatchlings claw their way from sandy nests to join a flood of water summoned by a hypnotic silver orb. *Blue Monk* struggles to regain her footing as Luna wanders across the heavens, washing the stars from the celestial dome and illuminating the shoal bright as a summer day. I stare into a brilliant sea, calm and transparent as rippled glass; the water, invisible; stalks of brown seagrass undulating gently over white sand; a submarine desert of crystal and magic. As the moon rights my craft, I rearrange the bunk cushions once again and drift into fitful sleep.

A few moments—or perhaps a few hours later—a bump of the keel on the bottom awakens me. It's too early to attempt escape but a purple glow to the east behind the silhouette of Elbow Cay heralds dawn's arrival.

I stretch my arms, step aft to untie my dinghy, pull it alongside and climb in, then grab the oars and let go of *Blue Monk*. Adrift, I yawn, rub my eyes, place bronze oarlocks in bronze sockets and sight *Zebra Dun* floating serenely beneath a sky of faintest lavender and black. Her dark bulwarks and white topsides still reflect the fading moonlight as dawn blooms behind the ragged outline of trees on Great Abaco's shore. I row quietly and slowly so as not to offend the morning, watching my grounded vessel recede into the aqueous landscape, relying on my 'rower's sense' to guide me blindly but unerringly toward the anchored schooner. The sky continues to purple, leaving only Venus to accompany the lingering moon.

John hears the slosh of water between my dinghy and his mahogany hull. He slides open the aft hatch and pokes his head into the new day. "Howdja sleep?" He smiles comically.

"Sleep?"

"That's what I figured." He rests his elbows on the rim of the hatch. "How about some coffee and breakfast? Let's get fueled up and then go see if we can't get you floating again."

I smile and nod blearily.

John emerges from his cabin through the hatch beside the main mast, steps across the mahogany-planked bridge deck, slides open the forward hatch, and steps forward to the galley in the bow of the schooner. Smells of coffee, eggs, and simmering flour mingle with sparkling rays of sun filtering through the portlights[46] into the low cabin.

After the meal, John follows me up to the deck. We climb into his dory, then row over a field of sand now well-saturated with the radiant azure color of Bahamian daylight.

Blue Monk floats almost upright. John steps aboard. "Do you have a pole of some kind—something we can stick into the bottom to use as a tide gauge? Slack tide lasts for about half an hour. A marked stick will help us tell when the sea's stopped rising."

I untie a red fishing spear from my cabin top. "This ought to be long enough—five-and-a-half feet. The boat only draws four-eight." I climb back into the dinghy, reach down, and poke the sharp end of the spear into the sand below, leaving the top of the shaft protruding from the sea.

---

46 *Portlights* - In some cases, a vessel's ports may be too small to allow practical viewing of the outside environment—some provide a rather uninspiring view of the inside of the rail—but such ports do admit light into the cabin and are therefore referred to as *portlights*.

"Let's set a hook over there," John suggests, gesturing off toward deeper water. "Bring the dinghy up forward. I'll lower an anchor to you so you can row it out. We'll snug the line up tight and try to get the bow to spin around as the water comes up."

I accept the anchor and a pile of chain that rattles against the floor of the dinghy. Rowing out toward deeper water, I haul the rode behind me as John pulls it through the hawsepipe[47] from the locker beneath the foredeck. He cleats off the bitter end[48] when the line runs out. "That's all the line," he calls. I reduce the pressure applied by my foot against the length of chain, rowing hard to help it pay out straight but metering the friction to keep the heavy links from flying too fast over the gunwale[49] and onto the shallow sea bottom in a tangled heap. Where the chain meets the anchor, I put my foot down tight, pull hard at the oars to straighten the rode, and then quickly flip the anchor into the water. "She's in," I call back to John who has already begun setting the flukes into the bottom, hauling in slack, and applying pressure to the bow.

I rinse black anchor chain rust from my hands, row back, tie off

---

47 *Hawsepipe* - Thick line used to moor or dock a ship is *hawser*. A pipe conducts line and chain from its storage locker through the deck to the bow. This was probably referred to originally as a "hawser pipe," before being shortened to "hawsepipe" and adapted to general usage on vessels of all sizes (for rodes of all sizes).

48 *Bitter end* - the end of a rope that is tied off. Inspiring the expression, "hanging on to the bitter end," the bitter end was originally that end of a line fastened to the "bitts" (cleats or bollards) on a dock.

49 *Gunwale* - pronounced *gunn'l*; the top edge of the side of a small boat

the dinghy, and return to the cockpit of *Blue Monk*. "Tide's almost up," says John. "Try your motor, too; every little bit helps."

I squeeze the bulb in the fuel line to prime the engine and pull the starter cord two or three times. The outboard roars to life, revving high and belching blue smoke before settling down to a quieter idle. Engaging the throttle, I push the engine's tiller-handle off to the side, hoping to spin the bow toward the anchor. "Let's both get up on the foredeck," I suggest. "The aft end of the keel is the deepest part; we might lose an inch or so of draft if our weight is all the way forward."

On the bow, I haul in more slack, tensioning the anchor line again. On the next bounce, *Blue Monk* spins a few inches closer to freedom.

I haul in more line.

"She's definitely moving," John assures me. "Tie a float to the anchor. As soon as she's free, I'll toss the line overboard. You jump in the dinghy, pick, it up and meet me back over at the *Zebra Dun*. I've been watching the spear. We're either getting off now or you'll have to find someone with a big motor to drag you off at high tide tonight. It's gonna be close."

"Let's get the sails up and sheet them in tight," I suggest, grabbing a winch handle from its holster at the base of the mast. "Whether we get free or not is a tossup at this point, but I'm not likely to get more stuck than I already am." I clip a halyard to the mainsail's head and winch up the sail. *Blue Monk* heels a few more degrees, bounces and spins some more. I adjust the anchor line again, then attach the jib to the forestay, gesturing to John to haul the canvas aloft. He walks to the mast and pulls the halyard, then walks aft to winch the sheet in tight from the cockpit. The boat heels even more.

Blue Monk bounces...

Spins slightly...

Bounces again.

"We're sailing!" calls John. I toss the buoyed end of the anchor line overboard and jump hastily into the dinghy. I coil the line neatly, piling the anchor on top of the chain on top of the rope between my feet on the dinghy's floor. Extracting the spear from the sand by the rubber loop attached to its red fiberglass shaft, I place it forward of the seat.

The morning blossoms—an exploding opium poppy. I look up to see my little sloop sailing across an expanse of sparkling turquoise accompanied by a blast of radiant green forest under a sky supersaturated with pastel blue, highlighted by the carbonated glow of shimmering, submerged sand. She's graceful, flying like a joyful flamenco dancer with her skirts cascading about her, the contours of her hull singing with the curves of her canvas. *Blue Monk* has been my home and sturdy traveling companion for two years. Today, she's more than that; she's a living creature, beautiful and proud. I watch her sail off to deeper water with John at the helm.

I take a breath and for the second time this morning, aim my bow toward the *Zebra Dun*.

In spite of my sleeplessness, I am charged with strength and vitality. The warmth of the sun surges through me. The clear water and white sand below me are exquisite! I grab my oars and pull the dory vigorously across the shoal, sprinting over the waves, reeling in the vivid blues of the sky, the greens of the shore, the whites and beiges of the sea bottom. The world comes alive with a vibrancy and intensity I have never before experienced.

What is this?

I wonder if I'm not overreacting to the sight of seeing my boat under sail, but the experience is clearly more than that. Groundings in these shallow waters are commonplace and inevitable. I'm not one to get excited about something as mundane as getting unstuck.

I draw closer to where John has hove *Blue Monk* to,[50] waiting in deeper water to hand her over so we can finish our journey to the anchorage at Marsh Harbour on the other side of the point.

"John, I just had the most unbelievable…"

"Yes, I know; a sudden wave of beauty. I felt it, too."

We look at one other with acknowledgement but not surprise. Whatever this is, it's much bigger than we are.

John rows back to where *Zebra Dun* waits at anchor.

---

50 *Heaving to* ~ a method of balancing the sails to "park" a sailboat. The boat will drift slowly and comfortably, even in heavy weather.

I take the helm and adjust my lines.

The wind catches my canvas.

Blue Monk heels gently and leaps forward.

The Blue Monk

Jungle Signs

October, 1989

O N A COOL MORNING in Marsh Harbour, I row over to join John Nation for a pancake breakfast on the deck of his schooner. "Carl Jung," he explains, "said certain symbols in dreams are archetypal; they always mean the same thing to all people. Water, interestingly enough, is an archetype for consciousness."

I consider this information. "If that's true, it helps explain the joy we experience here and the revelations we're having." I give his raised eyebrow a moment to settle. "If water is consciousness and archetypes are universal, we can assume our subconscious minds react to the various symbols around us, especially water. We live in and on the water every day. We derive our food from water. Water surrounds us when we sleep. We travel great distances across it. We see water when it is angry and dashing itself against the rocks, and when it is clear and calm. The clarity of the water here—just being able to see the bottom—must have an effect on the psyche. Is it far-fetched to assume that while we live this way on the waking plane, our spirits might be growing in consciousness, nourished by this powerful symbol dominating our external lives? As we embrace our experiences, could some Newtonian opposite inner reaction also be happening? Are we experiencing inwardly as we live outwardly?"

John twists his chin, test-fitting my concept into his worldview while brushing the pancake crumbs from his chest.

"Can we also assume there might be other places where people get by well enough on a conscious level," I continue, "but where the symbolic content of the environment is oppressive to the spirit? Are the symbolic signals jammed in some places? These islands have no bright lights or radio stations or microwave towers filling the air with static. There are no neon signs or highways filled with a million bumper stickers and license plates and obnoxious advertisements your mind must filter out to keep you from going mad with information overload. Here, you can drop your blinders, open your eyes, and bare your soul. You can drink in the world around you and get drunk every day on your surroundings. The Bahamas inspire an unchaining of the spirit, an unfurling of the sails of the psyche.

"Water is consciousness. We are living in it."

John closes his eyes, allowing the yellow light of the morning and the slight chill of the early October air to soak in. He takes a deep breath and smiles. "I also pay attention to smaller, more personal symbols," he says, observing a dragonfly alight on the rail to sun its iridescent wings. Kipling, the ship's cat, glares at it predatorily.

"Dragonflies are always lucky for me. I have a few other personal totems; I call them 'jungle signs.' Open your mind to the irrational. You'll find certain things are significant for no particular reason. Let them speak to you; you may hear some meaningful messages.

"Primitive cultures believe certain animals and things embody spirits. You may be more comfortable believing your subconscious speaks to you through whatever you project onto these symbols, but either way, they're worth paying attention to. The whole concept of *meaning* has little place in a strictly rational world...but who wants to live in a strictly rational world?"

I smile at John's obvious pride over his citizenship in the irrational realm before contributing my view of things. "Before I came to these islands, I would have described myself as a rational pragmatist, but I've encountered so much meaningful coincidence and magic; my perspectives have expanded. The human spirit is like a bottle of champagne. A lot of gas is dissolved in the liquid. The bubbles are invisible but when we pop the cap and release the pressure, the gas comes out of solution. These are the symbols and jungle signs we're talking about. Even when they're dissolved in the waters of the subconscious, the bubbles add a certain zing; they add a pleasing burn to the taste and tickle the inside of your nose. Keep the cork in; the gas is contained but you can't drink the champagne. No bubbles mean either a corked bottle or wine that's been allowed to go flat before it can be drunk."

John chuckles and raises his cup. "This morning, my coffee will have to suffice, but I like your analogy."

We put feelers out for odd jobs to keep us in rice, beans, flour, and fresh vegetables. Late in the afternoon, a small powerboat approaches bearing a lightly built, officious Chinese woman. "I'm Connie. I hear you two are looking for work?"

As she holds on to the cap rail of the schooner, a two-foot shark circles her boat at the water's surface. We point but Connie finds nothing remarkable about her mascot. "Just a little shark," she shrugs. Connie goes on to tell us about a house that needs varnishing, carpentry, and electrical work on Foote's Cay, a private island. We agree on terms and she speeds off.

"How about that shark?"

"Definitely a jungle sign," says John confidently.

We finish dinner early. I row home to sleep.

The morning is calm and still. We're both broke. I'm out of fuel on *Blue Monk*. I catch a towrope from John and cleat it to my foredeck. Together, we cut a slow ripple across the smoked glass of the sleeping sea, motoring toward a small island that looks from a distance much like an old battleship; tall clumps of casuarina trees appear as smokestacks extending from a hull of distant coral.

We swing around between Foote's Cay and the large, neighboring island of Great Guana Cay, where we anchor in clear water a hundred feet from a rickety wooden dock.

The island becomes our home for the next few weeks. Connie is here to supervise the project, but as soon as she sees we need no prodding to work productively, she tells us what needs to be done and leaves us to it.

When not working, we dive in the coral garden on the far side of the island or stalk snapper among the rocks adjacent to the anchorage. The island offers an orchard of fruit trees. Some of the Haitian workers grow okra and other vegetables that they generously share.

We eat well.

We work hard.

Two coats of varnish dry.

We install ceiling fans and wire them up, making indoor work more pleasant.

John and I look for things to fix or paint or upgrade, hoping to find productive ways to extend our time in this small, profitable paradise.

The afternoon sky fills with white streaks and trails. John gazes at the clouds contemplatively, but says nothing.

The next morning, I awaken after sunrise. Above me, the sky is blue and clear but past the northwest end of Great Guana Cay, out through Whale Cay Cut over the deep North Atlantic, a dark gray cloud advances like a curtain, consuming the Bahamian sky. I shout to John on *Zebra Dun*. His hatch slides back and in response to my gesture, he turns to face the ocean. "Get ready, buckaroo," he calls back. "We're going to have ourselves a gale."

The cloud boils in from the ocean; the leading edge collapses downward—a black waterfall in the sky. "That cloud is a big mass of cold air from the Arctic," explains John over a hastily prepared breakfast. He's compulsively pedantic, even in times of crisis. "The dramatic leading edge is where the cold northern air is diving under the warm tropical air. Imagine putting a glass of ice water out in the sun on a tropical day. The glass..."

"The glass sweats."

"Exactly—and that very large, very cold glass is now on its side, about to roll over us."

I wolf down my eggs and row back to *Blue Monk*. A few minutes later, the first cold gust from the northwest clutches our two sailboats and jerks them back against their anchor lines. "Let's get some extra hooks set before the wind starts honking," I shout across the water.

The shore behind our anchorage is composed of what Bahamians call "moonrock." Many thousands of years ago, these islands were coral reefs. The remnants of this submarine history have been eroded and contorted by waves, time, and wind into rocky teeth that can easily penetrate the hull of any boat that blows ashore. Between our own two boats and this inhospitable coast, Connie's wooden sharpie tugs impatiently at its mooring.

I let out more line to increase the holding power of those anchors already in the water, then carry a third anchor and its tail of chain out in the dinghy for additional security against the blow. John makes similar arrangements aboard the schooner.

Ocean swells driven by the storm begin to roll in through Whale Cay Cut.

The weather grows angry and turbulent.

The temperature falls.

Our boats bounce and pitch.

The dark sky wall passes overhead and continues southward, leaving a gray blanket behind. Our clear sand-bottomed anchorage transforms into a field of frothing milk. Spray flies over and around our boats. John shouts something to me but the north wind carries his words across the Sea of Abaco.

I sit alone in my cabin—it's rather like sitting inside a working cement mixer—for several hours until I notice my outboard motor sitting askew on its bracket. I run to the cockpit to straighten it. A large swell passes beneath my boat, lifting the bow and then almost submerging the stern of my boat. The engine is torn from its mount and left hanging in the water by its safety line.

The engine cover latch somehow releases when the engine falls; the wind seizes it. I grab for the cover just as another swell arrives to tip me overboard into the water. Sputtering, I toss the engine cover into the cockpit and, shivering, climb back on board. Suspended from its rope, the engine bangs violently against my hull until I am able to haul it from the water.

By late afternoon I've had enough bouncing. I'm salty and hungry and not in good spirits. I whistle loudly to John and with hand gestures, indicate my intent to dinghy ashore, implying he should keep an eye on my progress in case anything happens—not that I know what he might do for me if anything does.

John is not one to abandon ship either, but all our anchors are in the water and set; little else can be done out here. He follows my example, timing the swells to step precariously from his pitching deck into his lunging dinghy.

Moments later, we're safe on the dock, watching our trusty steeds bucking in the pasture.

Walking down the conch-shell-lined path, we enter a different world. Aboard our boats, the wind and water are hissing and spitting and howling. Ashore on Foote's Cay in the shelter of the casaurina pines, we encounter nothing more than a pleasant, breezy day. We continue walking toward the house, grateful to have our feet on *terra firma*.

I pause and look seriously in John's eyes to capture his attention. "Wait here for a second," I tell him. "Don't go *anywhere*. I'll be right back." I sprint for the house, unable to suppress a laugh. He pauses for a second, confused, and then realizes he's been played. "Damn you!" he shouts, "If you use up all the hot water, I'll kick your ass!"

Through the night, the wind continues to shriek.

Dark clouds billow across the moon.

Not a star is seen.

Inside, all is comfortable and quiet except for the clattering of palm fronds against the shutters, but I sleep uneasily. Periodically I awaken, put on my sea jacket, and climb the stairs to the widow's walk atop the house, a lookout platform so named for sailor's wives who would, in days gone by, ascend to their roofs to scan the horizon for sails that often never reappeared. From this windy post, I shine a spotlight over the treetops into the anchorage.

The anchors hold. *Blue Monk* hobbyhorses violently, tugging at her lines. The schooner pitches and hops like a firewalker who has lost the faith, but both vessels stand their ground.

Morning arrives tentatively. The wind clocks around to the north and then to the northeast where Guana Cay offers us a better-protected lee.

Connie's sharpie is not so lucky. Her modest plywood vessel broke loose and blew ashore on the moonrock during the night. She's salvageable but her hull is breached. John and I help carry Connie's wet belongings up to the house. We wedge plywood between her boat bottom and the rocks to prevent further damage. Still, the sad task of wringing the ocean from your soggy life is a personal and largely private affair. There's little we can do apart from offering sympathy and help with repairs when the storm is passed, but Connie is stoic; she knows this lifestyle comes with hazards. She accepts the consequences along with the joys.

"Remember the little shark in Marsh Harbour?" I ask John.

"I thought of that, too. Do you think...?"

"Best not to draw firm conclusions. Maybe the shark was a sign? Maybe the shark was just a little shark? Maybe it was neither or both? Having answers distracts us from the joy of pondering life's good questions."

John laughs. "I agree but I'm glad it was a tiny nurse shark and not a twenty-two-hundred-pound Great White!"

The next day, the wind finally abates. We go about the business of patching and refloating Connie's sharpie, and of getting the salt water out of my engine while we enjoy the reemergence of the sun.

The arrival of the winter gales marks a change of season.

Our time here is over.

Southern latitudes beckon.

Connie settles her accounts with us. By our humble standards, we earned quite a bit of money. Living as we do, a few hundred dollars easily lasts a month or more, and each of us now has a personal treasury approaching four figures.

Zebra Dun takes the bridle of the *Blue Monk* in her teeth and tows her back to Marsh Harbour. We refill food lockers, purchase new spears, and even splurge on a cracked conch dinner at the Tiki Hut. I top off my fuel tanks. We visit our teacher friends at the Marsh Harbour Mission and bid them farewell.

It's time for *Zebra Dun* and *Blue Monk* to part company. John's friend Veronique flies in from Dinner Key to voyage with him to places south. He raises his big gaff sails and leaves Marsh Harbour with a wave. I remain behind to await the arrival of my cousin Dan who will accompany me on my own journey to the Exumas.

Until he arrives, I'm alone on my tiny boat in this world of literal beauty and unconscious metaphor.

I stare into the transparent water.

I listen to the wind.

Overhead, a seagull makes a lazy circle around my mast before heading south, disappearing over the trees of Great Abaco.

Everything is a jungle sign.

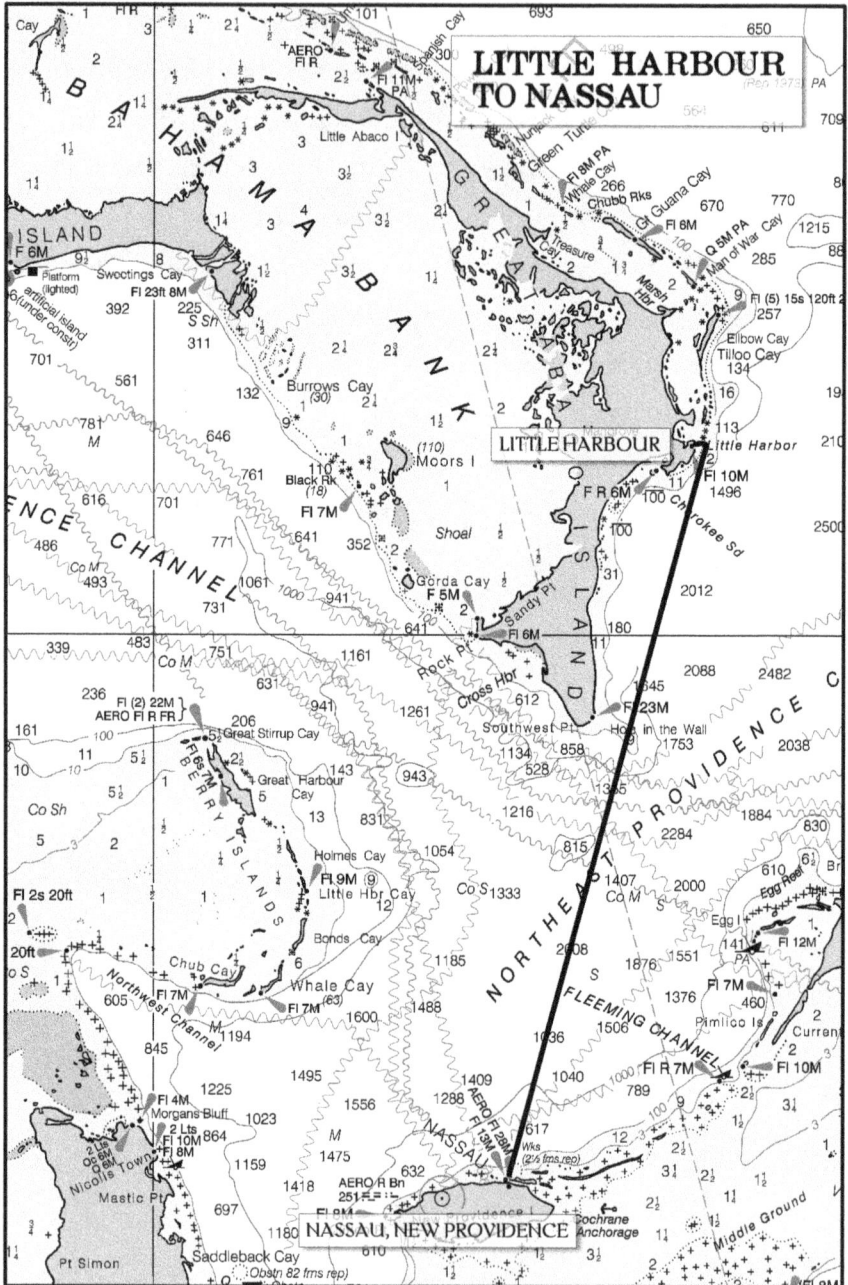

LITTLE HARBOUR TO NASSAU

I Just Am

MY COUSIN DAN AND I spend a night and the following day at Little Harbour. Here, the chain of out islands and the shallow Sea of Abaco end. Beyond this protected harbour, the coast of Great Abaco Cay turns southward into Northeast Providence Channel, an incursion of the deep North Atlantic that divides the Bahamas' two major banks.

We leave before sundown, bound ninety miles south to Nassau, New Providence Island, passing between two arms of coral reef into rolling offshore swells. The wind is light and easterly—an easy broad reach. After sunset, the flashing beacon high on the rocks at Hole-in-the-Wall on the southeast point of Great Abaco provides a handy bearing point from which to gauge our progress south through the darkness.

Out in the big ocean waves, Dan is queasy. I've done little offshore sailing before, apart from crossing the Gulf Stream to get to these islands, but tonight I feel fine. I'm in charge of getting my boat and my cousin safely from Abaco to Nassau. There's no "Sea Daddy" aboard this time; debilitating seasickness is not an option.

≊ The Blue Monk

Who am I, some twenty-four-year-old kid, to be piloting a small boat on a moonless night, beyond sight of land? With a passenger who knows *nothing* about sailing?

We pass within a hundred feet of a northbound sailboat. I illuminate my sails with a searchlight to make sure they see me. The tossing motion of the other vessel's masthead light relative to ours reveals the size of the seas as we fly comfortably southward, but *Blue Monk*, in spite of her small size, is perfectly content out here in the ocean swells. We wave at one another before each vessel disappears into the black void astern of the other.

"How are you holding up, Dan?" I ask.

"I've felt better but I'll be okay," he tells me. He forces a weak smile and nibbles a soda cracker to calm his stomach.

The wind freshens. I turn *Blue Monk* into the wind. Dan takes the helm while I go on deck with a safety harness on to tuck a reef[51] in the mainsail.

Dawn.

The sea changes from black to gray to deepest blue.

New Providence Island rises gradually above the wave tops.

An immense cruise ship enters the harbour ahead of us. The thought of sharing a channel with a vessel that size is intimidating, but now I know where the entrance is.

---

51 When a boat carries too much sail to handle easily in high wind, its sails must be *reefed*. Reefing the mainsail is accomplished by lowering it partway. The resulting flap of sail is tied to the boom with small pieces of line (reef points) built into the sail for that purpose. The term has no relationship to reefs of the coral variety.

At eight o'clock in the morning, *Blue Monk* rounds the breakwater into Nassau's busy, industrial harbour. A police boat cruises around the entrance, its blue strobe light flashing. Passing the cruise ship docks, we make our way east through the busy port toward the arch of Potter's Cay Bridge.[52]

"Over here is where the resorts and casinos are," I explain to Dan, gesturing at Paradise Island moving slowly by to port. "Paradise Island was originally named 'Hog Cay'—probably a less-than-ideal name for marketing a vacation spot." Dan chuckles. He's already feeling better now that we're out of the swells and inside the sheltered harbour.

Anchorages in Nassau Harbour consist of small groups of boats tucked in along the sides of a wide channel, protected from ocean swells by the lee of the islands but exposed to the constant wakes of passing powerboats, the booming bass of tourist barges dressed up in loosely piratical style, and a tide that rips one way or the other through the channel four times a day.

A wooden fishing smack[53] tacks up the harbour against wind and current, its mainboom fashioned from a crooked tree branch. I'm sorry we didn't get here in time to watch her navigate under the Paradise Island Bridge without an engine, but I'm grateful to get a

---

52 Potter's Cay is a thin strip of island that lies between Nassau and Paradise Island. The bridge that crosses over it is referred to either as the Potter's Cay Bridge or the Paradise Island Bridge

53 *Smack* - a traditional wooden sailboat set up for fishing

glimpse of what this historic harbour looked like decades before. The voices of the dark fishermen working the lines on the ghost sloop are swallowed by the din of Nassau's commerce and development.

Zebra Dun lies at anchor not far from the bridge on the north side of the harbour. John and Veronique wave from her deck.

I anchor, row Dan over, and make introductions. Though I've been at the helm all night, I elect to accompany everyone to shore. Better, I think, to forgo a nap and force myself to return to a normal sleeping cycle.

My visit to Nassau is a blur of fatigue. Dan and I hike around town. We buy supplies. I purchase a new spear at a dive shop and some new music to listen to. I encounter a breadfruit tree and pick one of the strange cannonball-sized fruits. Street merchants charge me white man's prices for vegetables and conch at the Straw Market under the big bridge. A steel drum plays for the tourists through a tinny amplifier. Coconuts, papayas, and fresh fish abound. The sad, legless, clawless bodies of live landcrabs sit stacked in crates waiting to be sold; I never knew they were edible. Someone blows an impossibly long note on a conch shell trumpet. Cruise ship visitors cheer and offer tips. After a few hours, I've been offered all the T-shirts I care to be offered. Enough of Paradise's hotdog stand.

We return home and tie a bucket behind the dinghy so the current can grab it, preventing the tender from beating into the hull of

Blue Monk when the wind and tide pull the two vessels in opposite directions.

John and Vero sail off the following day at first light; she has a plane to meet in Georgetown in two weeks. Dan and I need another day of rest after our ninety-mile offshore passage. We wait until the following morning to head south to the Exuma Cays.

At dawn, as I fire up the engine and haul up my anchors, a familiar voice sings, "Ahoy, *Blue Monk!*" Two boats from Dinner Key Anchorage circle around me. Keith is here on *Ritmo.* Charlie is sailing his tiny blue sloop with no name. We are all headed south across the Yellow Banks. Our impromptu flotilla motors east under the bridge, past the rusting wreck of an old freighter adjacent to the southwest channel.

A single-engine seaplane takes off in the harbour, just before passing *beneath* Paradise Island Bridge. I look at Dan and laugh; try a stunt like that in the States and you'll never fly again. Dan chuckles along with me. He's from Colorado; he knows "Old West" when he sees it.

Blue Monk slowly leaves New Providence Island behind. The clanking of civilization fades upon our return to the clear, tranquil shallows of the Bahama Banks. "Hopefully," I tell Dan, "the wind will fill in as the sun gets higher so I can shut down this noisy motor."

The Exuma Cays lie forty miles southeast across the Yellow Banks—a day's sail. The guidebook advises us to be vigilant and steer clear of coral heads, but we don't see any particularly large ones. The shallow water is clear and blue again. The bottom rolls lazily by beneath us.

The wind—already light—diminishes to an occasional puff.

Sand, sponges, corals, and grass patches meander by ever more slowly.

Well before the tops of the Exuma islands peek over the horizon, the wind dies altogether.

The sails hang limp.

The engine drones.

The sky is hazy and white.

We take down our clattering sails and motor across a sea of glass.

Dan spots an object in the distance—a sailboat motoring through the white zone where the sea blends with the sky, skating above its own rippling reflection, trailing a long, thin ribbon of wake.

Sailing across an endless field of tidal currents, navigating with compasses and watches, it's hard to tell which island is which by the shapes that appear on the horizon. Other sailors have electronic navigation equipment much more sophisticated than ours. Maybe this boat can give us an accurate position?

Our courses converge.

Dan recognizes John and Veronique on *Zebra Dun* before I do. Five miles west of the northern Exumas, we idle our engines and enjoy a gam[54] on the Bahama Banks.

---

54 *Gam* - a social visit or friendly interchange, especially between whalers or seafarers.

"Looks like some weather's coming down," says John as he waves his hand across the streaky sky. "We just left Allen's Cay. We're heading south to Norman's Cay for better protection. Allen's is a beautiful place but nowhere I want to be in a gale."

The fleet presses on together.

After a few more hours of motoring, *Blue Monk* slips around the south side of Norman's Cay to anchor in eight feet of clear water fifty feet from an old dock.

The sun descends. All hands are tired from the journey. We tie obligatory buckets to the sterns of our dinghies (a practice that becomes standard in this land of fast moving tidal currents) and retire beneath a shower of stars.

The anticipated cold front blows through. Though not as severe as the gale at Foote's Cay, gusty winds cause our boats to strain at their anchor lines. When the wind is at odds with the tidal current, *Blue Monk* rolls awkwardly. I'm grateful for the protection of the island's lee; it must be rough out on the banks.

Norman's Cay is the site of a former hotel and resort that became a haven for drug smugglers until the Bahamian defense force shot it (and I assume, the smugglers) full of holes. A ditched DC-3 cargo plane sits largely exposed at low tide on a shoal in the center of the harbour. Bent propellers describe its final landing on the soft seagrass. We snorkel around coral-encrusted engines and landing gear, hunting for fish. In the cockpit of the wrecked plane, I mug for a photo. Dan strikes a surfer's pose atop the fuselage.

We remain at Norman's Cay for four days while the wind continues to blow.

Beyond a dilapidated dock, weathered steps lead up a hill to an old hotel. I lift a trap door in the porch and discover a cistern full of sweet rainwater beneath it—*treasure*. Nassau water tastes like a waste product from a frog breeding program. I filled a few jugs with the ghastly stuff as a precaution before leaving New Providence but opted to sail south with my main tank almost empty in hope of finding *anything* better.

After discovering the cistern, I pump my Nassau water into the sea (with apologies to the fish) and top off my tanks with the good stuff. Hauling jugs down the stairs, across the dock, and out to the boat is hard work. When we're finished, as a reward for our efforts, we lower our bucket-on-a-rope through the hole in the porch once more to enjoy a freshwater shower and shampoo.

The wind clocks around to the east and continues to blow hard, but the sky is clear; the days are beautiful. At slack tide, we prowl the harbour for conch, climb and dive on the wreck of the airplane, row over to the tiny islets adjacent to Norman's Cay, and, in the evenings, sit on deck playing music and telling sea stories.

I snap a photograph of John and Vero. They are two comic book heroes, standing next to a palm tree on a postcard-perfect tropical islet. The wind blows Vero's hair and skirt. John smiles with his bronze chest bared to the sun. They glow with strength, power, and vitality.

The winter wind continues unabated.

"I have to get Dan back to Nassau," I explain to John. "His plane leaves the day after tomorrow."

"I have the same problem," he responds. "I need to deliver Vero to Georgetown to catch her plane. I'm running out of days, myself; we have to get out of here. Keith and Charlie are going to accompany me south in the morning."

"I don't mind admitting I'm scared to head back to Nassau with the wind howling like this," I confess to John. "It must be rough out there."

He thinks silently for a moment and looks at me paternally. "I hate to throw a cliché at you, but if you weren't scared I'd be worried about you."

At dawn, our four boats round the southern tip of Norman's Cay out into the waves and wind.

My three companions head south.

I head northwest.

It will be a long time and many miles before I see any of them again.

On the way back to Nassau, the wind is behind us all the way, a rowdy downhill run. Our course is true. The trees of New Providence rise on the horizon before us just where they're supposed to.

The Blue Monk

Blue Monk shoots beneath the bridge under wind power to drop anchor off the Nassau police station at sundown, exactly where we were moored a week before.

The next morning, I hail a taxi on the VHF.

Cousin Dan returns to the Rocky Mountains.

I linger a few days in Nassau to meet up with some of the teachers from the Abaco Mission who fly down to join friends on holiday. For the weekend, it's me and five beautiful young women knocking around Nassau town, exploring Fort Charlotte and swimming off the beach on the ocean side of Paradise Island.

A conch boat anchors close to *Blue Monk*. It's just an old fiberglass powerboat. Once somebody's dream, she's now an ugly hulk loaded high with seaweed-covered shells. Downwind of it, the stench is overpowering. The fishermen must have seen me rowing with my entourage. "Hey, mon. Set me up," they call as I row by.

"They all flew home," I explain. "Sorry. Maybe next time."

I'm grateful to have been spared an uncomfortable diplomatic exercise by the ladies' departure, but it's not like I got "set up" either. I'm a freak who lives alone on a tiny sailboat. They're all going home to jobs, boyfriends, and grad school.

I breathe and sigh. "Loneliness is the cost of living," suggests my inner voice; time to get on with my journey.

I bake whole grain bread in my oven the night before departing. I have no autopilot; keeping good bread aboard makes it easy to prepare and consume mid-day sandwiches without abandoning the helm.

In the morning, I quietly extract my anchors from the Nassau Harbour mud, motor under the Paradise Island Bridge, and aim my bow southeast toward the Exuma Cays.

The breeze is moderate—just right.

I turn off the engine, adjust my compass course, and trim my sails.

Who am I, some twenty-four-year-old kid, to be piloting a small boat alone, beyond sight of land, across the Bahama Banks?

I don't know.

I just am.

The Blue Monk

Fear and Freedom
October, 1988

IN THE DINNER KEY ANCHORAGE, Mike, a stocky white-haired man with a stern brow, anchors next to me for several months, flying Canadian colors over *Peapod*, his home-built steel boat. We pass each other often enough to become friendly. *Peapod* is cleverly put together; Mike tells me with a smile that her mast is actually a salvaged aluminum telephone pole. I know my way around, so I help him to find what he needs in Miami. When he's ready to sail on, he invites me over to thank me for being a good neighbor. To my surprise, his wife Betty is with him; I have never seen her aboard. "I like living on the boat," she explains, "but I don't like it when the wind blows and the rigging starts rattling. I'm happier when it's calm, when we're at anchor and the boat isn't heeling over."

Having come down the Intracoastal Waterway from Montreal to make final preparations in Miami, Mike gets *Peapod* ready to leave for the Bahamas as soon as the weather is right for a Gulf Stream crossing. "We'll be staying at Dove Cay in the Exumas," he tells me.

"It's a private island; we'll be the caretakers. Stop by for a visit if you get down that far south."

November, 1989

Winter is a time to watch the sky for telltale signs of cold fronts racing down from Arctic latitudes, a time to stay close to sheltered harbours. But I've crossed these Yellow Banks twice already, once in rough weather. I'll shoot down from Nassau and then island-hop south. Though I'm not sure how far I'll go or where I'll end up, I make Georgetown in the southern Exumas my goal; it's one of the places Trimaran John always talked about.

The Exuma Cays are of a different character than the comparatively lush Abaco chain to the north, where a large main island and a chain of out-islands define the boundaries of a protected bay. These islands are a battleground where ocean and land fight for dominion. Though the waters are clear and colorful and vibrant, bleakness lives here, too. Gone are the pine forests and hardwood hammocks. The Exumas are rugged and desolate, an intimidating landscape both exotic and remote, where thin scrub vegetation clings to tortured rock formations. Twice daily, the tide pulls unfathomable quantities of water on and off these banks. With no large mainland to moderate the current, the islands take the brunt of shifting tides. The cuts between them are subject to fast moving currents and wandering shoals; it's prudent to traverse them when the tide is slack.

Allen's Cay is the northernmost anchorage in this chain of islands that stretches southward from a point forty-two miles southeast of Nassau to a latitude just south of Havana. Uninhabited except by a species of Bahamian marine iguana, Allen's Cay is actually a cluster of small islands that encircle the white sand bottom of a pristine lagoon. Over millennia, tidal currents have carved a deeper ring of blue around the shallower middle. The southernmost islet— U-shaped with a small beach inside its curve—marks the end of this gorgeous, otherworldly anchorage. Colors are supersaturated. The sand bottom provides good holding ground.[55]

I row to the beach. Three iguanas crawl from the foliage to greet me. I neglected to bring an offering so I'm grateful to read in the guide that they're vegetarians.

Back aboard *Blue Monk,* I prepare a simple evening meal—chopped vegetables and rice—but I enjoy my hot supper way out here so far away from everything and everyone.

I light the kerosene lamp that illuminates my cabin and look over my chart to plan tomorrow's route.

Dove Cay appears beneath my finger.

I remember Mike's invitation.

---

55 *Holding ground* - Some anchorages offer better holding ground for anchors than others. Sand and mud admit the flukes of an anchor more readily than dense seagrass or flat, rocky bottom.

The tiny island is right on my way and slightly off the path more frequently taken by yachtsmen—a perfect next stop.

After a half-day's easy sail, I drop a hook in the seagrass next to *Peapod* with her waving maple leaf ensign. On shore, a charming Bahamian cottage stands behind a wooden dock among palm trees and mangroves.

Mike is pleased to see me. He invites me to stay a few days and introduces me to his son, Roy, an amiable, dark-haired man in his late twenties.

I enjoy meals with them, catch up on old times and attend to chores on the boat. Roy helps me work on my outboard motor. Most likely, some piece of dirt is clogging the fuel system and causing it to run rough. We accidentally drop the engine overboard while taking it off its mount, so after diving down to retrieve it, we end up having to tear it apart anyway to clear out the seawater.

I scrub three weeks worth of dirty laundry in a big galvanized tub with a washboard and sweet rainwater from the cistern under the house. Hermit crabs scatter as I walk the beach followed by two playful dogs. I string my hammock between two coconut palms and relax with a book and a pillow.

Mike shares news of misfortune. Betty took her own life a few months before my visit. He motions solemnly to a far corner of the island where she is buried in a secluded spot.

The water clears.

When we were in Miami, months passed before I even knew she was aboard. When I finally met her, she spoke only of fear—fear of the sound of anchor chains rattling, fear of the boat heeling over under sail. Betty hid in the small floating shelter her husband built, away from noise and disturbance, and still she was afraid. Mike carried her to this quiet and peaceful island, to a sanctuary where nothing threatened, where she could walk in the sunshine along a white beach shaded by coconut palms, listening to the chuckling of the waves, to a place where she could free her spirit from fear.

But we carry our demons with us. Behind her reflection in these peaceful waters, Betty saw only sharks, stinging jellyfish, and spiny, poisonous things. Having left the loud noises, bright lights, and angry people behind, she heard only imagined vitriol whispered by a cruel sea, carried on an ill wind, and distorted by a troubled spirit. With nowhere else to run to quiet the howling torment, she fled in the last way she could.

Her body lies under the palms beneath a mound of coral rock and conch shells, consigned to this tranquil place. Perhaps her spirit can now celebrate freedom from fear and embrace a world of serenity and peace. There could be no more beautiful heaven.

Clamped securely to its mount on my transom, the outboard runs better—not perfect, but better. Good company and land underfoot have been restorative. The sand and coconut palms and crystal blue water are sublime.

⤷ The Blue Monk

But Dove Cay is only a stopping point, a temporary destination, a place to absorb the shock of the last passage, regain balance, and prepare for another leg of a longer journey.

The morning is cool.

The wind is fair.

The sea beckons.

I lash my oars to the cabin top, haul the mainsail aloft, and stow my sail covers. Anchors release their grip on sand and seagrass. I secure them on the bow.

Past the tip of the island, the wind increases.

Blue Monk heels and accelerates.

I ease the mainsheet to take pressure off the helm.[56]

Sailing alone into the unknown, across shallow waters hiding corals and currents, I too, am afraid.

It is the price I pay to feel alive.

---

56 *Weather helm* – If the mainsail is too tight, the helmsman must fight the boat's tendency to turn into the wind. Letting the sail out balances the boat and relieves pressure on the tiller, reducing *"weather helm."*

Good Company

"Twenty years from now you will be more disappointed by the things
that you didn't do than by the ones you did. So, throw off the bowlines.
Sail away from the safe harbor. Catch the trade winds in your sails.
Explore. Dream. Discover."

—*Mark Twain*

I sail on for another day with a stiff easterly wind on my beam, dancing across an abstract quilt of blue and teal to Staniel Cay, hoping to catch up with the *Zebra Dun* at Georgetown in Great Exuma, a hundred miles to the south.

This breeze is excellent for making headway south, but to enter Staniel Cay Harbour, I must turn my bow into the tide and wind. My sputtering outboard still hasn't quite recovered from being submerged, first at Foote's Cay and again at Little Dove Cay— and I don't trust engines under the best of circumstances. The cruising guide advises me to land here with caution; the shoals are treacherous.

I've had too perfect a sailing day to ruin it by running aground. I opt out of fighting my way into the harbour, and turn about to anchor in the lee of Big Major's Spot, an adjacent island offering comfortable shelter from the wind. I'll wait here for the easterly to subside.

Confident my anchors are well set, I head to shore in the dinghy, rowing hard against the current to find a phone and buy supplies. Somewhere along my journey, I lost an oar. My spare is not quite as long as its predecessor. I hobble in slowly, pulling harder and faster with my shorter oar to keep my bow on a straight course into the rushing tide.

Close to the harbour lies "Thunderball Cave," used as a set in the 1965 James Bond movie. The cavern appeared large enough on film to serve as a secret lair for the movie's villains. Hardly more than a coral arch, the actual cave is too small to accommodate my dinghy.

I tie *Artemisia* to the town dock and walk through the settlement to find a phone station. Staniel Cay's dwellings vary in style. Most are simple wooden structures painted in island hues, but a few "real" cinderblock houses stand among them with satellite dishes, air conditioners, landscaped yards, and plate glass windows.

In a tiny grocery store, I restock on flour and other basics. I telephone my mother from the local BATELCO[57] station to let her know I'm still alive.

---

57 BATELCO - the Bahamian Telephone Company

My errands complete, I stroll back toward the dinghy dock. An American family hastily throws bags and suitcases into the bed of a pickup truck; they're preparing to depart via Staniel Cay's airstrip. I offer a friendly "hello" and smile as I walk by. A girl about my age stops me. Dressed for travel, she's clearly bound toward civilization, not the beach. "Are you the guy on the little blue sailboat out by the island?"

"In the flesh."

"By yourself?"

"Yes." And because I suspect she's looking for more than a simple confirmation, I add, "It was time to go sailing. Everyone else was busy doing other things. If I'd waited for them, I wouldn't be here."

"I really admire that," she returns. "I'm Lauren. My sister should meet you."

Meeting Lauren or her sister or anybody else's sister sounds fine by me. There is much to be said for the shared experience. Having left all the too-busy people behind, I'm alone on a grand adventure in an exquisitely magical and beautiful place. The only thing this movie is missing is romance.

I'd love to meet your sister. I'd love to watch the glow of amazement in her eyes as we sail at night across a moonlit sea, to show her my secret beaches where a person can walk for miles without seeing another soul. We'll climb the rickety stairs of the old lighthouse at Little Harbour to gaze at the mighty blue Atlantic through the window while the surf thunders below. Jump up on my shoulders;

we'll pick that big, ripe papaya hanging just out of reach. We'll steal lobster from under the ledges on the reefs, swim among dark schools of mojara[58], brilliant yellowtail, and shimmering jacks. Dine with me on conch and homemade bread from my oven. Let the yellow lantern light illuminate...

Lauren calls for Kym who emerges from a nearby doorway with a bag slung over her shoulder. "This is the guy from the little blue boat out by the far island," she explains. "He's out here all by himself."

"Dave," I offer, extending my hand to the two young women.

Kym is thin—perhaps a little too thin. Despite having been on vacation, her eyes betray fatigue, but an obvious beauty and spark of intelligence glimmer behind them. Dark hair frames a charming asymmetrical smile. "I really admire what you're doing," she says. "I work this terrible, terrible job; I'm running on a treadmill and I can't get off. I don't know how. I don't know what to do. I wish I could just...get away...like you."

Behind her, the rest of her family finishes putting their luggage on the truck. They perform a final check to see if anything important was left in the rental cottage. Our meeting is quickly drawing to a close.

I'm seized by an almost overpowering urge to say, "Hop in the dinghy. Let's go," but I know she'll either jump on board and traumatize her family, or fly home and feel terrible about the missed

---

58 *Mojara* - a gray reef fish that makes good eating despite its tough skin

opportunity for the rest of her life. A trip together could make a wonderful story—or it could be truly unpleasant sharing life on a tiny boat in the wilderness with a disoriented stranger.

"Aren't you scared out here by yourself?" she asks.

"I'm no hero," I say, still reeling from the unexpected feelings triggered by this simple encounter. "I'm just doing what I need to do to continue to like who I am. I get scared and lonely like everyone else. I have the same needs and desires. But why not ask yourself what you really want and go after it? You'll be terrified and uncomfortable at times, but at least you'll be honest. You can't eat goals and aspirations but you can live pretty well on them."

I recall a night not so very long ago in the swells of the Gulf Stream when I was afraid of finally having the dream I'd wanted for so long. In the Abacos, I was afraid to acknowledge the strange coincidences and magic all around me until they overwhelmed me and forced me to surrender control, to accept my own inability to explain or understand that which clearly existed but made no sense. I was afraid the gale at Foote's Cay would take my little boat and break her on the rocks. Sailing south from Abaco to Nassau over five-mile deep water, I imagined sinking through a cold sea of blackness. Today, I'm afraid I'll always be alone in Paradise.

But there are worse things than being afraid. I remember the little mound of coral rocks on Dove Cay.

I am afraid every day of my life, but I use my fear to propel me through a world where I have come to trust my body, my skills, my instincts and intuition.

"I don't believe you're scared of anything," Kym says.

"Want to hear something really scary?" I ask. "Think of dying without ever having lived. Think of being miserable your whole life and believing all the while you don't have the *right* to be unhappy because you did everything you were *told* to do to find happiness. Think of throwing your life away because of a crazy world's empty promises. *That's* scary."

A horn honks.

The truck engine turns over a few times, sputters, and starts.

"Will you write me?" she asks, scrawling a Washington, DC address on a piece of paper napkin.

I tear a scrap from the napkin and borrow her pen to return the gesture.

"I'll be in touch," she says.

The horn honks again.

We shake hands. Our fingertips slowly part.

The truck lurches and disappears over the hill in a cloud of dust.

The row home is easy with the wind and tide behind me. Alone in this far corner of heaven's desert, I cleat my dinghy's painter[59] securely to the aft deck, climb aboard, and make some bread dough.

---

59 *Painter* - The line used to attach the bow of a dinghy to a boat

I am by myself but somehow I am not alone.
While the bread rises I compose a letter.

The Blue Monk

And Then You Gybe

LITTLE FARMER'S CAY could pose in an exotic South Pacific postcard. Coconut palm trees lean from the sandy shore over
rich, turquoise water. After a half day's run south from Staniel Cay,
I anchor in the racing tidal current I've become accustomed to and
dinghy in to explore.

A cave yawns at the water's edge, partially submerged at high tide.
I wander in, stooping to fit beneath the ceiling. Bats flutter and squeak
around me. I want to explore farther back but I carry no flashlight
with which to penetrate this curious world of perpetual shadow.
I return to my dinghy and continue toward the dock.

The word "settlement" suggests something tentative—some
compromise that was "settled on." Though families and neighbors
may occupy such places for centuries, the word "town"—or even
the more humble "village"—is an affront to the gods of storm
and sea at whose whim they are lived in. Little Farmer's settlement
stands adjacent to the beach on the western shore. Its fifty inhabitants—all descended from Chrisanna, a freed slave who bought the
island for $30 in the 1800s—are friendly and welcoming. A Bahamian

family invites me to sit on their wooden porch with them to enjoy a rare luxury, a cold drink. I ask them about the fruits that grow here. The sapodilla trees are bearing fuzzy brown orbs the size of a plum; given time to ripen, they taste a little like a sweet pear. Sugar apples on another tree look like a cross between a giant acorn and a hand grenade. The flesh around their seeds tastes like tart cinnamon applesauce.

I call my father from the island's BATELCO station. My stepmother tells me about her cousin in New York City who wants to hire me based on what she's told him about my graphics skills. I can't imagine a place more different from Little Farmer's Cay than Manhattan. I call Steve in New York and tell him I'll let him know. "If you don't hear from me in a week, don't think I'm not interested; assume I'm stuck waiting on weather somewhere with no phone available."

Though I'd like to stay another day to explore the cave, the wind favors my southward course. At dawn, I continue on the inside passage, with the Exuma Cays between me and the ocean, negotiating shoals and rocks until I run aground on a mid-tide. I don't trouble myself to do anything more than set a single anchor in deeper water—the rising tide will eventually free me—but I will make no more progress today.

Mares' tails[60] streak the sky; a cold front is heading this way.

---

60 *Mare's tails* - wispy cirrus clouds full of ice-crystals that often portend the arrival of a high-pressure system moving down from the north.

The outboard still runs rough. I might as well try again to solve the problem while I wait out the weather. I consult the cruising guide for a place to spend the night.

When I float clear of the bottom, I head back north about a mile to anchor in the lee of Cave Cay. The island is rocky, desolate, and scrub-covered. The narrow entrance to its protected, interior harbour runs between two rocky cliffs, but the guidebook tells me the channel is too shallow for *Blue Monk.* That theory holds true until another sailboat larger than mine passes me to disappear between the cliffs. I consider following them, but I already have two anchors down and I'm comfortable where I am.

An hour later, a middle-aged couple dinghies out to visit me. "You might want to move," they suggest. "A norther's coming down. You'll be a lot more comfortable inside when the wind picks up."

"But the entrance is too shallow. How much does your boat draw?"

"Probably about the same as yours," the man assures me. His wife smiles and nods agreement. "There's plenty of water. Follow us in."

I haul my anchors and motor slowly between rocky walls taller than my mast, following the strip of darker blue that indicates the narrow corridor of deep water in the center of the channel. Inside, I turn to port to anchor in a shallow lagoon over a seagrass bottom, surrounded by beaches and twisted rocks covered with scrub. A high hill stands between the lagoon and the ocean. Covered with cacti, the terrain is more of a desert than a tropical paradise.

A fisherman's shack of driftwood and rough timber squats at the edge of the shallow lagoon.

The norther arrives. The wind blows and the temperature drops but inside the island's interior lagoon, the gale is barely noticeable; hardly a ripple disturbs the water.

Two days later, my neighbors move on.

I remain in the sheltered anchorage at Cave Cay waiting for the north wind to surrender to the easterly trade winds. Though Georgetown would be an easy reach southward, the best route from here to there is through the deep water on the windward side of the islands. Alone and on no particular schedule, I have no reason to hurry. I prefer to do my blue water sailing in moderate weather.

Two days later, when the wind abates, I motor out of the harbour. The outboard still sputters—yet another carburetor overhaul did not solve the problem—but I can't stay alone at Cave Cay forever. I push out from my sheltered world, emerging between the two cliffs onto the Bahama Banks, my sails already hauled aloft to assist should the engine fail.

I motor slowly around the south side of the cay, aiming my bow out through the cut toward the blue Atlantic. The inbound current piles and surges against a rocky islet that stands in the middle of the channel like a strange cubist sculpture defying the sea. The tide pushes me sideways as I fight my way off the edge of the banks. The rock appears to drift around me.

Battling the current with my sails up and my engine revved as high as it will go, I push my way slowly toward deeper water. The outboard finally swallows whatever was choking its fuel system. When I need power most, the motor runs strong again. With renewed vigor, the propeller pushes me past Picasso's lost masterpiece out into the swells.

I clear the cut.

My sails fill.

I turn south but angle slightly east to put sea room between my vessel and the rocky coasts of the islands.

I'm alone in the cobalt swells. When I pull the tiller, the whole earth obeys my command, swinging around me to align my destination with my path.

The sun arcs slowly across the sky.

I sit at the helm listening to the recordings I bought in Nassau.

Silhouettes of the southern islands of the Exuma chain sail by. I mark their progress in the guidebook. Late in the afternoon at Great Exuma Cay, I pass back onto the Bahama Banks. I follow the sketch chart in the book, using my compass binoculars to navigate around the reefs by taking bearings on landmarks ashore. I sail down a crystal bay into Elizabeth Harbour to drop my hooks in a crowded anchorage.

My trip from Nassau to Georgetown has taken almost a month.

The following morning, I dinghy ashore to buy supplies. Georgetown is the remains of a slave settlement abandoned along with its inhabitants to subsist off the land and whatever could be salvaged from shipwrecks when a cotton-growing venture went bust after the American Revolutionary War. Today, the descendants of those early castaways make a modest living from conching, fishing, and providing services to hundreds of yachtsmen who crowd their protected anchorages each winter. Georgetown is another "settlement," its wooden houses painted the pastel colors of the sand, sea and sunset. Chickens roam the streets. Goats are tethered to trees in yards. Diesel generators grind constantly in the background. A few architecturally incongruous banks service transient yachtsmen and a growing community of Americans who build vacation homes on Great Exuma Cay.

I visit the payphone at the local BATELCO station. Inside, someone has scrawled a graffito: *life's a reach and then you gybe.*[61]

Landing at Georgetown involves dinghying from the anchorage to the dock via a tunnel under the main road. The current rushes either in or out depending on whether the tide is filling or emptying saltwater Lake Elizabeth on the other side. For most cruisers, this is no problem; engine-powered inflatable dinghies are unhindered by the rushing water. In *Artemisia Gentileschi*, my little soapdish dinghy with unmatched oars, attaining the dock is a struggle. I catch an oar tip on the side of the narrow tunnel and find myself

---

61 *Reaching* is sailing with the wind abeam, an ideal point of sail. *Gybing* or *jibing* (contemporary spelling) is the opposite of tacking. It involves changing course across the wind with the wind behind the boat. An uncontrolled gybe (caused by a wind shift or an inattentive helmsman) can send the mainsail boom flying dangerously from one side of the boat to the other.

spinning and bumping back out. More than once, I fall back into someone else who entered behind me. To complicate matters, the popular Bahamian equivalent of Russian roulette involves blasting a twenty-foot powerboat through the tunnel at high speed under the blind assumption that nobody else is traversing it at the time.

Stocking Island lies a mile across a small bay, offering protected hurricane anchorages and an unusual monolith perched on a high hill. I spend a few days exploring, and hike to the top where the concrete salt beacon[62] gazes upon a blue horizon. On the ocean side, the beach is inspiring. White ribbons of sand connect the sea to dramatic rock formations.

But after a week in Georgetown, I've had my fill. Christmas is almost here; yachts arrive for the holidays at the rate of a dozen per day. Georgetown rapidly becomes a social drinking station for retired yachtsmen twice my age who seem bored with paradise.

We made some money. The kids moved out. We sold the house. We closed the business. We bought a boat. We made it to the islands.

Now what do we do?

I commend these sailors both for their financial success and for following their dreams to these southern latitudes. But their dreams aren't mine. Perhaps they never valued the wildness, risks, and challenges of the journey; perhaps for them it was always about

---

62 The Monument is called the *Salt Beacon* because it was originally used to guide cargo ships into Elizabeth Harbour to pick up salt mined at various places on Great Exuma and Little Exuma.

arriving—about conga lines and limbo contests and tropical drinks. These yachtsmen are here at the ends of their voyages; I am in the middle of mine.

A gray Bahamian military launch cruises through the anchorage just before sundown, stopping at various boats. The boat eventually pulls alongside *Blue Monk*.

"Good evening, sir," says a uniformed man. "The Bahamian Defense Force requests permission to board your vessel for a routine inspection." He points his machine gun down and off to the side.

I consider whether or not the request is actually a request. "Of course. Welcome aboard. I'll fetch my passport and ship's papers."

The men look down from the cockpit through the companionway into my cabin but don't step inside. One of them opens a cockpit locker but doesn't pull out the sail bag that obscures his view of whatever's stowed behind it.

Why bother to search if you're not going to look? I hold my tongue.

I return to the cockpit with my documents. One of the soldiers scans them quickly, nods and hands them back.

"You're sailing by yourself?" asks one officer.

"Yes, sir."

"Where is your wife?"

"I'm not married."

"Do you have a girlfriend?"

"No girlfriend either; just sailing by myself."

The soldier looks confused.

"Are you gay?" he inquires after a pause, looking at me with a side-long stare.

"Just single."

The soldiers take pity on me. "Come to the hotel tonight," says their leader. "I'll buy you a drink."

"Thank you," I say, attempting to sound grateful. "That's kind of you. I'll try to get over there tonight."

The officers step back aboard their launch and move on to the next boat.

They searched for nothing.

They found it.

I had forgotten about that other world. I'm naïvely surprised and offended to encounter it here in this remote wilderness. "At least they were friendly and polite," I tell myself—though I don't believe it.

I reflect on my life alone on a tiny boat in a strange land. Perhaps the name painted on my hull has had unintended consequences: I—the rational pragmatist, the skeptic, the doubter, the questioner, the non-believer—am pursuing ideals that stand on invisible foundations. I wouldn't be living in the wilderness on a 26-foot sloop if I wasn't on a pilgrimage of some sort.

By myself in this blue wilderness, I've honored a calling stronger than my human desire to be with others. I have never felt so empowered or free. These past five months, five hundred miles from my home port, away from traffic and noise and bright lights, the "real world" I encountered here feels a lot more "real" than the "real world" I have always been exhorted to join.

Yet I find this loneliness grows old—like watching a movie by myself.

What about New York? The idea of living in a concrete jungle scares me far more than the idea of sailing alone in a wild one.

Perhaps that's reason enough to try?

I step to the mast and raise the mainsail.

The Road Home

I PULL MY ANCHORS from the Georgetown bottom and sail away from the ever-expanding fleet of drinking yachtsmen, negotiating the passage between the reefs, filling my sails with clear, clean air from the great Atlantic. The trade winds blow from behind me.

This is the downwind trip said to make the climb south worthwhile. Offshore in the blue ocean swells, I watch the islands slip by my port side and look for landmarks that match those in the cruising guide.

In the afternoon, the sky grows streaky. It's uncommon to get so many cold fronts this far south but the wind favors me as the gale approaches, clocking slowly behind me. I duck into Cave Cay as I did on my way down, passing Picasso's lost sculpture in the cut. Seen from the ocean side, it's an unremarkable rock. I enter between the two coral cliffs into the island's interior lagoon.

Carrying a second anchor out in the dinghy, I set my hooks wide apart to minimize my drift as the wind changes—to keep my keel out of the shallows.

The sky is white and hazy.

The temperature falls into the 50s.

I'm the only one here but I'm comfortable and safe, sheltered by steep coral shores and sand beaches on all sides. Hardly a ripple violates the surface of the lagoon when the gale arrives.

I read, bake bread, play music, read some more, play more music. After a day or two or maybe three aboard, I explore the lagoon in the dinghy and then land to investigate the scrub-covered island.

I encounter one of the caves the island is named for. I'm tempted to climb inside but think better of the idea. This would be no place to get injured or stuck. Who knows when someone else might visit here? When they do, will they question why my boat is empty and my dinghy is tied ashore?

I row across to the other side of the lagoon, tie my dinghy to a small dock, and climb a dirt path through low scrub grass up a sandy hill. A few gnarled seagrape trees cling to the earth but the land is open, barren and dry. A tall sentry plant stretches its thorny arms next to the trail, thrusting its central stalk twelve feet skyward. Small cacti—prickly pear and other varieties—are oddly nontropical; they're desert flora. I walk a short distance to stretch my legs; it's refreshing to be on land, but I feel like I'm trespassing. Technically, I *am* trespassing; a sign on the dock says this island is privately owned. Though the odds of anyone either caring or catching me are slim, being an unwanted guest sullies the experience. I head back to the boat to read, cook, practice guitar, and read some more.

A second gale blows through.

I've never spent an entire week alone before.

The trade winds clock around to the southeast again.

In the morning, I haul my anchors, start my motor, and exit between the cliffs.

The chop is light in the lee of the islands. The wind is fair. The sea bottom is tideswept sand, a submerged blanket of shifting turquoise and beige. I pass a few other boats—most of them headed south—but continue on alone across the sparkling wilderness.

Without an autopilot, I am bound to my tiller but with some adjusting of the sails, I can get *Blue Monk* to balance herself and stay on-course for a few minutes at a time. I go below to make myself a sandwich with bread I baked at Cave Cay.

By early afternoon, I've sailed just over twenty-two miles—not far—but I find no reason to push myself. After more than four hours in the cockpit, with fair weather expected tomorrow, I'm happy to take a break, dropping anchor at Big Major's Spot near Staniel Cay for the night.

Already, I have stories and memories attached to these islands.

I consider rowing in to let my family in Miami know I'm alive but I'm still dependent on my mismatched oars. I don't know what to tell Steve about the job in New York. The tide is running; that means a fight going one direction or the other. Better to sit tight.

I am rewarded for staying aboard. From my anchorage off the sand beach near the island's westernmost point, I watch a wild pig come out of the trees to walk at the water's edge.

At sunrise, I'm under weigh again, this time completing a thirty-five mile passage to Dove Cay where I stopped to visit Mike and Roy on my way south. The anchorage is pretty—a blue, seagrass-bottomed channel between two green islands scoured deeper than the surrounding banks by the ever-racing tide.

Mike's boat is gone.

I'm alone here, too.

The house is locked up; they must have sailed to Nassau for supplies. Still, this is a sheltered place to anchor. After sundown, the stars are magnificent, reflecting in the transparent water to reach my eyes alone. The vision is surreal—so much more vivid and vibrant than it rationally could be—in the most literal sense of the word, 'supernatural,' as in 'transcending the merely natural,' overloading the senses.

This is a different world.

Soon, I will only be able to see the brightest of these stars.

Do I want to leave them behind?

Will knowing they are here be enough?

The next day's twenty-two mile passage to Allen's Cay is easy. The temperature is mild, the wind moderate. I fly my big jib and round the rocks at the entrance to the island group's interior anchorage by early afternoon.

I am once again the only boat in the anchorage. I moor *Blue Monk* over white sand encircled by natural channels of sapphire blue cut by swift currents flowing on and off the banks. Beyond these narrow channels, the islands are low, scrub-covered, and rimmed by sparkling beaches punctuated by gray outcroppings of sharp, coral "moon-rock." I row to the beach to call on the resident iguanas and stretch my legs. As on my first visit here, when I leave the dinghy, several of the four-foot lizards crawl from the underbrush looking for a handout. They keep a short distance from me but remain watchful and unafraid.

In the low jungle, I discover the ruins of a house. Not much remains, only a foundation and crumbling walls covered with crudely painted names of visiting yachts. The blue water and white sand are serenely inspiring here but this is a place of wild beauty—no place that should be marred by the presence of blocky human habitation. Succulent vines consume a pile of cinder blocks at one side. A seagrape tree grows through a crack in the deteriorating concrete floor. Two iguanas crawl across the rubble. Nature reclaims her own.

After my walk, I return to *Blue Monk,* cook dinner, and listen to ZNS radio from Nassau forty miles away. The date is December 23rd; I'll be in Nassau for Christmas. The Nassau Weather Service predicts the wind will blow from the south. Perfect! With a long northwest passage across the Yellow Banks ahead of me tomorrow, I plan to get going early.

⊰ The Blue Monk

Night falls on the home of the iguanas. The reflection of wispy gray clouds scudding swiftly over a brilliant moon dances on the water.

Something isn't right.

Did the ZNS weather forecaster bother to look up at this sky?

Tempest in the Lizard Kingdom
December 24, 1989

I awaken before the sun. The night sky purples beyond the dark silhouette of the island to my east. I flip on the radio and listen to ZNS out of Nassau. Someone has died; a five-minute list of survivors—it must be half the population of the Bahamas—follows the obituary. Today is the anniversary of the publication of Charles Darwin's *On The Origins of Species.* The announcer derides it as "a book that proposes man descended from monkeys." Several more minutes of not-even-anthropologically-interesting filler follows before the desired weather report is finally broadcast.

Nassau radio clears me for takeoff.

A light rain falls. Humidity condenses out of the warm tropical air. The southerly wind suggests the approach of a cold front. I prepare to depart but my gut tells me not to. *I don't need a weatherman to tell me what these clouds mean.*

By sunrise, the wind increases, clocking around to the south-south-west. A powerful tidal current, rather than the wind, determines my vessel's orientation; I sit beam-to the weather. Machine gun raindrops pelt my vessel's starboard side. Opposing winds and currents create a large, uncomfortable swell in the anchorage. If the wind blows from the north before the tide changes, I could end up riding stern-to the blow; not a comforting proposition.

Allen's Cay is hardly the same peaceful anchorage I fell asleep in last night.

I'd love to get out of here.

Radio zns's disregard for accurate weather forecasting betrays Nassau's long history as a seaport. I passed a protected harbour at Highburn Cay yesterday and proceeded here with no advice about a coming front. This morning's early broadcast reported only southerly winds at twenty knots; it's already blowing twenty-five at Allen's Cay. If this wind holds, I could enjoy ideal sailing conditions for a run north to New Providence, but the clouds are streaky. In these latitudes, winds from anywhere south of southeast foretell the influence of high pressure air swooping down from the Arctic to overpower the Caribbean trade winds. In these latitudes, winds from anywhere south of southeast are capricious and unstable. I balance nature's warnings against the lack of any broadcast by man. I listen to the radio one more time before pulling anchors.

The forecast has changed.

Winds are expected to be out of the north today at twenty to thirty knots with gusts to gale force. That's the forecast for Nassau's protected harbour; conditions here at Allen's Cay will be worse.

I let out scope on my windward anchor and then, with the dinghy and my unmatched oars, haul up and reset my second hook in the center of the island group; the soft sand will provide good holding ground. I wrestle a third anchor, a length of chain, and a strong line from a cockpit locker and install them on the foredeck—in case I need an emergency brake.

The rain pauses. Dark, streaky clouds scud across a white sky overhead. The wind diminishes. The ride becomes more comfortable. I enjoy the relative calm while it lasts. A gale can blow for days, and because of the strong tidal current streaming between the islands here, the guide book warns "Allen's Cay can be extremely rough in a norther."

I can handle "rough." Though staying aboard will be uncomfortable, I'm equipped with sturdy anchors and plenty of heavy chain[63] —good insurance considering the ragged coral shores around me. Beyond the entrance channel downwind of me lies a sandy beach. If I should break loose or drag anchor, its soft sand will be my target landing spot.

The iguanas here, or perhaps some other swarm of unseen inhabitants, have a malevolent laugh. The noise began after midnight last

---

63 *Chain* ~ When anchoring, a length of chain is placed between the anchor and the anchor line attached to the boat. Mechanical advantage improves the anchor's holding power; a boat must lift the entire length of chain off the bottom before it can pull up on the shank of the anchor. The anchor is therefore pulled across the sea bottom, an action that tends to bury it more deeply.

night when the wind first came up and the temperature fell—a raspy, demonic cackle straight out of a horror film, resounding across the islands from a chorus of hysterical devils.

The wind clocks southwest.

The sky fades to a uniform gray.

The air is cold.

A tide-driven swell surges through the turbulent anchorage. Held beam-to the waves by the wind, *Blue Monk* rolls nauseatingly.

After a few hours, the tide slackens; the boat rides bow-to the wind again. I prepare lunch. Eating my sandwich, I calmly and helplessly await the approaching tempest, experiencing a strange mix of fear, anticipation, resignation, and boredom.

My boat is prepared.

My anchors are set.

My sails are lashed down.

My oars are lashed to the cabin top.

Negligence is no part of this equation. Whatever will happen is up to forces beyond my control.

I consider running south four miles to better shelter at Highburn Cay but, at low tide, I'm not sure I can carry my four-foot-six draft over the sand bar at the entrance. Today would not be a good day to get stuck aground.

I call Highburn Harbour on the VHF but get no response.

Best to sit tight.

Though the word "gale" conjures up images of crashing waves and wind-driven spray, I've sailed in 30-knot winds before. The technical definition of "gale force" specifies wind of over 34 knots—a significant, but hardly awe-inspiring wind speed—and I should be at least somewhat protected in the lee of the islands.

A fine line divides disregarding the strength of nature's fury and taking a storm too seriously; I'm just not sure where that line is.

With time to wait, the impending gale looms larger. By late afternoon, the wind backs to the west—unusual. The rolling swell in the anchorage returns with the tide. The island demons are at it again, cackling in the cold rain.

Daylight fades. A last minute boat, *Kokonot,* arrives in the anchorage ahead of a line of dark, low, ugly clouds and even harder rain. They must have had a bumpy day sailing across the banks.

The latest radio update says the gale will arrive tonight. Had I known I had this much time, I would have tried to make Highburn Cay, but at this point, I'm staying put. In better weather, I'd rather be here than in Nassau's crowded, industrial harbour for Christmas.

Outside, the night is cold and wet. I'm grateful for my guitar, my stereo, my books, and my warm, dry cabin.

By ten o'clock, the wind howls under a coal-dark, starless, moonless sky. The gale turns northwest, blowing across rather than between the islands; I have better protection in their lee now, but the current and the roaring air fight savagely over my tiny vessel. She tacks awkwardly on her anchor lines. Accustomed to riding bow-to the wind, my instincts respond to the feel of the boat, telling me I'm dragging anchor when I'm not. Mooring lines creak, stretch, and strain. Stays and halyards hum. Rain pressure-cleans my hull and deck. Sleep is impossible.

Midnight on Christmas Eve: The howling wind is demoralizing. I turn up the volume on the stereo but find it difficult to summon up a festive holiday spirit.

At 3:30 in the morning, the rain pauses. I grab a flashlight, braving the dark and the wind to inspect my foredeck. I'm hanging on one anchor; I haul in slack on the other so it can share the strain. *No chafe on any of the lines; good.*

Upwind of me on *Kokonot,* my neighbor is on deck for the same reason. He waves at me in the loom of his spotlight. The night is so dark I can hardly see the islands, but judging by the position of his light relative to mine, we're both in the same places we originally anchored.

At certain wind speeds, my halyards vibrate at a low frequency. The mast, a hollow aluminum tube, vibrates sympathetically, causing the entire boat to moan and pump dramatically. I don my foul weather gear and adjust the tension on the halyards to calm the "music." When the wind finds a new note to play, I adjust them again.

An hour later, it gets *really* bouncy; I'm caught between wind and tide again. My oven flies from the galley, almost landing in my bunk.

The current holds my stern forty-five degrees off the wind. Waves attempt to board my cockpit; they explode against my transom. Each chilling gust heels me thirty degrees.

Enough of this already! What am I doing alone on a tiny boat, getting knocked around in a remote, wet, freezing wilderness? Am I crazy? *This* is Paradise?

Night's blackness succumbs to dawn. I venture again to the fore-deck and find everything in order. The anchors hold tight. The lines haven't chafed. But my astonishment at witnessing the spectacle around me transcends all fear of being in the middle of it. A gale does in fact involve crashing waves and wind-driven spray. Wave tops fly off in steaming streaks of spindrift. Sheets of mist blast over Allen's Cay's highest hill, the fleeing ghosts of waves detonated against the windward side of the islands. As if a firehose is trained on it, the island that sits between me and the north wind appears to be covered with rising steam. The cut, once clear and transparent aquamarine, is a seething cauldron of furious green water and stirred up sand. Waves driven from the shallow banks boil through the entrance, undulating madly without consistent direction, spitting foam and hissing invective.

Yet, in spite of the cold and the uncomfortable motion, the sinister laughing of the iguanas, the vibrating groans of the rigging, and the ominous creaking of the anchor lines, my life is richer for having experienced nature's power from within.

⑤ The Blue Monk

A voice on the VHF—a yachtsman sheltering at Highburn Cay—announces the wind is expected to calm somewhat by nightfall.

By afternoon, the wind passes through north—still blowing, but less forcefully. "Comfortable" would be an exaggeration, but I welcome any lessening of the storm. Tentative spots of blue peek through gray cotton skies.

Nightfall on Christmas Day: The wind blows steady and cold, but conditions are lighter. After staying awake for almost forty-eight hours, I sleep well.

In the morning, the harbour remains rolly as the gale opposes the tide. My hatches are shut tight against the cold. Tomorrow, I'll make my run to Nassau. I've spent enough time by myself these past few weeks. I'm ready for some company and a change of scenery.

My neighbors on *Kokonot* hail me on the VHF radio to invite me over for a day-after-Christmas lunch—a kind gesture. They have a big boat, hot tea, and a warm meal to share. I'm grateful for the hospitality and for the company of others who can recount this unimaginable experience. We are creatures of the story; when we encounter the remarkable, we find solace in knowing others have seen it, too. In some small way, nobody else will ever quite understand who we are. We are bound together by common experience.

Long after dark, I thank my new friends for an enjoyable day of commiseration and row back to *Blue Monk*.

The wind has subsided to fifteen knots.

The sky is starry and clear.

A brilliant moon illuminates the white sand bottom of the anchorage.

The only sound worthy of mention is that of the waves gently lapping against my hull.

It isn't so bad here.

Tomorrow, I leave the Lizard Kingdom to cross the Yellow Banks to Nassau.

I retire and sleep the deep, satisfied sleep of one who anticipates a day under the Bahamian sun, navigating the clear waters of Paradise.

The Blue Monk

Gulf Stream Crossing II

January 1990

Nassau is hardly my favorite place in these islands but it's on the way home. Broke and tired, I'm ready to see my friends in Miami again. My voyage continues to be a grand adventure but I have eaten all I can at this sitting; I'm ready to return home, digest my experiences, and earn some money.

I call Steve in New York to tell him I'll give the job a try. If I'm going to return to the States to work, I might as well accept his offer. If I can live alone on a boat in this wilderness, how hard can it be to live in a city full of people where there are grocery stores on every corner?

As confident a sailor as I've become, I'm hesitant to cross the Gulf Stream alone, especially without an autopilot. My mother calls Winston for me; he's a friend from Dinner Key who works as a professional delivery captain. Winston is a tall, black Jamaican man in his mid-thirties with a strong brow, a cheerful, musical voice and a gentle smile. Two days later, he waves at me from the Nassau dock.

"Dave, how are you?" he sings, giving me a crushing hug.

"My trip has been incredible, but when it's time to go home, it's time to go home."

Winston has done his share of sailing. He smiles and nods his understanding.

"Do we need to pick up anything before we leave?" he asks.

"I'm a bit low on stores but I'm broke. The fuel tanks are full and we have enough food on board to get us home. Our trip won't be a gourmet cruise but we won't starve, either."

Winston reaches into his pocket, pulls out his wallet, grins and hands me an American hundred-dollar bill.

"Thanks, that's kind of you but I hate borrowing money; I have no idea when I'll be able to pay you back."

"No, Dave." He puts the bill in my hand. "Take it. Your mom paid me $400 to help you sail home. Let's make a quick trip to the store and buy some good stuff to eat; you don't have to pay it back."

I can't blame Winston for asking to be paid—he's a professional sailor—but part of me feels cheated. After having come so far on my own meager resources, I prefer not to sail my journey's final leg with "hired help." It's as if my mother paid someone to push me over the last hill of a six-month race. I expected a business arrangement of some sort but imagined I'd negotiate the terms myself.

Winston reads the disappointment on my face. "You're out here sailing just fine by yourself, Dave, but your mother has no idea what cruising's like. As far as she's concerned, her boy's in danger. If she can put a "professional" on board, she can sleep better. You know I'd do this for the cost of the plane ticket, but I did your mom a favor. The fact that I'm a licensed captain makes your mom secure; the fact that she paid me means she doesn't have to be afraid. This is not about your sailing ability; it's about your mom's insecurity."

My gaze drops as I consider his words. "You're right, you know?"

"Yeah, I know. Take the money. Let your mother sleep. Unless you say otherwise, I'm here as your crew, not as your captain. Now, let's buy some chow and go cruising."

An hour later, we climb aboard with bags of groceries. I stuff apples and oranges and ripe plantains[64] into the food hammock over the bunk in the main cabin. Snacks, pasta, onions, potatoes, cabbage, and canned tomato sauce are packed with care in the lockers under the galley.

The sun is low in the sky. Winston looks over my tiny boat and sniffs the air. "This wind is blowing pretty hard. Are you sure you want to leave tonight?"

"She's a small boat but she's a sturdy one. We'll be fine," I reply. "Let's take advantage of this southeasterly, make a fast, easy run, and not get stuck waiting for the next norther to pass. A little bit of Nassau goes a long way."

---

64 *Plantains* - a type of cooking banana best eaten when ripe to the point of being black on the outside.

With anchors lashed on deck and the dinghy secured on the cabin top, we exit through the north end of the harbour, pass the break-water where the big cruise ships come in, and sail into the deep, powerful North Atlantic.

Night falls.

We charge rapidly and vigorously northwest toward Chub Cay, thirty-five miles to the north. With a brisk wind behind us, we run downwind with a full jib and a reefed main.

Winston shoots me a look; he's hesitant to impose his experience on me. "Dave, do you think we should put up a smaller jib? The wind and seas are picking up...and it's blowing a lot harder out here than it was in the harbour."

"Let's watch her for a while," I suggest. "She's sailing along well enough. Plus, I confess I'm not exactly thrilled at the idea of going out on the bow to change sails in these seas."

Minutes later, *Blue Monk* flies over the crest of a ten foot roller, trips on the next wave, and rolls sideways in the trough. Ocean water pours over the starboard coaming, flooding the cockpit. The mast spreaders dip within six feet of the water's surface before she rights herself and continues on—a knockdown.

"Maybe you're right," I suggest with humorously feigned matter-of-factness. "I'll go forward and bend[65] a smaller jib."

"*This* is why we always sail with the hatches closed in heavy weather,"

---

65 *Bending sails* - traditional sea-talk for attaching sails to the boat.

Winston explains. "A single rogue wave could fill and sink this boat—
instantly—right out from under us."

On the foredeck with a safety harness on, I clutch fluttering wet
sails with one hand and grip the stainless steel bow rail tightly with
the other. I steal a gulp of air, then blow bubbles to keep the sea
water out of my nose as the plunging bow dips me and my bundle of
rope and canvas repeatedly under the waves. When the swells heave
me skyward again, I continue working the bag gradually over the
sail. I hank on a smaller jib, hand the ends of the sheets to Winston
in the cockpit, and then make my way carefully back to the mast to
haul the smaller sail up the forestay.

We proceed at a less reckless but nevertheless exhilarating pace
through the starry night and windtossed seas.

After rounding the Chub Cay lighthouse at the southern end of
the Berry Island chain, we pass into the relative calm of the shallow
northern Bahama Banks.

I have never been to these islands. Sailing within sight of them
without stopping seems a waste, but I say nothing; this isn't the time.
We continue westward across the shallows as the wind decreases,
picking up the silhouette of Ocean Cay at dawn before running
aground a mile from the edge of the Gulf Stream.

The grounding gives us little cause for concern; the tide is rising.
In fact, finding the location of the shoal on the chart provides us
with an accurate fix on our position.

The Blue Monk

I drop a single anchor. We sleep for a few hours before crossing the Stream. We'll sail overnight and plan to arrive in the morning.

Late in the afternoon, we round North Rock in a perfect calm.

The brilliant turquoises of the Bahama Banks yield quickly to bottomless blue as we pass into deep water.

The outboard hums without complaint.

The sails are furled; not a breath of wind blows to fill them.

I am grateful to find the wind asleep and the Gulf Stream in a gentle mood. Though I prefer to sail, I am content to listen to the engine today. Winter winds are capricious; this is no place to explore the spectrum of their temperaments.

Winston and I chat in the cockpit.

The Bahama Banks recede beneath the horizon.

We are alone on the sea.

Being beyond sight of land inspires a sense of wonder, independence, and vulnerability—a disconnection from the universe of man. No law applies here save for the law of the jungle. Money has no value. The very concept of insurance is a fantasy. No culture exists beyond that which you create with your co-conspirators. A voyage offshore is a journey into timelessness and reverie and oneness with the world.

The feeling fades.

We are not alone.

Behind us, a white ship appears. As the vessel draws near, I see the red stripe across her bow.

"Coast Guard," I say to Winston, who holds a soda can in one hand and the tiller in the other.

Wonderful! Here's a tiny boat motoring from the Bahamas to Miami with a 24-year-old kid and a black yachtsman aboard. Nothing suspicious here.

The Coast Guard's tender brings six uniformed storm troopers alongside. Their bright orange inflatable dinghy sports what appears to be some sort of roll cage—as if bars could somehow protect the soldiers in the event of a rollover at sea. Two guardsmen wearing pistols and flak jackets stand behind the steering console while four others sit in formation, each perched on one knee in the bow— science fiction at its finest.

Four men board *Blue Monk* with clipboards and cases containing tools and equipment.

They begin to inspect the boat.

They empty my dirty laundry bag (God help them) and use a fiber- optic device to search the inside of my forward water tank.

They check my papers.

They open and search my cabin drawers.

My forward hatch is dogged shut for offshore sailing; the cabin is hot and stuffy. After two hours dripping sweat all over the inside of my boat, the two guardsmen doing the inspecting report to the two

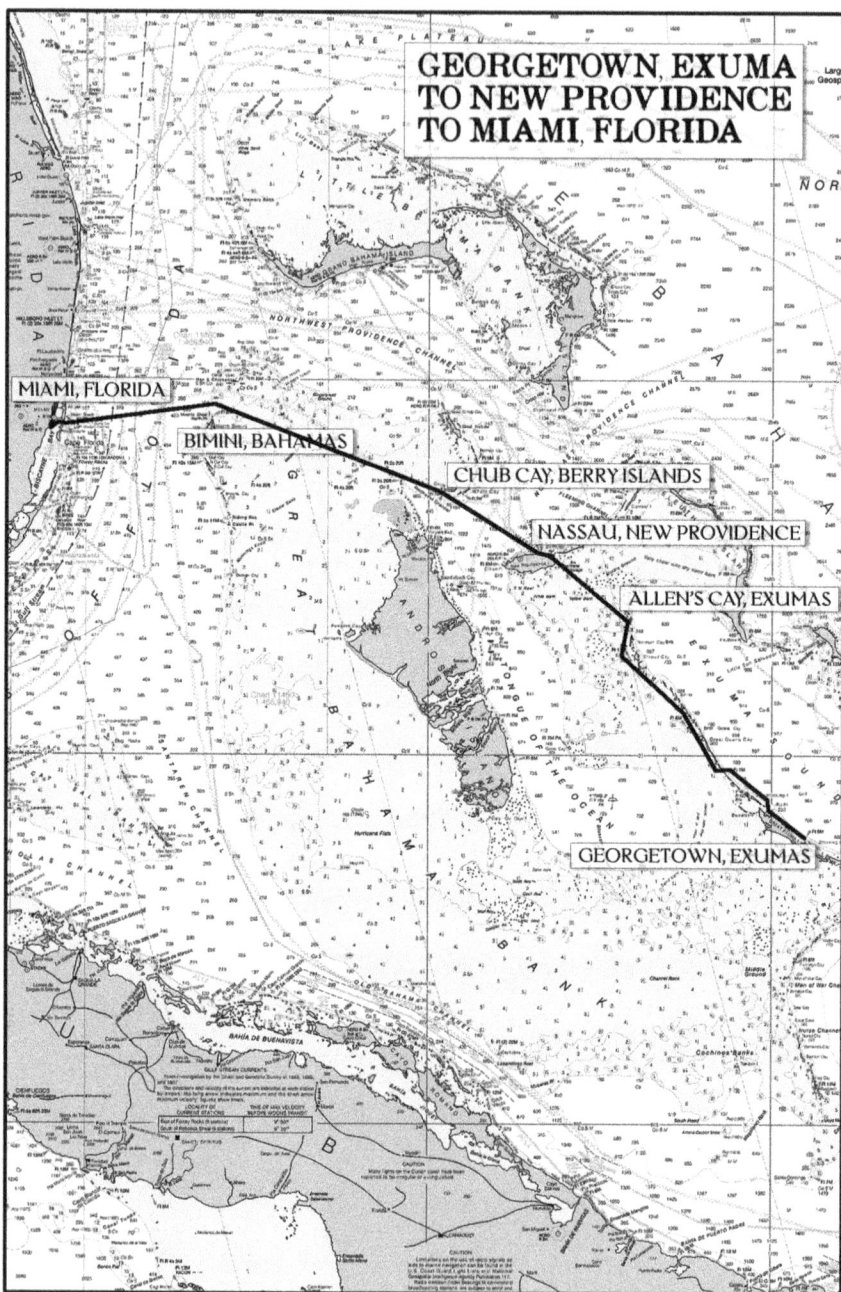

GEORGETOWN, EXUMA
TO NEW PROVIDENCE
TO MIAMI, FLORIDA

MIAMI, FLORIDA

BIMINI, BAHAMAS

CHUB CAY, BERRY ISLANDS

NASSAU, NEW PROVIDENCE

ALLEN'S CAY, EXUMAS

GEORGETOWN, EXUMAS

who guard us in the cockpit that all is clear. After presenting asinine recommendations about life jackets, they summon their tender to return them to their ship.

I sign a form agreeing that the search was conducted with "courtesy and professionalism" and then, after having searched every inch of my boat except for two cockpit lockers that could easily have held hundreds of pounds of contraband or four cramped illegal immigrants, they thank me for my cooperation and leave.

I'm impressed when people who carry guns thank me for my cooperation.

The ship fades into the darkness.

Night falls.

The horizon over our destination glows, illuminated by a billion lights.

The stars fade.

Tops of radio towers rise into view.

Buildings appear.

Hours drone by.

We continue westward.

At three o'clock in the morning, we enter the big ship channel at the Port of Miami, motoring quietly past huge freighters tied along the seawall. Gigantic loading gantries tower over us like immense insects in the darkness. We motor down the channel, awash in brilliant light.

At the end of the port, at the mouth of the Miami River, the big city slumbers—buzzing and crackling at some detectable yet inaudible frequency. Powerful energy emanates from this intersection of sea and city—impersonal, mechanical, electric. All is chrome, glass, and glitter. Something about it revolts me. In my fatigue-induced stupor, I look up at the towering skyscrapers, trying to understand my aversion to this concrete leviathan I have returned to.

Turning south down the Intracoastal Waterway, we pass under the Rickenbacker Bridge into open, familiar Biscayne Bay.

Though we're exhausted, U.S. Customs requires us to make a detour to Crandon Marina on Key Biscayne; a special check-in phone is available there for inbound yachtsmen to clear in. I give the operator our passport numbers and another number given us by the Coast Guard.

The exchange is uneventful.

By sunrise, we're on our way across Biscayne Bay again. Masts of boats anchored in front of the Dinner Key spoil islands are in sight.

The wind fills in lightly. Though we have only a few miles to go, it would be a shame not to complete my voyage under sail. I walk forward to the mast, raise the sails, and grab the tiller.

Ready for Anything

HOW MANY HIGHWAY LINES are painted on Interstate 95 between Miami and Washington, DC? The scenery never changes; trees and billboards float by the window of my rented moving truck as the highway snakes its way northward. Every once in a while, the color of the pavement lightens or darkens, signaling passage into another county whose asphalt differs slightly from the one I just drove through.

I'm northbound, somewhere in Georgia, passing "Pedro's South of the Border" billboards with increasing frequency. As I draw closer to the truckstop from hell, my thoughts drift. A plot to blow up this blight upon the landscape would make a good novel. I imagine Pedro's exploding in a blinding flash, followed by a cacophony of whistles, shrieks, and pops from the fireworks stand. In unison, hundreds of billboards stretched out for a hundred miles north and south of the crater that only moments ago was a tacky roadside attraction begin to smolder. With a dramatic *whumph*, they burst into flames. Painted sombreros wither and turn to smoke.

Much too hostile, I gently reprimand myself. I've been without billboards and highways and corny amusement parks long enough to have forgotten about them. Reentry into the atmosphere of Planet America with its noise, traffic, advertisements, and television is more difficult than I'd imagined. My heat shields aren't in good condition.

I grab a bag of chips and pretend they're a real lunch; I don't want to waste time stopping except to refuel.

Country music oozes from the radio. I flip through the stations, hoping to catch something worth listening to, but I find only an audio version of the truckstops and billboards I'm already saturated with. I opt for silence and twist the volume knob firmly to the left until it clicks.

The afternoon drifts on a calm cloudy sea of green and gray. I drive in place on a world that rotates beneath my wheels. Hunching forward in my seat, I steer with care when the big semi-trucks rumble past in the left lane, their slipstreams pushing me sideways. *Damned powerboaters. Always making a wake.*

In the islands, I drank in everything around me with all my senses. I still do; I take in every license plate, bumper sticker, and advertisement. I lost something at sea; my bullshit filters disappeared. I no longer subconsciously scan and refine the contents of my environment to determine what sounds and images should pass to the conscious part of my brain.

Is it me or is civilization full of trash?

The walls and filters will go back up; I'll have to learn to wear blinders to live in this world where the quantity of meaningless information is staggering.

I place my left foot on the gas pedal and stretch my stiff right leg off into the footwell of the vacant passenger side of the cab. I sing a few odd tunes to myself.

No letter awaited me at the Great Exuma post office, but I wasn't surprised. I knew I wouldn't be hearing from her for a while. Her missive arrived in Miami shortly after my return.

> Dear Dave
>
> Sorry I didn't write earlier. Our meeting at Staniel Cay inspired me.
>
> I quit my job, took some time for myself and went to Italy! I have Italian roots and wanted to reconnect with the motherland.
>
> Get in touch when you return to the States. I'd love to visit you and hopefully do some sailing.
>
> Warm regards
>
> Kym

I hardly recognized the pretty girl I picked up at the airport in Miami. The bags under her eyes were gone. Her smile was radiant.

Such a delight to see her spirits so improved since our brief meeting at Staniel Cay.

The following morning, we took off down Biscayne Bay aboard *Blue Monk* with a light easterly wind abeam.

A front blew through, making our anchorage at Elliot Key choppy, but good food and conversation compensated for gray weather. Our time together passed all too quickly.

Pedro's is behind me now; the "You Have Just Meesed Pedro's" signs grow sparser. I press on with sympathy for the poor souls headed the opposite direction.

The promised New York opportunity evaporated the moment I stepped on American shores; I suspect it was contrived to lure me home. But my two-week visit to Washington, DC was interesting and fast-moving. Manhattan didn't want me, but DC opened its arms and so did Kym. I found a job and a reasonable apartment a block from hers, a short walk from the subway station.

Jungle signs pointed to an open door—a break from boating to explore other frequencies of the spectrum of life.

Why not?

If I can sail the Exumas solo, I'm ready for anything.

Low on fuel, I pull off at the next exit and lean against my truck full of furniture, crates of record albums, musical instruments, clothing, and books. Dazed and road-weary, I watch the fumes from the gas pump nozzle distort the gas cap cover. I'm well into North Carolina now. Three or four more hours of traveling lie ahead.

Darkness is coming on fast. I grope around in the cooler for some sort of sugar bomb to keep me awake.

I remind myself to be open-minded about my new adventure. Millions of people live in the city and love it. They work, ride the subways, and enjoy the intensity of urban life. I'll adjust. The city offers music, art, culture, educated people. Kym is there.

Stop being critical of crowds and noise.

Let things be.

Be patient with yourself.

I still navigate like a sailor. I don't remember what end of town my apartment is in, but I know the old brownstone is not too far from the Capitol building on the side opposite the Washington Monument. I take a bearing on the two structures and soon find myself driving between the skyscrapers, past China Town, past the galleries and museums of the Smithsonian to C Street.

Exhausted, I grab my guitar and a few valuables from the truck, pray the rest of my belongings will still be there in the morning, and step inside.

At dawn, I drag my furniture out of the truck, hang pictures and stock the kitchen with old standby basics: yeast, sugar, and flour for bread, rice, various beans, pastas, and split peas. I ate well in the islands. Fresh fish, lobster, and conch will be scarce here but I won't be switching to hot dogs and Chinese takeout.

I hang my guitar on the wall next to a five-string banjo I bought from John Nation but never spent much time learning to play. No longer buried in a locker under *Blue Monk's* vee-berth, the shiny instrument with its unusual high-string-on-the-bottom[66] is suspended in easy reach where it will inspire me to practice and study.

I wire up my stereo first; music makes unloading the truck easier. A day of moving, unpacking, and decorating gradually transforms the basement apartment into a home.

Standing in the brick-walled living room, I take inventory of the symbols around me. Home is symbolic of self. Aboard *Blue Monk*, I lived surrounded by water. Here in this basement, I am surrounded by earth. If the sea is not present, perhaps this subterranean apartment will provide motivation to continue on my introspective path?

For the first time in years, I lock my door.

I brush my teeth, undress, and turn off the light.

Noise from passing cars, police sirens, and other city sounds presses against my window as I fade into sleep.

---

66 The five-string banjo is tuned differently than most instruments, on which the strings are arranged from low to high. On the banjo, the highest pitched string is on the bottom; the thumb of the right hand alternates between playing bass notes on the fourth string and melody notes on the fifth string closest to the player.

Washington, DC

EVERY DAY, I ride the train downtown to work; nobody ever seems to smile on the subway.

The romance with Kym is short-lived. She—along with everyone else in DC—is preoccupied with terrestrial obligations I haven't thought about for an eternity. After six months alone, I want to bask in my new romantic connection. But Kym focuses on practical matters—paying bills, buying groceries, performing at work. And I am now a subway-riding electronic prepress technician,[67] no longer a free-spirited, sun-tanned Tarzan who once boldly escaped this very realm. Passion and romance yield quickly to the politics of scheduling time and balancing commitments. I am crushed.

Adjusting to my new environment is a daily struggle.

I have never been depressed before. Melancholy sits upon me like a thick fever, but if I wallow in my apartment alone on weekends,

---

67 *Prepress* – Future readers may wonder what prepress is (was). In the early days of digital printing, documents were created on-screen and then rendered to photographic paper or negative film with an imagesetter for subsequent transfer to a printing plate. Contemporary methods often skip these photographic "prepress" processes; the digital document is sent directly to the printer.

I will die. My spirit is sick; I have failed in some profound yet inexplicable way.

I nurture myself.

I take banjo lessons after work.

I bake bread every week as I did in the islands.

On weekends, I rise early, eat breakfast at the Eastern Market and walk up Capitol Hill to the Smithsonian museums or the volleyball courts near the Lincoln Memorial where I play all day before walking home exhausted enough to sleep.

Some weekends, I ride a train and then take a bus to teach sailing lessons at a marina on the Potomac River—a chance to get back in my element and meet new people—though the brown river is a poor substitute for the clear waters of the Bahamas. When the egotistical manager of the sailing school declares, "You've got a lot to learn about boats," I say nothing but don't return.

I engage fully with a beautiful, lonely world. Every Sunday, I choose a new museum to explore. I visit art galleries or the Museum of Natural History or the Air and Space Museum. Some of the lesser-known ones like the National Portrait Gallery fascinate me. Free lectures offer insights into art and history. The National Art Gallery shows free foreign films with subtitles.

Washington, DC

Sunday night after a day of volleyball and museums, I lay my head down on my desk.

I float, neither asleep nor awake.

Sparkling waters roll beneath me. I fly low, skimming over tropical seas. Mangrove Cay, Great Sale Cay, and the rest of the Abaco chain roll by, illuminated by a brilliant moon.

At Man-O-War Cay, I enter the harbour and bank to the right.

The boats tug gently at their moorings.

The water is brilliant and clear.

I search for *Zebra Dun* but the schooner is not in her usual spot.

I find her at the southeast end of the harbour.

Her aft hatch is open.

I drift down the stairs into the low cabin.

It's not late, but John Nation is asleep; he retires with the sun.

So good to be in the islands again, if only for a spontaneously imagined moment.

The vision fades.

I am in Washington, DC, alone in my room at my desk.

I survived another weekend. Time to get some sleep.

"Dave?" John Nation's voice sounds tinny on the telephone. "Sorry to call collect. I was worried about you. I had a dream you came to my cabin last night; you seemed upset. I don't know if it means anything but I figured it was worth a call to find out."

The dream must have been pretty vivid to inspire him to row ashore and hike a mile down the Queen's Highway to the phone.

I relate last night's experience to him. "Did you move *Zebra Dun?*" I ask tentatively. "Are you farther down the eastern harbour now, near the Lee's dock?"

"Exactly." His voice is oddly unsurprised. "I moved there a month ago. It's quieter; not so many powerboats blasting by."

The next evening, I explain the coincidence on the telephone to my friend Bill in Miami.

"Do you believe in ESP?" he asks.

I pause to consider the question. "I believe in the inexplicable. Most people are disempowered by not knowing, but I prefer to enjoy the mystery. As soon as you attempt to explain the inexplicable, the odds are overwhelmingly in favor of arriving at a false conclusion."

Saturday.

The sun is setting.

I'm exhausted after playing volleyball next to the Lincoln Memorial all day.

I walk home past the Eastern Market, carrying a sandwich in a bag for dinner and a few items of clothing in a backpack.

Suddenly I have company.

Strutting and bopping cockily beside me are two young ghetto kids.

I size up the situation.

A hundred yards away is another group these two hope to impress. The kid on my left is about fourteen years old; the other is probably nine. I shift my sandwich bag to my left hand. If I need to take action, the best course will be to use my right hand to clobber the left kid. The other one is too young to be much of a threat; he's just trying to act tough.

I continue walking.

My thoughts race.

Rage against the city wells up in me; anger at the disintegration of my romance with Kym, regret over having exchanged a perfect, happy life in the islands for a world of Coast Guard cutters, banks, traffic, noise, and these punks who have no idea who they're dealing with.

I'm afraid—but not for myself; I'm afraid for *them.*

I have never been quite so enraged and out of control before. I don't lose my temper or come unwound easily, but I'm *this* close now.

"Hey, what you got in the backpack, man?" says the youth on my left.

"Nothing for you," I say with a tremor in my voice.

We continue walking.

I focus on his hands. If he makes any sudden move, he's *dead.*

A voice inside my head urges me to strike first, before he does.

I hold back.

"Whatcha got in the other bag?" he asks.

"That's my dinner. It's not for you, either."

We're far enough from the rest of his gang now. I could knock this punk down and make a run for it.

I wish they'd quit this. They're going to get so much more than they're bargaining for. I'm going to end up having to justify to some judge why I came unglued on some poor teenager.

"Yo! Leave that guy alone. Get back over here," calls one of the kids from the group down the street.

I inhale deeply.

My companions laugh and peel away to rejoin their friends.

I return to my apartment, shaken and upset. I am so disconnected from this world, so incapable of understanding why *anyone* would behave this way. Visions of violence, and fear that I might inflict real damage to these wretched people intrude upon my consciousness. I almost destroyed those poor dumb kids who are probably venting the same rage and frustration, hoping to win some minor confrontation—some tiny, hollow victory to color a gray landscape of defeats, unscalable obstacles, desperation, and decay.

Am I any different in this place?

Sunday morning.

I'm half asleep, lying in bed late, letting my thoughts drift.

My bedroom door creaks open.

A hand enters.

"Kym?" She's the only other person who has a key.

The hand withdraws.

The door shuts.

I fly out of bed, motivated neither by reason nor fear. I am an animal, a creature of the jungle. An intruder is in my den.

I land in the living room an instant later, ready for battle. A dark figure slinks out the window, moving gracefully as a ballet dancer, oozing like an evil fluid up the steps, over the fence into the neighbor's yard, a ghost disappearing into the ether.

I'm trembling.

I call the police and warn my upstairs neighbors.

I inspect my apartment for missing articles and find only two were taken: my oven mitt—I imagine to prevent leaving fingerprints—and my kitchen knife.

I just leaped out of bed naked to do battle with a guy carrying a kitchen knife!

I fill out a police report—a futile response perhaps, but one that provides a needed channel for reaction.

A cop drives me around the neighborhood. He harasses an unsavory-looking street kid and pokes through his duffel bag, but invading this guy's privacy just because someone tried to rip me off offers no solace. I don't imagine we'll find anyone on the streets carrying around a dime store kitchen knife and a floral-patterned oven mitt.

I call the landlord. He sends someone out to re-weld the bars on the back window.

Friday, five days later.

Mara, the new supervisor, asks me to stay after work again.

What's it about this time? Another write-up for some trivial, contrived offense?

I sit down with her and the boss. He smiles smugly. "Regrettably, we need to terminate your employment here. We have evidence you stole money from the company."

"Show me," I reply. "I've stolen nothing. I don't handle company money."

Bastard! These people are framing me.

"The evidence is incontrovertible but we don't have to show you anything. Please sign these termination papers before you leave."

I scan the papers for a moment, put them on the desk, lay the pen on top of them and walk out of his office without signing. But instead of slinking quietly out the door like a guilty employee who's been caught doing something wrong, I visit each of my co-workers and explain calmly that I was accused of stealing and fired.

All are shocked and angry. Morale in the office plummets. Several of them assure me their résumés will be going out on the street Monday morning.

I decide to let fate choose my path.

I advertise in the newspaper for a tenant to take over the lease on my apartment.

I call my former employer's competitors. They're happy to set up job interviews.

Either a suitable new position will keep me in Washington, DC or an exit door will open.

I receive an inquiry from a qualified tenant within a day of placing the ad in the paper.

I'm forced to cancel two job interviews because of a cold and fever that keep me in bed for three days.

The Blue Monk

A week later, I rent a truck, load my belongings, and drive south to Dinner Key.

Light Blue

A LIGHT CHOP sparkles on Biscayne Bay.
The wind is against me.

I feel like rowing today—for the sheer pleasure of it. Donovan's Light at the end of the Dinner Key Channel is a mile out.

Dinghies circulate around Dinner Key Anchorage like pennies. *Artemisia Gentileschi* is a good horse—we've traveled many miles together; but when the opportunity to buy the dory-skiff for $200 shows up, I jump. She's thirteen feet long, hard-chined,[68] and built from plywood bent around a set of frames. Fastened with fiberglass strips on the inside, she's glassed over completely on the outside.

A Charlie Strayer design based on the classic Chamberlain dory-skiff, she's drawn up and built by the anchorage's own resident naval architect, but as is the case with most anchorage dinghies, she needs

---

68 A *hard-chined* boat has flat plank surfaces that approximate the rounded curves of a smooth hull.

fixing up. New bronze oarlocks and strips of oak to reinforce her worn gunwales restore her to serviceable condition.

I buy a couple of Sitka spruce 2x2s from Shell Lumber and carve a pair of strong-but-light ten-foot sweeps[69] with a spokeshave, leaving more wood behind the oarlocks, next to the handles, to keep them better balanced. With epoxy and veneer, I laminate a curved blade for each oar. A band of layered fiberglass prevents chafing between the bronze oarlocks and the soft wood. Six coats of spar varnish add a final touch of elegance.

I christen her *Light Blue*—like *Blue Monk*—after a Thelonious Monk composition.

My new tender gets a new coat of blue topside paint with a white bootstripe and two sets of oarlock sockets—one pair aft of the center seat for rowing solo and another pair forward to balance the load when I have a passenger in back.

She glides through the water, slices through the wind, and never ships a drop of water in a sea. I can pull three passengers and their gear out to the anchorage in one trip. *Light Blue* is my missing piece.

Unlike tubby Artemisia, *Light Blue* is slender, long, and fast. She's tippy but with practice, I find my balance. After a week of rowing her, I can step from her sole to her front seat and from her breast-hook[70] to the dock.

---

69 *Sweeps* - traditional oars with curved blades

70 *Breasthook* - a wedge shaped piece of wood fitted inside the point of a small vessel's bow. It's too small to qualify as a foredeck.

I lend *Artemisia Gentileschi* to someone who lends her to someone who lends her to someone. Such is the way of the anchorage.

Several dinghies are stolen from the dinghy dock. *Light Blue* is not among them but the anchorites are naturally upset. We don't like losing our boats. We especially don't like the idea of living with locks and keys. Dinghies can be replaced but our lifestyle is sacred.

Concerned the thieves may strike again, Ray Montana contrives an expendable dinghy from a single sheet of ¼-inch plywood. Always a comic, he names his simple blue box the *William F. Buckley* after the famous conservative commentator.

A few miles north of Coconut Grove on the Miami River, Haitian freight boats are loaded with hundreds of bicycles. The bicycles are obviously stolen and they're clearly visible from the I-95 overpass, but the police don't do anything about them.

Dogpatch Danny works on a towboat on the river. He finds the dinghies stacked up with the bicycles and lets everyone know where they are.

The police, as usual, refuse to help.

A small army of anchorage residents bands together and heads for the Miami River.

They offer the Haitian captain a compelling proposition.

The freighters are docked directly under a high bridge.

The Haitian freighters are built of wood.

Wood is flammable.

It's a no-brainer.

The sailors return with their dinghies.

Donovan's Light isn't much to see; it's just a channel marker—three pilings with a light, two cormorants, and a sign with a reflective number on top. It doesn't even remotely resemble a traditional lighthouse. It hardly deserves a name. The nondescript beacon actually isn't named on any of the charts, but everyone in the anchorage always calls it 'Donovan's.'

Who in hell was Donovan?

This is my turnaround point.

The tall buildings of Brickell Avenue and Coconut Grove spread out in front of me, stretching toward downtown. The marina's forest of masts peeks over the spoil islands. To starboard, the long arm of the Rickenbacker causeway with its high arching Powell Bridge connects Miami to Virginia Key, continuing across Bear Cut to cradle the northern end of Biscayne Bay.

I'm a mile from shore.

The wind is behind me.

I'm ready for the sprint home.

Pulling hard, I close my eyes. Soon, I will row *Light Blue* in the clear waters of the Sea of Abaco.

voyage the second

The Blue Monk

Gulf Stream Crossing III
August 1990

HE GULF STREAM divides the North American continent from the clear shallow waters of the Bahama Banks. On a calm night, the Stream is beautiful and serene, but when the wind opposes the northward flowing current, its waters grow tempestuous. Though only forty-five miles across, the Gulf Stream is not to be taken lightly; its moody waters have claimed many mariners. But crossing the Stream is a rite of passage for Florida sailors. As the River Styx separates the land of the living from the land of the dead, the Gulf Stream also divides two realms.

Things are different on the other side.

So are those who cross over.

Six miserable months working in Washington, DC lie behind me. Upon returning to Dinner Key Anchorage, I found *Blue Monk* in good order in spite of having left her unlocked and open. Though often characterized as a "den of thieves," Dinner Key is probably the only place in South Florida I could have left my home so vulnerable and exposed.

I pull the outboard motor from its (unlocked) locker in the cockpit and clamp it onto its mount on the transom. I convert meager savings into gear, groceries, and supplies for a journey. On the morning of the new moon high tide, I beach *Blue Monk* on the north spoil island, scrape off a thick layer of marine growth and coat all but the last few inches of her bottom with red anti-fouling paint. I regret not having sufficient tidal drop to paint the entire keel, but I'm consoled by the knowledge that barnacles can't live in the Bahamas; they're unable to filter enough food out of the pure waters. Ray Montana helps me build a new forward hatch. Over the course of a month, my boat is made ready for passagemaking.

Ray lives on a small Amphibicon[71] sloop he sailed down the Intracoastal Waterway from New Hampshire. This is the first time Ray will see the Gulf Stream and the enchanted islands he's heard so many stories about. Working in a sailboat rigging shop in Coconut Grove, he hears everyone's Bahamas adventures from the other side of the shop counter; he's eager to know firsthand what they're talking about. Ten years my senior, thin, wiry, and balding, with an artist's goatee, Ray Montana has a dry, New England sense of humor; he's always ready with a bad pun. We are kindred spirits, captivated by things nautical and the call of the islands.

---

71 *Amphibicon* – The *Amphibicon* was designed from scratch as a trailerable cruising boat by E. Farnham Butler and Cyrus Hamlin.

We wait to depart until the weather radio foretells favorable conditions, pulling anchors on a September afternoon with *Light Blue* in tow. The red brick lighthouse at the end of Key Biscayne slips past our port side. We aim our bow offshore. Our destination—West End, Grand Bahama Island—lies forty-five miles north and the same distance east. Traveling at four knots for just over ten hours, we'll be carried that far north by the current. We set a compass course a few degrees south of east.

The lights of the Florida coast recede into a yellow glow behind us. *Blue Monk* dances lazily over the offshore swells. A certain uneasiness accompanies my return to these big ocean waves after a long hiatus, but the nervousness is soon replaced by a sense of delight. *Blue Monk* handles the seas with an easy grace that reveals the centuries of seafaring and experimentation behind her design; her seakindly lines are the footprints of great mariners past. *Whoever designed this hull spent time out here in these swells.*

Lights flash on the eastern horizon.

We press on.

Three hours out, I get a "third person" feeling—as if I'm inside my head looking out through my eyes but not truly present. A few small burps bubble up from my stomach. Seasickness: I know it's coming on. "Ray, can you take the helm a while? I feel a tiny bit pukey; I'm going to go below and lie down. Holler when you need a break and I'll trade the bunk for the tiller."

The wind is light and the swells are large; the boat rolls. It's difficult to keep from getting tossed out of the bunk. I lie fitfully with a small bucket on the sole next to me—just in case.

Raindrops drum on the deck. Ray puts the dropboards in the companionway to keep the water out. Down below, in the dark of the cabin, I listen to the sounds of changing weather.

The hull vibrates.

Our speed increases.

More flashes illuminate the ports.

The dull boom of distant thunder punctuates the sounds of waves and wind.

Reluctantly, I rise, vomit into my little red bucket, don my foul weather gear and join Ray in the cockpit.

He smiles at me sympathetically. "What should we do about this storm?"

It looks worse ahead of us.

"Let's get the jib down," I suggest. "If the weather gets heavy, I'd rather not have to go out on the foredeck in it. The wind is changing. We'll make decent time under mainsail alone on this tack."

Ray agrees, and as I'm not well, he snaps on the safety harness and makes his way forward to lower the jib. It comes down easily. He leaves it hanked to the forestay and stuffs the canvas into a sail bag, which he lashes securely to the bow rail.

The end of the jib halyard escapes, flies free and streams ahead of us like a kite. Ray shrugs and climbs carefully back across the bouncing deck to the safety of the cockpit.

I shrug back at him; there's little we can do.

Generously, Ray suggests I go down below to rest. He knows I'm miserable, and I take his advice, but I feel worse leaving him in the cockpit to stand my watch.

Rain.

Wind.

Our ship hums, flying through the waves.

A deafening explosion accompanies a blinding flash.

Are we struck?

"Ray?"

Close!

The sail luffs as we come into the wind.

The main hatch slides open. "Dave, you'd better get out here."

The waves have grown swollen, turbulent, and disorganized, driven by a strong cool wind. Another bolt of blue-white lightning strikes the water fifty feet from us. A sharp, electric crackle introduces the shotgun report. A circle of luminous green light appears in the waves at the impact point, lingering like the flash of a strobe in our eyes after the lightning disappears. I heave once more into my red Ace Hardware bucket.

My aluminum mast is the tallest object for miles.

"I want to go back, Dave. This stinks! We're out here in a storm, miles from shore—and now we're taking on water." Ray points his flashlight into the cabin where a flood laps over the floorboards. Fruits and vegetables dislodged from their fishnet storage hammocks tumble around in the water on the cabin sole.

I'm still queasy, but I summon up my strength. I speak calmly and put a hand on his shoulder. "Ray, it's three in the morning. We're eight hours out; we can't be very far from West End. We're definitely a lot closer to the Bahamas than we are to Florida. Heading back would be a long, uncomfortable trip; the current will set us far north of Miami. But there's no reason to assume we're off-course and the wind is behind us now. Let's push on."

As we talk, the rain and wind subside; the squall is moving past us.

"I'll pump the bilge and find where the water is coming in, Ray. Try to bail some of the water out of the dinghy while we have a break in the weather."

When you're afraid in the middle of the ocean, you can't call for help. You can't pay to get off. Once you've boarded the roller coaster, you can't stop the ride no matter how terrified you are. At some point, after all options are exhausted, practicality trumps the panic instinct. You get your head together and focus on making the best of a bad situation.

I remove the companionway steps and insert the handle into a manual bilge pump installed beneath them. It's hard work at a gallon per stroke, but the water recedes, stranding soggy bananas and apples on wet floorboards.

On deck, with the squall past, Ray manages to get a respectable amount of water out of the dinghy with a five-gallon bucket on a rope. He tastes the water in the bailing bucket; it's fresh. The dinghy has done a valiant job negotiating the big seas, taking on more rain-water than seawater.

He comes down below to look around. Our situation seems less desperate with the floorboards no longer afloat. "Here's your leak," he says, pointing to a small stream of water coming through the deck on the starboard side. "Your chainplate's broken; when the waves wash over the deck, the ocean leaks in."

Chainplates attach the mast shrouds[72] to the boat. On many boats, with a bad chainplate, you can't sail without the mast coming down, but *Blue Monk's* are bigger inside the boat than outside. The chain-plate has separated from the heavy stringer to which it was secured, but it can't pull all the way out. We are saved by clever engineering. The problem is a simple broken bolt—nothing that can't be fixed easily. Fortunately, the deck can take the strain for now.

---

72 *Stays and shrouds* - supporting wires strung between the mast and the hull or the edge of the deck.

We squeeze caulking around the chainplate and continue on.

We're no longer sinking.

"Must be hell on shore on a night like this," Ray jokes.

His spirits have improved.

Slowly, slowly, the eastern sky lightens.

Waves turn from turgid black to oily gray to cobalt blue.

We're still offshore in big, deep water, but I can see the radio tower at West End.

Only a few more miles to go.

Flying fish scatter from our bow.

Casuarina pines on Grand Bahama Island rise from the sea ahead of us.

"The cruising guide says to watch out for coral heads near the coast." I point out the page to Ray. "Let's tack back out a short way and enter through Indian Cay cut a mile or two north of here." I can't tell if we're looking at waves breaking on coral or just the foamy tops of swells rolling in from deep water to stack up on the shallow Bahama Banks, but we'd best not take chances.

Ray puts the helm over.

Without a jib, in this light air, the boat won't cross the wind.

Without a jib halyard, we can't raise the jib.

"Try falling off to get some speed and then put the tiller hard over."

Blue Monk comes into the wind and stalls but still won't tack.

I lower the motor and pull the starter cord.

Nothing.

We try tacking again with the main boom pushed over to back-wind the sail.

Nothing.

Finally, we fall off the wind the other way, gybing the boat around to let the wind cross behind us. "Here she comes." We wallow for a long moment in the swells, fend off the dinghy as we circle and gather speed.

The morning is bleary after a long, sleepless night. Time flows quietly and unsteadily but the hours deliver us past the broken light tower on Indian Cay Rock onto the Bahama Banks. The color lightens dramatically as we sail over the dropoff into the shallow sea—*baja mar*—for which the Spanish named these islands.

Once behind the rocks and past the sand shoal, we adjust our course south to West End Point to anchor, rest, and clear Customs. I lower the outboard once more, pump the bulb in the fuel line, and pull the starter cord.

Nothing.

Pull.

Nothing.

Pull. Pull. Pull.

Nothing. Nothing. Nothing.

Ray smiles and shakes his head.

But wind and tide are in our favor. We sail to the point, round up into the wind, and drop anchor, joining a handful of other boats.

A faulty engine is the least of our concerns. We made it across the Gulf Stream to our destination and the dinghy—miraculously—survived, too. In the calm of the anchorage, Ray reaches up with the boathook and retrieves the wayward jib halyard.

I open the forward hatch, haul up the windscoop to get air moving through the stuffy, wet cabin, and then go on deck to raise a yellow quarantine flag to the mast spreader. As the night's ordeal fades from experience to memory, we mark the passage's final cross on our chart.

We have traversed the mighty Styx. Tomorrow, we'll continue eastward across the Bahama Banks, eager to face what the sea may bring. As with any boundary between here and the mythical beyond, those who cross arrive transformed on the other side.

Across the Banks

A FEW HOURS after arriving in West End's calm anchorage, my seasickness passes.

Ray and I prepare a simple breakfast.

The flywheel came loose somehow during our Gulf Stream crossing. I pull the cover off the engine, tap the wheel down and tighten the nut that secures it. One pull of the starter cord and the motor runs again. Things are already 'Better in the Bahamas.'[73] Ray rummages through my hardware collection and finds a stainless steel nut and bolt suitable for re-securing the chainplate.

We weigh the anchor, motor into the marina, and tie to the Customs dock.

"I figured we'd get everything sorted out once we got anchored up," I explain to Ray. "The Bahamas has some sort of magical energy field. If something breaks, someone will come along with the part you need. If you're hungry, someone will invite you to dinner or drop off a fish because they've caught more than they can eat. If you get

---

73 During the 1970s, the Bahamas' official advertising slogan was, "It's Better in the Bahamas."

stuck somewhere, it's inevitably to experience something wonderful you would otherwise miss. I may sound crazy but the coincidences stack up here to a point where you have to acknowledge something is happening. It may or may not have a logical, scientific explanation; you don't have to get on your knees and pray to it, but I find a certain spirit of generosity and boundless possibility here that's worth honoring."

Ray smiles. He's not sold yet but he's lived on boats long enough to accept possibilities others might dismiss.

I always expect to get fleeced by Customs officers but this one takes pity on us when I show him our tiny boat. "You boys come cross de Golf Stream in dat bod weadder las' night in *dot* l'il boat? You guys *crezzy*, mon!" He stamps our passports, charges a minimal fee, and spares us the indignity of searching the boat.

I tell Ray about the last time I landed here, when Ron and I hiked through the jungle to the airport Customs office because that was the only one indicated on our chart.

My supplies, stored under the starboard bunk beneath the leaky chainplate, are waterlogged. We place cans and plastic bags of food on the dock to dry in the sun.

An overnight stay in the marina provides us with needed rest but leaves me with twenty-five dollars.

By first light, we've cleaned and organized the boat, stowed mostly-dry food and gear, enjoyed a good night's sleep, and eaten a hearty breakfast of those eggs that survived our rough passage. The rising sun beckons from a glittering horizon. Storms and ocean swells lie behind us, relegated now to the trophy closet of memory. Getting here was our big challenge; last night's Gulf Stream crossing marked our successful initiation into the Secret Order of Salty Florida mariners. This shallow wilderness will be easier going. We proudly set a course for Mangrove Cay across the blue-green Bahama Banks.

A light wind blows south of east.

We make slow progress but we're in no hurry.

Something is *different* here, and as we sail, silently adjusting to this other world, our focus shifts from clock to compass. In the afternoon, I climb the mast rungs to the spreaders and call, "Land ho!" to Ray in the cockpit below me. The trees of Mangrove Cay peek over our blue-green horizon. Two hours later, we anchor in its lee. Though the water here is shallow, we can't see bottom; the sea is silty or somehow stained dark by the mangroves.

We prepare a hot supper, enjoying the isolated wilderness. Neither land nor civilization are all that far away, but with no other soul visible within the circle of our horizon, we are alone in the world.

Darkness falls.

Stars appear.

We laugh in the cockpit, relaxing after a good day's sail.

"What the hell is *that?*" Ray points to a burst of orange on the western horizon. A fiery glow in the clouds spreads quickly. This is no sunset. A yellow triangle of flame climbs skyward through the center of the conflagration.

Did we sail away just in time to avoid a nuclear disaster?

"Ray, that's the space shuttle; there must be a launch at Cape Canaveral. The spaceport is just about due west of us."

A stream of fire and incomprehensible power gushes from beneath the rocket, which climbs higher and higher as the river of light slowly dissipates under the rising flame. We observe the stages of the launch in fascination as the shuttle ascends into the sky.

A bump awakens us hours before dawn; we're bouncing on the bottom.

The tide is ebbing.

Groggily, we pull anchors, start the engine and move a hundred feet farther from the island.

We return to our bunks.

The tide drops and strands us again.

"Must be close to dead low by now," I assure Ray. "The bottom is soft sand; we're in no danger. Let's stay in our bunks. When the sun comes up, we'll take a row while the tide floats us free."

A few items are still damp from our Gulf Stream crossing. I hang shirts from the boom and leave some food on deck to dry. After breakfast, we explore tiny Mangrove Cay by dinghy.

As expected, Mangrove Cay is comprised of mangrove trees. The island offers no beach or land to speak of, only a patch of green a half-mile long and a quarter-mile wide, perched on a labyrinth of roots through which the water flows freely. We discover a narrow, natural channel into the mangroves and row inside, using *Light Blue's* long oars like canoe paddles so the narrow waterway can accommodate us. Inside this outer ring of island, thick foliage forbids the intrusion of wind; all is quiet and calm. Snappers chase small fish through the endless maze of algae-covered roots beneath the shallow waters.

This is isolation. How long might it be before anyone else comes in here?

With no room to turn about, we paddle backward out of the channel, continuing around the island to where something is beached on a shallow shoal—a small airplane. The engine is gone but the rest looks almost new; the clean white plane rests its wings on the tropical mud. An emergency landing? Maybe—or perhaps a planned stop at a secluded place to transfer a South American cargo worth much more than the sacrificial vehicle used to carry it? We climb out of the dinghy to inspect the plane, stepping on the sparse seagrass clumps to prevent the thick, gray mud from sucking the sneakers off our feet.

As I row us back to *Blue Monk*, Montana Ray reaches over the side to retrieve a bunch of floating bananas. "You meant what you said about being magically provided for here," he jokes. Other drifting items cross our path as *Light Blue* makes her way round the island to return to our ship. *Blue Monk* is hard aground, heeling severely—which is why the fruit fell off her decks; I underestimated the range of the tide and the water's depth. There's nothing we can do, but the day is young. We climb into our bunks and read while the rising water rights us and floats us free.

A few hours later, we head for Great Sale Cay on a tight reach in light winds with the engine providing most of our forward progress. Mangrove Cay disappears quietly behind us. Endless blue horizon encircles us; a tapestry of sand, sponges, and seagrass passes below. Occasionally, we sail over murky areas that appear to be shallow flats—"fish muds" where schools of feeding fish stir up the bottom.

We reach our destination late in the afternoon—a bay formed by the open arms of two thin peninsulas extending from Great Sale Cay. We drop anchor over sand and sparse seagrass, this time choosing a spot not-too-shallow to accommodate us at low tide.

Two other sailboats share this anchorage with us. Aboard one is an older couple on their way back to the States. Seeing that we're two young guys on a tiny boat, they assume we could use some money. A white-haired gentleman motors up in an inflatable dinghy to ask if he might contract me to clean the grass and algae off his boat bottom.

An hour later, I'm shivering for having been submerged too long in cold water, but the swim is a baptism, a return to the embrace of these special seas, a reaffirmation that through some mechanism beyond my ability to understand, I am provided for. I say nothing to Ray—I'm not selling anything or building a case for a cause—but

I'm grateful to have an extra forty dollars in my pocket. I can stretch that money a long way here.

Barney and Barbara are aboard the anchorage's other vessel. They're young cruisers like us, making their way home to Florida. Barney is a guitarist and singer. I bring my guitar over; we trade songs late into the evening. They share a hot dinner and tell us of friends to look up at Man-O-War Cay.

Before retiring, we sit in *Blue Monk's* cockpit and marvel at how many stars can be seen this far from the urban glow of Miami.

In the morning, our neighbors raise their sails and depart with a wave, leaving the anchorage to us. We row *Light Blue* to a rickety fisherman's dock on the north side of the cove, then walk across the peninsula on a meandering footpath through the scrub grass to a white beach on the north coast. Any tourist would love to frolic on this sand, but in this less accessible part of the world, ours are the only footprints. After coming from a place where people crowd the beaches, competing to stake a claim on a patch of sun, we step lightly under the coconut palms. We are privileged to be here, and privileged to know such places exist for those willing to weigh anchor and believe in something better. We walk along the wave line where the wet sand is harder for a half-mile, then hike back to the dinghy.

We row around a coral ledge rimming the cove, cross to the other side where the water shoals, and then follow the rocky shoreline toward the southern peninsula of the island where the water deepens to four feet. We don masks and hop overboard, towing the dinghy behind us as we hunt for fish with spears in hand. A big pufferfish with two-inch eyes startles me with its gaze from the shadows, but hoped-for lobster and snapper are elsewhere.

After a few hours, we return to our boat fishless. But determined to live off the sea, we scrape a collection of whelks and chitons off the rocks. They look like Devonian fossils, but they're *seafood;* how bad can they be? Boiling water quickly transforms the unfortunate mollusks into a pot of boiled erasers. "I wonder which one was Lawrence?" Ray asks solemnly, looking at the whelk shells in the pot.

"How about I whip up some pasta?" I suggest. "I have a can of tomato sauce in the locker that got sea water on it; I need to use it before it rusts."

The meal is humble but here in this beautiful anchorage, after diving in crystal water and walking along a pristine beach, spaghetti with canned sauce is a king's repast.

We're just two guys in a boat anchored off an uninhabited island, safe from storms, crashing waves, and hidden reefs. What we're doing isn't all that adventurous. But this is *everything*—an opportunity to observe the world not through a glass window or on a printed page, but to row across it, swim beneath it, and feel its soft sand under our bare feet; to enjoy a sky full of stars unobscured by the glare of civilization; to hunt for food not in a commercial freezer, but under a coral ledge. Possessing only primitive shelter, a cooking stove, bunks, books, tools, and a guitar—all means with which to reunite our humanity with the natural world from whence we came—we are happy with the here and now; we don't have to work or punch a clock. What remains is the pure, simple joy of living.

"Stay another day or head out tomorrow?" I ask Ray.

"This is a peaceful place; I could get used to it." He pauses and takes a deep breath. "But let's keep sailing. If the Bahamas is this beautiful here, I want to see the out-islands."

The Blue Monk

Saturnalia
Two Months Later

JOHN NATION AND I sit on the deck of *Zebra Dun* in Man-O-War
Harbour.

Diana rows over to visit. She and Richard have had a little too
much togetherness over on *Killer Tomato;* thirty-two feet isn't much
space to share sometimes, especially when you're not doing much
sailing. Man-O-War Cay is a perfect place to just sit and be, but
one can only tolerate so much sitting and so much being before one
develops an overpowering desire to go sit and be somewhere else
with someone else.

Diana complains for a few minutes. In her late forties, she's looking for a relationship where her role is more serious than being a
boating accessory, but having escaped her fiberglass confines, she
soon decompresses and reverts to her usual, bubbly self.

Diana points to *Rabbit,* a white sloop with an unusual rounded
stern anchored nearby. "Have you met Doc?" she asks.

We shake our heads.

The boat's been here as long as we have, stored on a mooring in the protected lagoon. We don't even notice *Rabbit* anymore, which is why we both missed that, today, someone is aboard; a dinghy floats behind her.

"I worked with Doc back in Palm Beach when I was a nurse," Diana explains. "He bought the boat to retire on but he hasn't gotten to use it much. He finally shut down his practice; he's here in the Abacos for a while. You'll like him; he's a really sweet guy."

On cue, Doc appears in his cockpit. Diana calls to him and waves him over. Soon a short, silver-haired man with permanently hunched shoulders joins us on deck. Quiet and intelligent, Doc shows all the signs of recent arrival, like someone who went into the light not knowing what to expect and awoke in a strange world swathed in vivid blues and greens. He's still adjusting, opening his eyes—a process that takes some time; the land of clocks and calendars is not easily forsaken. "I hope..." he says slowly, "I hope I can stay here a while. I've dreamed of getting away, but my family thinks I'm crazy. 'It's not safe for someone your age,' they say. 'Surely, you must be lonely on a boat by yourself.' I worked hard for forty years, and now that I can finally get what I've waited so long for, my kids and grandkids can't stop coming up with plans to 'keep the old man entertained.'"

Sitting in a folding chair on the *Zebra Dun's* mahogany deck, Doc closes his eyes and breathes deep, traveling back in time, carrying his present with him. He smiles. For now, he's here, doing what he wants to do. He's been missing a simple, intangible something.

Like these islands, John's wooden schooner suggests a certain other-worldliness. I have no quarrels with fiberglass boats—they have their advantages and I happen to live on one—but the unique sounds, smells, and images associated with traditional wooden boats connect one more readily to history, romance, and tradition. A handcrafted wooden vessel has stories to tell, and suggests by inference that those who sail aboard her will, too. Many yachtsmen carry a Jolly Roger ensign but few fly those colors without an air of cheap costumery. When the skull and crossbones are hauled to the masthead of the *Zebra Dun,* the effect is striking and authentic.

In a former life, before he got a divorce and a wooden schooner, John directed a planetarium in Oklahoma. He describes how we are about to experience a rare triple conjunction of Saturn, Uranus, and Neptune. Such planetary alignments, he explains, have been blamed for wars and earthquakes, floods and famines, momentous political shifts, flashes of technological innovation, and bursts of creative expression. As we speak, astrologers sharpen pencils and put fresh ribbons in typewriters, scouring the news for important events and catastrophes to validate the profound effects of the celestial alignment. Astronomers polish mirrors and lenses in powerful telescopes. In Washington, DC, President Reagan is warned by top advisers not to make major policy decisions until the conjunction passes.

John never lost his boyhood fascination with the stars. He grows more and more animated as he holds court on deck, describing how the celestial bodies, with the exception of distant Pluto, orbit the sun in alignment, almost as a set of concentric, elliptical rings—though debate over the validity of Pluto's status as an official planet remains open. Each satellite orbits at a different speed; it's rare enough that any two are at the same point of orbit at the same time. Tomorrow night there will be three.

Today, whether at the simple peak of his enthusiasm or affected, himself, by the growing confluence of planetary gravity, John pauses to take a breath. "We are going to have ourselves a saturnalia," he proclaims.

"How much money you got, Bricker?" he asks. Many of John's proclamations are followed by this unfortunate question.

"About four or five dollars."

"That ought to do it. I have a few dollars left and a cast-iron Dutch oven stashed under the bridge deck behind the wood stove. Between us, we can afford a chicken and some brown sugar, some veggies and some fresh garlic. Tomorrow, let's sail over to Shell Island where it's dark and the viewing horizon is low. We'll build a fire and roast us up a chicken to honor the pagan gods.

"Doc? Diana? Join us? Richard's welcome if you can get him to move, Diana."

"I'm in," says Doc without hesitation.

Diana nods over her shoulder at the *Killer Tomato* and rolls her eyes. "Not much chance of getting mister I-never-sail-on-the-boat-I-happen-to-be-retired-in-the-Bahamas-on to do much of anything. I'm afraid it's going to be a bachelors' night out for you guys."

After lunch the next day, *Blue Monk* follows *Zebra Dun* out of Man-O-War Harbour through the narrow, rocky cut. Doc is not far behind on *Rabbit*. We turn to starboard, heading northwest across the Little Bahama Bank. A mild norther is blowing. The wind on our beam should make for ideal sailing but we're in the lee of the out-islands much of the time; the breeze is light. We motor-sail to ensure we reach our destination with daylight to spare. Leaving Man-O-War Cay behind, we pass the low, rocky islets of the Fowl Cays Sea Park, privately-owned Scotland Cay, and the comparatively lengthy coast of Great Guana Cay, which accounts for almost half of our thirteen mile journey.

At the end of Great Guana Cay is Whale Cay passage; a deep-water entrance from the North Atlantic Ocean to the Abaco banks. No place to be in unsettled weather, the seas in this cut pile up in ten-foot swells even when the wind is light. Local folklore says many boats lie on the bottom here. Whale Cay is a barren, rocky hump, swept clean by angry waves. Undeterred by big seas, enormous cruise ships make their way through the cut onto the banks into a sheltered, dredged mooring area. The cruise lines have developed the northwest end of Guana Cay into a private beach paradise with bars, t-shirt stands, and calypso bands—everything a sun and alcohol-seeking vacationer might desire.

But no ships are moored here today. Party beach is not our destination. Neither will we traverse Whale Cay Passage on this voyage.

A half-mile southwest of the ship mooring area, the dredge spoils from its creation form a small, sandy islet, unofficially dubbed "Shell Island" by cruisers. As with Pluto's bid for planethood, Shell Island has not been around long enough to be awarded official "island" status by cartographers. The unpretentious mound of sand mixed with millions of seashells and covered with scattered, scrubby grass patches, appears as little more than a shoal on our charts, but the tiny cay offers an excellent anchorage for our purpose. Shell Island is primitive, secluded, and remote—the ideal place for our saturnalia; it provides shelter from the swells rolling through the cut, has neither trees nor high hills to obscure our view of the sky, and is far from any lights that would interfere with our night vision. Apart from those we carry aboard our boats, the closest man-made lights are two miles away. This is a wild place, a speck of sand frequently passed and seldom visited. Here we find no tourists, no fishermen, no Haitian refugees, no Customs officials, no traffic lights or grocery stores—only three disparate planets brought together by happenstance and fate.

The sun falls below the pines of Great Abaco.

The wind picks up.

The temperature drops.

We drag my dinghy to the top of the beach and prop it on its oars behind us to serve as a windbreak. John had the foresight to gather dry firewood back at Man-O-War Cay. We add to his collection a few pieces of driftwood we find on the beach. Behind our dinghy shelter, a small flame begins to consume our branches and wood scraps.

Yellow sparks crackle and fly high into the fast-darkening night.

Stars gather overhead.

John points into the brilliant sky. "See the three planets grouped in a small triangle there? They're what we've come here for. They won't appear this close together again for over a thousand years."

It honestly doesn't look like much. On a moonless night in Abaco, the sky is one massive cluster of stars, anyway. But one excuse for being here is as good as another. A conjunction of planets is but the magic stone in our experiential soup, imparting mysterious flavors and mystical healing properties as surely as our own presence renders sacred this simple hill of dredge tailings at the edge of a shallow sea. Painted orange by firelight, our three spirit-faces hover before the darkness. The north wind is cold, but we are warm before the flames in the shelter of the propped-up dinghy.

The chicken, cooked with sliced carrots and onions in the iron pot over our humble fire, is delicious. Like happy savages, we strip the bones and toss them into the fire.

The celestial event brings no floods, earthquakes, or political revolutions, no grand strokes of insight, no bursts of creative inspiration. We are but three small men huddled before a flame atop a tiny mound of shells beneath the Milky Way.

Doc is quiet and reflective.

His eyes sparkle in the firelight.

This is a moment imagined and waited for since childhood, a long-awaited escape, a hoped-for connection to the deeper and simpler, a purification, an unlearning, an ascension to the mountaintop, a peeling away of layers to expose the core. "I have a heart condition," he says softly. "I'm not going to live forever. If I am to go, why not tonight beneath these stars?"

We sit together in silence as the flames die down.

The chill wind overpowers the warmth of the waning fire.

It's late.

A red moon rises above the horizon, brightening the sky and washing away the dimmer stars.

A hundred feet off the beach, our vessels bob quietly in the loom of their anchor lights. We launch our dinghies, return to warm, waiting bunks and sleep as one can only sleep after a day of sailing and a full plate of dinner.

In the morning, Doc pulls his anchors and heads back to his mooring at Man-O-War Cay. John and I wave and set a divergent course across the Sea of Abaco to Marsh Harbour on the mainland.

A week later, we return to our usual anchoring spots at Man-O-War Cay.

Rabbit sits peacefully on her mooring but no dinghy is tied behind her.

"He had to go home for a while," Diana explains. "Family matters."

We don't see him again.

Journeyman

JOURNEYMAN commanded my attention the first time I entered Man-O-War Harbour in 1989 during my first cruise to the Abacos. Sitting on her mooring under a canvas sun cover, her varnished hull and traditional lines stood out proudly against the fiberglass vessels anchored around her.

"Tell me about *Journeyman*," I say to John Nation. "No sleight to *Zebra Dun* intended, but she's got to be the most beautiful boat I've ever seen."

"A German sailor named Gerhard built her," says John, "and you're right; she's a museum piece."

Each time I row to town, I can't help but admire her. I sneak alongside to steal a peek over her bulwarks. Every inch of her is perfectly crafted.

What an experience it would be to sail a vessel like this!

On this, my second cruise to the Abacos, I find *Journeyman* still asleep on her mooring, waiting for Gerhard in the shelter of Man-O-War Harbour.

One day, I spy him aboard removing the sun-awnings from over his decks. I knock on his hull and offer to help.

I must see this extraordinary boat.

Introductions are easy here where eccentricity is the norm. Gerhard is in his mid-fifties, thin and gray-haired with hollow cheeks. I can't tell if he's outwardly friendly with a hardened interior or calloused on the outside and warm underneath. Here is a man who knows how to push aside obstacles and get things done. *Journeyman* is a monument to German efficiency. As with the rest of us, years of life aboard have catalyzed a reshaping of his personality into an array of concavities and convexities and disparate, quirky, even contradictory qualities. Gerhard is an engineer, a European craftsman, a sailor, a bitter divorcé, an ex-oil rig worker, a cynic, an overgrown kid, and an empiricist trying to understand the currents of magic and coincidence flowing through life. His plan to sail back to Florida for work contradicts his soul's desire to stay in these islands aboard his beloved boat, but Gerhard is a doer, not a dreamer; he will serve his sentence in the world of fences and grids, bend his sails, and return to the realm of wind and waves.

Gerhard's facility with English far exceeds his confidence speaking it, but he explains how he designed and assembled *Journeyman* in Belize twenty years before, living in his joyful memories as he relates her story. She's a double-ender inspired by traditional Colin Archer designs of the North Sea. Gerhard ventured into the Central American jungle himself to hand-select and harvest the trees to build her. Each rib is fashioned from an eight-inch thick mahogany branch grown naturally to the curve of its hull station—and each rib is doubled. The planking—long-leaf yellow pine below the waterline and granadío, a dense tropical rosewood above—is precision-cut; every board fits perfectly into the one below. So exact is this construction that she requires no caulking. Once launched, the swelling of the wet wood seals her hull.

Journeyman's planks are trunnel fastened. Derived etymologically from "tree nails," trunnel fastening forgoes the use of corrosible metal screws or nails in favor of hardwood dowels hammered into holes drilled through the planks into the ribs. The outside end of each dowel is notched to receive a wooden wedge. The hammered-in wedge is covered and sealed with a glued wooden plug. The resulting hull is one hundred percent cellulose.

deadeyes

All *Journeyman's* hardware is homemade; Gerhard fabricated his own bronze hatch hinges and latches. The deadeyes and belaying pins[74] in her rigging are hand-carved from lignum vitae, a fantastically strong hardwood originally used for wooden clock gears because its natural oils gave it a self-lubricating quality.

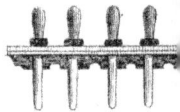

belaying pins

But mere technical description is insufficient to convey the scope of Gerhard's achievement.

Journeyman is warm, charming, a Black Forest cuckoo clock gone to

---

74 On a traditional vessel, *deadeyes* are wooden blocks through which the rope rigging is roven to adjust tension on the mast. Instead of securing halyards to cleats, they are traditionally fastened around *belaying pins* that serve the same purpose. (See figures)

sea. Her bulkheads are festooned with artistic woodcarvings. Like her exterior planking, her cabin glows with varnish and natural wood. Massive quarter knees[75] along the deck-hull joint attest to her over-construction. An 85-horsepower Perkins diesel provides more than ample power for windless days.

None of this work was accomplished in the name of vanity. Though she could be a millionaire's showpiece, Gerhard created *Journeyman* to prove to himself how far he could take the shipwright's art. After decades of regret over not being able to complete his boyhood carpentry apprenticeship, he committed to a personal goal—to design, build, and sail a forty-two foot yacht. Completion of this self-imposed final examination justified his assumption of a title, not of Master Carpenter—that might be seen as arrogant—but of humble Journeyman.

A few weeks after our meeting, I help Gerhard sail *Journeyman* to Fort Lauderdale. With a light wind behind us, the islands fall slowly away. Beyond sight of shore, we are but a speck plodding across a blue desert of water and sky.

We make excellent time until we run aground on a sand shoal while taking a shortcut over the Bahama Banks; the chart said the water was deep enough. Gerhard is fuming mad, sputtering expletives, wishing we'd chosen a different route, but with help from

---

75 *Quarter knees* - connect roughly perpendicular surfaces such as the deck and hull of a boat. They look and function much like wooden shelf brackets.

the rising tide and *Journeyman's* big diesel, we extricate our keel from the mud, reach the edge of the Banks, and continue across the Stream.

Experienced mariners, we understand the respect the Gulf Stream is due, but Poseidon offers no challenge to test our resolve or break our spirits. We motorsail across in light winds over gentle seas, an easy passage.

Once safely inside Fort Lauderdale inlet, we lower our sails and tie up on the Intracoastal Waterway to clear Customs and rest. After the requisite paperwork is complete, we continue inland up Fort Lauderdale's New River, waiting for bridge tenders to respond while the current pushes us toward the spans; I'm used to maneuvering in open spaces. Gerhard has arranged for a berth behind a private home; he'll live aboard at the dock while he works to replenish his cruising account.

With less than a mile to go, an old submerged line wraps around our propeller. Gerhard spends a few minutes in the cold and murky water, swearing, with a dive mask and a sharp knife, removing the obstruction and a tiny piece of his thumb before we complete the last half-mile of our voyage.

What a strange transition—to board a boat in the Abaco out-islands and disembark in a suburban backyard.

"I'm sorry I yelled at you when we went aground on the Banks," Gerhard confesses.

"Heat of the moment," I reply. "No big deal. I let it go back on the other side of the Gulf Stream."

"It was a pleasure sailing with you. You're a good sailor. I hope we will get a chance to sail together again."

"I'd like that, Gerhard. I'll look for you in the islands."

Water

"WATER," said Carl Jung, "is the commonest symbol for the unconscious." In these islands, the sea is clear; the bottom is visible. In a realm so potent with symbolism, water bends perspective as readily as light, inspiring visions powerful, moving and transcendent.

Cathy's Island

I anchor at Powell Cay, a less-traveled island northwest of Green Turtle Cay. Uninhabited, it's serenely quiet, with beaches devoid of human footprints and a grove of tall, wild coconut palms. On the lee side, dramatic coral cliffs shelter tropicbirds nesting in their season. Affixed to the rocks near the anchorage is a small, bronze plaque—"Cathy Swedenborg Loved This Island"— a shrine to a young woman who died here with her boyfriend in 1979 when their boat burned. Her epitaph is unconcerned with what was lost. Instead, it connects her forever to this special place she found and appreciated, and to her enduring suggestion that I might love it, too.

⮂ The Blue Monk

Late at night, I awaken and step into the cockpit. Unadulterated by urban incandescence, untinted by the azure hue of day, the nocturnal world projects its magic for those fortunate to bear witness.

The moon is high and bright; the white sand bottom illuminated like a stadium; the lunar light brilliant enough to read by.

I step astern, grabbing the backstay for support.

A diamond shape moves in the water below me.

And another.

Giant Atlantic stingrays glide over the bottom: dozens of them. Their dark forms undulate, slow and graceful against brilliant, subaquatic sand; an Escher woodcut brought to life; a moving tapestry of figure and ground; a dream landscape.

Such sights may be common. Stingrays may congregate here regularly on moonlit nights—or perhaps—only once—tonight. It doesn't matter; I am blessed to witness a secret world of shadows and light.

Cathy Swedenborg loved this island.

I understand.

Swimming In the Light

At night, especially during summers when the ocean is warm, the sea is alive with bioluminescence. Microscopic creatures glow firefly-green where the water is agitated. On a dark night, swimming is an otherworldly experience—my body emanates sparkling fire; propellers leave trails of light; swirls of green remain where oars are withdrawn from the water.

Tonight, in the lagoon at Man-O-War Cay, the phosphorescence is particularly potent. On awakening, I ascend to the deck to marvel at the stars above the silhouettes of the jungle-covered hills that protect this anchorage from ocean swells.

Not a breath of wind disturbs the lagoon.

The sea crashes against the rocks on the far side of the island.

Something breathes deeply—something close—a quick exhalation followed by an inward breath.

Ripples spread across placid water.

A glowing green dolphin glides beneath the anchored boats, leaving a phosphorescent contrail behind her. Dolphins frequently venture into shallow anchorages to swim among our boats.

How must we appear to them? With their sophisticated hearing and echolocation systems, they can surely observe us in our strange wood and fiberglass nests. I wonder what they think, these creatures who live in the sea yet breathe air, of those who live in the sky yet sleep beneath the water.

I watch in rapture as she crisscrosses the lagoon. Periodically, she surfaces to breathe among the sleeping vessels. Man-O-War is a small place, and no bountiful fishing ground compared to the barrier reef thriving with life a short mile away. Why would she even be here if not to dance in the light?

Clarity

Daylight skies are blue. Sunlight is yellow or orange at dawn and dusk, and pure white at noon. Under these influences, the natural hues of the diurnal landscape are a feast of color but the nocturnal realm is illuminated by no such chromatic vibrancy. Uncolored by the pastels of daytime illumination, Bahamian water untouched by sunlight takes on even more remarkable clarity. White light from stars and the bleached surface of the lifeless moon render the world of night a sonata of contrasting silvers and blacks. Brilliant reflections dance on shimmering seas, yet are subject to manipulation by changes in viewing angle. Each observer perceives a landscape uniquely decorated by his own proximity to the light.

With the moon approaching the horizon, *Blue Monk* lies at anchor with a few other boats near Great Guana Cay. As I row, neither the tiniest breath of wind nor the faintest eddy of tidal flow disturbs the surface.

The water is transparent as air.

I am not rowing; I am flying.

The boundary between atmosphere and sea is indistinguishable. Ribbons of reflected light curl from my bow, dissipating into nothing as I glide across the water. Like my dinghy, our anchored boats hover rather than float over shadows undisturbed by the refractive effects of moving waves. Adrift in the atmosphere above dangling anchor lines clearly visible in the sand below, my senses warn me to avoid falling even as logic assures me the invisible water still holds me up. How odd, magical, and surreal to find such clarity in darkness.

Blue Holes

Little Harbour is the last stop on Great Abaco before the ninety-mile long island elbows southward into bottomless abyss. Beyond the small reef where the chain of out-islands ends, the North Atlantic embraces the island's coast directly. Little Harbour is a world of its own, with a protected lagoon, caves full of bats, an old lighthouse on a sea cliff stationed above a place where ocean waves detonate into foam against the rocks below, and even a bronze sculpture foundry.

West of Little Harbour lies the Bight of Old Robinson, a shallow, oval bay rimmed by rings of coral. We snorkel among the rocky ridges at the perimeter, hunting for fish and lobster.

While swimming across the shallow sea floor, I encounter a yawning cavern—a blue hole—a forty-foot wide, infinitely deep subterranean passageway connected in some distant place to the greater ocean.

Richard, a French sailor on *Klodokat*, a steel sloop, joins us today. His second anchor line parted in a storm on the Bahama Banks a year before. He was in the water retrieving the first anchor at the time. He swam for days before dragging himself up on a desolate rock at the edge of the Gulf Stream. Thirsty and sunburned, Richard was rescued by a passing yachtsman while his girlfriend waited, despondent, in Bimini, having reluctantly given up the search for lack of fuel and hope. Upon being reunited with him, she offered him anything she could afford to give. Today, he wears his chosen gift; a pair of freediving fins as long as your arm from fingertip to shoulder. He takes a deep breath, then dives deep into the eerie gloom below me to explore the ledges along the hole's perimeter.

Blue holes like these dot the Bahamas. A few, like one not far from Marsh Harbour, are landlocked and possibly of some utility; what goes into a blue hole *stays* in a blue hole; nothing incriminating need ever be found. One can only imagine the nature of countless furtive missions to the bottomless pond in the Abaco pines since the Lucaya Indians inhabited this place centuries ago.

Depth

In the Bahamas, where the bottom is not visible, the water is deep— *really* deep. After passing through the cut in Little Harbour's reef before sundown, I sail overnight to make Nassau in the light of morning, daylight arrival being a prudent practice for calling anywhere in these shallow and poorly marked islands. About two thirds of the way between Little Harbour and New Providence Island, the chart shows a wide, conical depression in the ocean floor—4,762 meters—almost three miles deep. Falling that distance from the sky to the ground would take eight minutes. Add water resistance to that descent and you have time to think while you sink. The pressure at the bottom is 473 times what it is at the surface and yet, living creatures inhabit that inky blackness. That world is better imagined than experienced but it inspires no less wonder.

I check my compass heading again, adjust course, and consider the thin fiberglass shell that contains only myself, my humble effects, and enough air to buoy me high above the distant bottom.

Sailing here is as profound as staring into the Milky Way.

≶ The Blue Monk

Water *is* a symbol of the unconscious. Floating over miles of blackness, riding the invisible boundary between sky and sea, I traverse many planes. In the infinite depths of the ocean, I confront my own fathomless mystery. In transparent shallows, what lies beneath the surface is both revealed and obscured by reflection. Travelers across an aqueous landscape of deep oceans, peaceful calms, explosive turbulence, vibrant color, and sparkling contrast encounter visions no less beautiful, moving, and inspiring than any dream—visions illuminated by an inner force as powerful as the light of the stars.

Strangers in Paradise

EVANS RETURNS TO HIS SLOOP, *Arcturus*, after a year captaining a ship back and forth from the United States to the Persian Gulf to supply the U.S. military in Kuwait. He loves sailing. He even rigged a set of sails on the cargo booms of the immense freighter he had charge of, saving fuel and gaining sufficient speed to shave days off halfway-round-the-world trips. Evans's brother Phelps is aboard helping make *Arcturus* ready for more passengers. Their sister and her two teenage daughters will arrive tomorrow along with Karen, a friend with whom Evans apparently has some sort of romantic history. "It's complicated," he explains.

The next morning, I awaken, as I often do, to the muted sounds of John Nation clattering away at the keys of his old Royal Manual inside the mahogany cabin of his schooner. After our traditional corncake breakfast, I leave him to his writing and follow *Arcturus* over to Great Abaco. Marsh Harbour's grocery stores are a lot better than Man-O-War's, and I'm happy to lend my oars to the task of ferrying Evans's passengers on and off the boat.

All goes mostly as planned, but as can be expected in the Bahamas, Karen's flight is several hours late.

"Can you do us a favor, Dave?" Evans asks after we finish loading passengers and baggage onto *Arcturus*. "We'd like to sail to Guana Cay and get anchored up so the girls can do some swimming before dark. Do you mind picking Karen up for me and meeting us later?"

"I'd be happy to." I have a few hours to wait but I've been in these islands long enough to know time is malleable. With practice, hours can be bent, stretched, compressed, or willed to disappear altogether. Time is as imaginary as distance.

The day is hot but the sun is past its high mark. I enjoy my walk. Past Marsh Harbour settlement, the road curves through the pine forest to a tiny airport, built a mile or so from town, probably as an excuse to develop a small taxi industry. The terminal is a nondescript cinderblock structure at the end of a single, short runway cut through the woods. I wait outside, listening to the chatter of the Bahamian taxi drivers against the insect buzz of the wooded landscape. A drone of engines announces the arrival of a twin turboprop aircraft. I can't see the plane over the thick pines, but soon enough, I hear wheels chirp on the runway.

Propellers spin down with a decrescendo whine.

A beige Gulfstream Airways plane rolls to the tarmac.

A half-dozen people disembark, then disappear through the door to get their passports stamped and their luggage inspected.

Inside the tiny terminal, the crowd is stressed by long lines, late connections, overweight baggage, and other inconveniences.

I wait outside.

Taxis line up to ferry tourists to their hotels.

Twenty minutes later, they've all driven off.

Marsh Harbour Airport is quiet again.

Somewhere, a woodpecker taps at a tree.

The forest continues to buzz.

I wait, absentmindedly rolling the minutes between my thumb and forefinger.

A second plane hums over the pine tops.

Eventually, a young woman with a floppy hat leaves the terminal, looking around for a familiar face.

"Are you Karen?" I inquire.

After responding to my question, she knows that I know that she's definitely Karen. In an American city, the response would be "Who the hell wants to know?" but this is not an American city. All the same, I'm a stranger who hasn't shaved for months, wearing a weathered straw cowboy hat and calling her by name. "I'm Dave, a friend of Evans," I reassure her. "When your flight was delayed, he took off with his sister and nieces. He asked if I'd sail you over to Guana Cay to meet them on *Arcturus.*"

Karen sizes me up but I've mentioned the right people and I haven't asked for money. She smiles at the absurdity of landing in a foreign country to jump on a boat with someone she's never met, and at the fact that I didn't approach anyone *else* to ask if *she* was Karen. Somehow, in these islands, you just know.

Certainly, there are clues.

Bahamians and American expatriates returning to vacation homes in Treasure Cay often chat with a neighbor who happens to be on the same flight. They're likely to be on a first-name basis with at least a few of the taxi drivers.

Visitors bound for charter boats try too hard to pose as seasoned sailors; an air of costumery surrounds them, like business people who ride Harley Davidsons and wear black leather jackets on weekends.

Snow birds escaping Michigan's Arctic winds or the blizzards of upstate New York typically overpack. They herd squabbling children and way too much luggage through the terminal door. Mom brandishes a squeeze tube of sunscreen and argues for full coverage.

Cruising sailors returning to their boats wear sun-beaten, well-loved nautical hats and backpacks. They carry shopping bags stuffed with groceries and boating gear packed in plain cardboard boxes. They don't want to pay import duty on their expensive, new 'used' or 'repaired' equipment, so they smile peacefully and try to appear invisible to the Customs man.

Escapees from cosmopolitan corporate cubicle farms are stuck in high gear. The women bring with them their competitive, glamorous office theatrics. Ready to drink and play on a beach, they arrive wearing bikinis under loose shirts that advertise their loyalty to the latest fashion labels. Their men are either wound tight, prepared to do battle with the Customs agent and win, or they've regressed to frat boy goofiness. I wonder if they're disappointed when the Abacos don't turn out to be the nightlife casino cruise ship wonderland depicted in countless Bahamas travel posters. The shallow waters in these islands run deeper than expected.

Karen is about my age, lightly built and wrapped in a long cotton dress. She looks like she hasn't seen the sun for months; she's been hiding from winter in dry, heated rooms. Her appearance says 'mountain' or 'desert' rather than 'city,' and projects a humble, unpretentious bearing. Wearing no makeup and carrying a single duffel bag, she's obviously going to a place where closet space is minimal. But she can handle the road she's on; she assesses her surroundings with obvious intelligence. She's the only viable candidate for the Karen I've been sent for.

She breathes deeply, preparing herself for the next leg of her journey. "Is there any way we can get something to eat before we go? I've been flying since early this morning—New Mexico time—and I haven't had a bite."

I wave at a taxi. Soon, we're rolling down the two-lane road through the pinewoods. "Let's throw your bag in the dinghy. We'll row straight over to the Tiki Hut and get you a cracked conch sandwich. The restaurant is a short way down the harbour."

Karen laughs. Anyone else, anywhere else, would suggest we walk over, bicycle over, drive over, hell…even *skateboard* over, but here in this strange world that began to surprise her the moment her tiny airplane banked sharply over a tapestry of shoals and marshes and dived steeply into a barely visible slot in a tropical pine forest, we're going to row over.

"The tide is low," I explain at the dock, "so it's a bit of a drop to get down to the dinghy. I'll get in first, then reach up and grab your bag. After I'm in, you climb down the ladder while I stabilize the boat. Once you get down, the trick is to shift your weight all at once. You don't want to be halfway hanging from the dock ladder and halfway sliding the dinghy around with your feet. Get in and stay low so we won't tip."

"You're extremely reassuring," she says with a giggle.

I climb in and place her bag on the seat in the bow.

Karen climbs down the ladder between my arms as I hold the dinghy against the dock.

"I must warn you..." she explains from the bottom rung, extending a leg tentatively down toward the dinghy two feet below, "I'm a monumental klutz. My life history is a long series of bumps, bruises, crashes, accidents, and disasters."

"No problem," I say. "If you're going to fall, fall with conviction. The water's clear and clean. We're both waterproof. You'll be fine."

After some precarious rocking and a brief struggle, she's seated in the dinghy's stern.

Oarlocks slip into sockets with a familiar *clunk* that resonates through the wooden hull. I breathe, push off the dock, and look behind me once to get my bearings.

Pull and glide.

Pull and glide.

Karen sits stiffly in the back with arms locked straight against the gunwales. Gradually, she becomes accustomed to the motion of the boat, realizes we're not going to capsize, unlocks her elbows, and looks around at the thirty-or-so sailboats anchored around us. "Which one's yours?"

I point to the middle of the anchorage. "That little blue one over by the big white one with the maroon sail covers."

"Don't you want to stop and drop off my bag?" she asks as I continue toward the end of the harbour, pulling with big strokes of the oars, letting the dinghy glide across the calm waters.

"No need. Your bag will be fine in the dinghy; nobody will bother it. I never lock the boat up either; nothing gets stolen here."

Karen smiles again. A few minutes later, we're sitting in a floating restaurant, enjoying a sandwich and a cold drink. "I don't know why they call this a 'cracked conch' sandwich," I say to make conversation. "They don't 'crack' the conch; they just punch a little hole in the spiral of the shell, make a small cut and the snail slips right out. That's why whole uncracked conch shells are lying all over these islands. They do pound the crap out of it to make it tender, though. I suppose 'cracked conch' sounds more appetizing than 'conch with the crap pounded out of it.'"

After a half-hour in the Tiki Hut and another short row, we board *Blue Monk* and stow Karen's bag in the forepeak.

We tie the dinghy behind us.

The Blue Monk

I lash my oars to the cabin top.

We're ready to sail.

"Can I do anything?" she asks from the cockpit.

"Nah; I do this by myself all the time; I have everything covered. Your job is to enjoy the scenery, forget about the land of clocks and calendars, breathe some fresh air, and enjoy yourself."

"I think I can do that," she smiles. "I'll try."

I raise the mainsail and pull the sail bag off the jib, which is already hanked to the forestay. After letting scope out on the starboard hook, I haul us over to the port one, coiling line and chain into a canvas bag lashed to the bow rail before finally bringing the anchor aboard. "I have a system for this," I explain, pointing to an anchor shaped like a teardrop with the rounded end cut off. A triangular fluke extends from the straight edge toward the point of the teardrop. "These 'wishbone' anchors are unconventional but they set easily and hold tight; they might as well have been custom-made to fit on top of my bow rail. I hang one on each side, and keep the line and chain in these canvas bags; they're out of the way but always ready." I wrestle the second anchor aboard, hang it on the pulpit, and winch the jib to the masthead.

Blue Monk catches the breeze.

I trim the sails.

We heel slightly.

Karen grabs her seat.

Soon, we're reaching across the Sea of Abaco.

The wind is light but sufficient to move us along.

The sun sinks toward the top of the forest.

The water is brilliant swimming pool blue.

"See the island over there that looks like an antique battle ship?" I point at the strange shape on the horizon in front of Guana Cay five miles ahead of us.

Karen nods.

"That's Foote's Cay—about a mile from where we're going. We'll anchor on the other side of it where Evans is waiting."

We make small talk along the way. Karen runs a big university art gallery in New Mexico, which sounds like it should be fun, but apparently, she's doing the work of six people. As the sun slips behind the pine forests of Great Abaco, silhouetting the tree line against a sky of orange and pink, she's already reaching for her sketchpad and the box of colored pencils in her bag. Taken in through the eyes and expressed through the hands with a brush or a pencil, these islands are everything a creative spirit needs to cleanse her soul. Already, a short mile out into the Sea of Abaco, it is difficult to conceive that a world of unmeetable deadlines, unachievable demands, and meaningless tasks could coexist with this one.

I estimate the angle of the sun with my hand and gauge the distance ahead. "We'll get to *Arcturus* after dark," I explain. "When we get close to the anchorage, I'll furl the sails, start the engine, and ask you to stand on the bow and watch for rocks."

"Rocks?"

"Probably not, but there are a few off the point close to where we'll anchor. I want to keep an eye out and not come in toward shore in the dark at a slightly different place than we think we're coming in." In the waning light, I show her the guidebook and point out where the obstacles are. I reach inside the companionway to flip on the running lights.

Avoiding rocks is something you do routinely on a sailboat—like avoiding tall buildings while flying a plane or avoiding cars in the oncoming lane while driving; I think little of it. Karen masks her alarm at the prospect of a potential collision in the dark as we continue toward the island. Soon enough, we see *Arcturus's* masthead light rocking gently against the unmoving lights of Guana Cay Harbour.

After mooring, I row Karen over for a hot meal and a warm reception.

Over the next few days, I sail along with *Arcturus.* In the evenings, we anchor together. I play my guitar. We tell jokes. We swim with a pod of dolphins in the Sea of Abaco, enjoying good company and perfect weather.

Evans's niece sunbathes on the foredeck with her headphones on; being in this incredible place and tuning it out seems like a colossal missing of a colossal point. Driven by a capricious puff of wind, the jib sheet flies across the bow and deftly swipes the headphones into the water with the cassette player flying behind them; the line doesn't even touch her. The irony and precision suggest sentient design. If anyone were to attempt to remove those headphones with a piece of flying rope without hurting the person wearing them, they'd find the task impossible.

In the calm of Man-O-War Harbour, Karen tries rowing my dinghy with its oversized spruce oars. Like most first-time rowers, she splashes a lot, almost tips, and makes a great deal of circular progress, but only when her eyes begin to tear up do I notice the short fingers on her left hand. I feel bad, not about the fingers, but about the particular grippiness of the challenge she's confronting. I prefer the additional leverage of a longer oar; the balance points of mine are about a foot outward from the oarlocks. Rowing *Light Blue* requires good technique and some extra strength. Other boats are better suited to a novice oarsman than mine. I wish, at this moment, for a vessel that would inspire more confidence. Karen impresses me, though, in spite of her frustration. Up until now, her hand has been neither mentioned nor noticed. I find a quiet dignity in that.

After a few more days of island hopping, I hug her goodbye. "I really enjoyed meeting you," she says, taking my hand and smiling into my eyes. I'm not sure if her enjoyment is related to any unsuccessful attempt on her part to fan the cold embers of romance with Evans into a flame while surrounded by his family on a small boat, but that can't be anything but "complicated." Our connection is easier than that. We scribble our addresses on scraps of paper.

"Safe travels, Karen. I'm sure we'll meet again soon."

Neither of us questions the likelihood of that assertion. Sometimes, here in these islands, you just know.

Colors

February, 1991

VERDANT MAN-O-WAR CAY shines boldly against a turquoise sea on a blue-white winter afternoon. Gumelemi, seagrape, and poisonwood hammocks embrace white Colonial houses. High hills encircle the anchorage, protecting the harbour from the sea. On the sea bottom, the dark figure of a nurse shark at rest contrasts with the lighter hues of sand and seagrass. Where everything is remarkable, nothing is remarkable. These colors are the stuff of daily experience.

At anchor in Man-O-War's southeastern harbour, I regret my promise to care for John Nation's cat for two weeks while he visits his mother in Oklahoma. The paralyzing favor has just passed its fifth week when Drew sails into the anchorage on *Walden*. Recognizing *Blue Monk* (by coincidence, she belonged to him many years before), he rows over in his fiberglass Whitehall dinghy, a traditional New England rowing craft—a long glass slipper of a pulling boat with a graceful, swooping shear and a wineglass transom.

When I first met Drew at Dinner Key, he sailed a wooden, double-ended sloop named *Corentina*. Her planks ran stem to stern[76] without butt blocks or scarf joints. Drew cruised her up and down the

American Atlantic Coast and the Caribbean by himself. A capable navigator and a talented carpenter, he made a modest living with a Captain's license and a coping saw. Calling upon a wealth of sailing experience, his confident voice rumbled beneath his mustache over his brown beard, relating engaging stories of his many travels and adventures, punctuated by hearty laughter. I often joined him for morning coffee or an occasional moonlight sail. Sometimes, he'd disappear for months at a time but, like so many others, Drew always found himself called back to Dinner Key.

Beaufort, North Carolina was Drew's second home port. On a whim, he would journey into the Gulf Stream alone for the week-long passage as casually as most people head to the store for a carton of milk. He sold *Corentina* when he found a bargain on *Walden*, a fiberglass, cutter-rigged Westsail 32. He quickly hammered her into cruising shape and resumed his wanderings.

Like myself, Drew is an aficionado of the spruce oar as a mode of locomotive power. Most cruisers depend on outboard engines and inflatable dinghies for transport. But while such craft make for fast, convenient transportation, oars always start on a cold morning and require no petrochemical fuel. As with sailing, a seakindly pulling boat, responding to subtle changes in angle and pressure on the oars, inspires a unique joy.

---

76 *Stem* - The curved timber at the front of a vessel's bow is her *stem*. How often does one encounter an opportunity to make proper use of a cliché like "stem to stern?"

Rowing is a cultivated taste, a skill that comes with practice. Most people can't even stand up in a proper rowing dinghy, but a good oarsman can balance on the breasthook while he steps from his dinghy to the dock, or flip himself from the sea into his boat without shipping water. Internal combustion has its merits but a long rowing craft, like its canvas-bearing counterpart, compels one to slow down, to focus on the journey rather than the destination. Brute force has little to do with proper rowing. With polished technique, one can row at a swift and earnest pace for miles. As the musician's practiced touch squeezes the subtle, sweet essence from a string, an accomplished rower handles his sweeps and his vessel with an intuitive mastery that spirits him effortlessly across the waves.

Drew looks at *Light Blue*, my Chamberlain dory-skiff tethered behind *Blue Monk*. My tender is the same size as his Whitehall. He smiles mischievously. "Would you like to take a row?"

A northeaster is blowing. Even behind the sixty-feet-high coral hills that surround Man-O-War anchorage, brisk gusts of wind kick up a small chop.

"Sure. Where to? I imagine the seas are pretty choppy outside."

"Let's go to a beach, first," Drew suggests, "to clean the dinghies. I hate rowing with a dirty bottom and I still have a few Dinner Key barnacles to get rid of. Then we'll go rowing and end up where we end up." He pauses and grins before continuing. "We don't have to choose a destination to go rowing, do we?"

The question is rhetorical, but the suggestion to clean the dinghies is a good one. I do have some weedy spots on the underside of *Light Blue* though barnacles don't grow in these clear, clean waters.

We row northwest toward town, up the narrow lagoon, past moored sailboats and the docks of white-planked Bahamian houses trimmed with pastel shutters, past paths lined with conch shells and coconut palms, to a small beach where we drag our boats ashore and turn them over. A few minutes with a sharp putty knife and a coarse scrubbing pad consign scrapings of unwanted marine growth to the sand. We flip the dinghies back over, push them into the water and climb aboard.

Clean, *Light Blue* feels faster, as if freshly oiled. She rows easily, gliding with enthusiasm.

Drew pulls ahead, not quite challenging me to a race, but wordlessly suggesting we put our backs into the pace.

A rocky cut in the side of hairpin-shaped Man-O-War Cay provides a narrow gate for its well-protected anchorage. We exit into the Sea of Abaco.

"There's a coral head in the channel!" Drew remarks, looking down into water that's still fairly clear in spite of being stirred up by the chop.

"The locals know where the rocks are," I explain. "The channel is deep enough so most of them can go over it. The rest know to go around it. I doubt anyone will be coming by to install a marker, dynamite it, or file a complaint."

Drew smiles. He knows how it is in these islands. If you don't know where you're going and you don't keep your eyes open, you don't belong here.

The lee side of Man-O-War is scrub-covered coral—sharp gray rock covered by succulent plants with an overhanging shelf under-cut by thousands of years of wave action. The waves are bigger here than in the harbour; they slosh musically under the rocky shelf.

We continue, pulling steadily, breathing hard but working toward a second wind.

Drew looks over to see how I'm doing. *Light Blue* can handle herself in a sea. I row enough and swim enough to stay in good shape.

I'm doing *great*.

We continue around the point to head northeast into the wind, toward the reef and the mighty Atlantic Ocean.

The waves grow bigger. The north wind has put the distant reef in a rage.[77] The wind is lighter than expected, probably gusting to twenty knots, but these waves were sent by far stronger winds from higher latitudes. Driving into wind and sea, we pull up and over the crests. Atlantic swells roll in from the deep, trip over the drop-off

---

77 *Rage* ~ When the north wind drives the waves to break against the reef, the reef is said to be "in a rage."

and shatter against the coral ahead of us. A mile off the coast of Man-O-War, the reef line is a seething highway of white foam and exploding silver spray. Immense glass cannonballs detonate against a wall of impenetrable rock.

We pull harder, approaching the coral wall that demarcates the deep Atlantic from the shallow Bahama Banks—the third largest barrier reef on Earth. I wonder if we might not be engaged in a foolhardy contest, but our boats are dry, handling the waves as good pulling craft were designed to. We continue out over turbulent water, our bows facing a sky that fades from pastel blue to hazy white at the horizon.

The cut receives us—a sixty-foot deep, sixty-foot wide hole in the coral battlement worn by time, tide, and geological happenstance. To either side, rocky fingers of dull orange, brown, and green clutch at the sky through the foamy remains of spent waves. Black hills of moving water thunder spectacularly against unyielding coral, hissing and sizzling as they dissipate into rainbow mist. The power surrounding us is awe-inspiring. Many ships have met their ends on this coral; some of them lie in fragmented repose beneath us. How many people have witnessed nature's fireworks at this proximity and lived?

I look for Drew. He's two boatlengths away, on top of a wave, six feet above me.

Blue-black swells crowd through the cut, growing taller and closer together.

Drew drops below me as I ride up the crest of the next wave.

Inside the cut, the swells find no coral to break against. They pile up on themselves as they roll from the deep ocean into the shallow waters.

Where are we? The reef is difficult to make out through the big rollers.

Drew hooks his head to one side, suggesting we turn back. It would not be wise to row past the reef line and miss the cut coming back in; we'd never make it over the coral. We've seen what we came to see. Past this point lies nothing but miles and miles and more miles of cobalt swell.

Atop the next crest, I take a mental bearing on the houses and the white beach of Man-O-War Cay stretching off to the northwest. Hopetown Light guards the coast of Elbow Cay to the east where the Abaco out-island chain curves abruptly south. The next instant, I'm lowered into a valley surrounded by blue, foam-streaked mountains. I time my turn carefully so as not to get caught broadside by the big seas. Long, light oars give us leverage to work with our boats and the tremendous forces surging beneath them. I have an advantage with my higher freeboard. Drew ships an inch of water over his low shear but manages his turnabout.

We head back.

The seas move faster than our boats, but pulling hard, we can almost match their speed.

Drew synchronizes his pace with a wave.

I follow.

We're surfing!

The pounding reef falls behind.

On this side of the coral, the shallow water pulses with an impressionistic watercolor glow. We glide over sand patches, seagrass beds, and coral gardens, pulling hard, straining to keep pace with the racing seas we ride. The incoming tide runs with the wind, flooding onto the banks, carrying us back to shore. The swells diminish as we distance ourselves from the coral, but these blue horses are charged with the power of a North Atlantic gale. Large enough to carry us briskly, they are strong enough to capsize our boats if they can catch us abeam. We time each wave, surfing with extended oars to control direction and balance.

Drew stays one wave ahead.

I can't catch him.

We laugh and shout as we charge through the flying rollers.

Exhilarating!

I feel each incoming wave, gauging how the swell will lift; then pull and turn my tiny boat. By design, we row facing away from our destination. Atop the crests, I glance over my shoulder to take fresh bearings on Man-O-War's rocky southeastern shore. That coast is no place I'd care to land in these conditions, but our course around the island's point is true. After a long few minutes, we round the island to turn into Man-O-War's lee, into the gentle chop behind its rocky shore, over the coral head that sits in the middle of the entrance channel, and past the piling marking the edge of the shoal inside the lagoon.

Seen from the Queen's Highway—the jungle-shaded footpath that runs along the spine of the island—or perhaps from the white porch of a pink-shuttered Bahamian house on the harbour's edge, two sun-darkened figures rowing into Man-O-War harbour are hardly remarkable, even with a norther blowing and the reef in a rage. Where everything is remarkable, nothing is remarkable. These colors are the stuff of daily experience.

voyage the third

◫ The Blue Monk

Atlantic

July 4, 1991

AFTER EIGHT MONTHS in the Abacos, I am restless. I consider a voyage south to the Turks and Caicos Islands and the Dominican Republic. From there, who knows? On to Puerto Rico and the Caribbean?

But my plans are interrupted. *Journeyman* appears in Marsh Harbour. Gerhard hails me. "David, I was hoping I'd find you. I'm sailing *Journeyman* to Europe. Will you come as my crew? I can pay you and rent a mooring for *Blue Monk* at Man-O-War."

A trip across the Atlantic!

"When do we leave?"

Gerhard's daughter, Matina, is aboard. She's fifteen years old and knows not the first thing about sailing, but she's smart and eager to experience a new life with her father. A pretty girl, she blends her father's German facial features with her mother's dark Central American skin and hair. I launch Gerhard's wooden dinghy, put up the mast and give Matina sailing lessons in Marsh Harbour. I surprise her by jumping back aboard *Journeyman* when she's ready to solo. She's scared but manages to tack across the harbour through the anchored boats before docking gently alongside her father's boat to celebrate.

I make a two-day trip to Miami to purchase an autopilot and charts of Bermuda and the Azores before hurrying back to *Journeyman* in the Bahamas. My plane banks sharply over Green Turtle Cay, crosses radiant blue shallows, and noses down into a narrow slot in the Great Abaco pines. Wheels chirp on asphalt. The pilot shuts off the stall warning siren and feathers the prop as we decelerate down the short runway, past the remains of crumpled aircraft in the woods off to the side.

I consider hiring a taxi but elect to walk instead, carrying my guitar and duffel bag a little over a mile down the road through the pines into Marsh Harbour, past its single traffic light, and on down to the waterfront where my dinghy waits at the dock.

I park *Blue Monk* on a mooring at Man-O-War Harbour and move my gear to *Journeyman's* forward cabin.

July, 11, 1981

We raise *Journeyman's* huge, tanbark mainsail and shake the Bahamian mud from her anchors. *Zebra Dun* accompanies us as far as Whale Cay to wave farewell.

An early July departure is a late start for beating the Atlantic hurricane season. Fortunately, the tropics are clear. We turn to starboard through the swells in the cut, pointing our bow north toward Bermuda.

The Abacos fall below the southern horizon before day's end.

I study our engraved British Admiralty chart of the Azores.[78] Dramatic contour lines and ragged coasts suggest desolation appropriate to a place so remote. These islands appear tall and rugged—volcanic mountain peaks rising from the deep North Atlantic. I envision rocky cliffs and dry, inhospitable lava floes.

After a few days offshore, I practice navigating with a sextant given me by John Nation, working out calculations with an almanac and comparing my sun sights to coordinates read off the SatNav.[79] I average twelve miles from our true position; not badly inaccurate, I'm told.

The swells affect me. I develop a nagging seasickness and take to my bunk. After a day or two, Gerhard has had enough of it. He hands me a bucket and orders me out of bed. I heave a few times but recover gradually afterward, finally acclimating to my rolling

---

78 *Azores* – (Açores) are a group of volcanic islands about 1,000 miles west of Portugal

79 *SatNav* – SatNav was an early satellite navigation system that predated GPS. The SatNav provided a position fix every hour or so until it was phased out in the early 1990s.

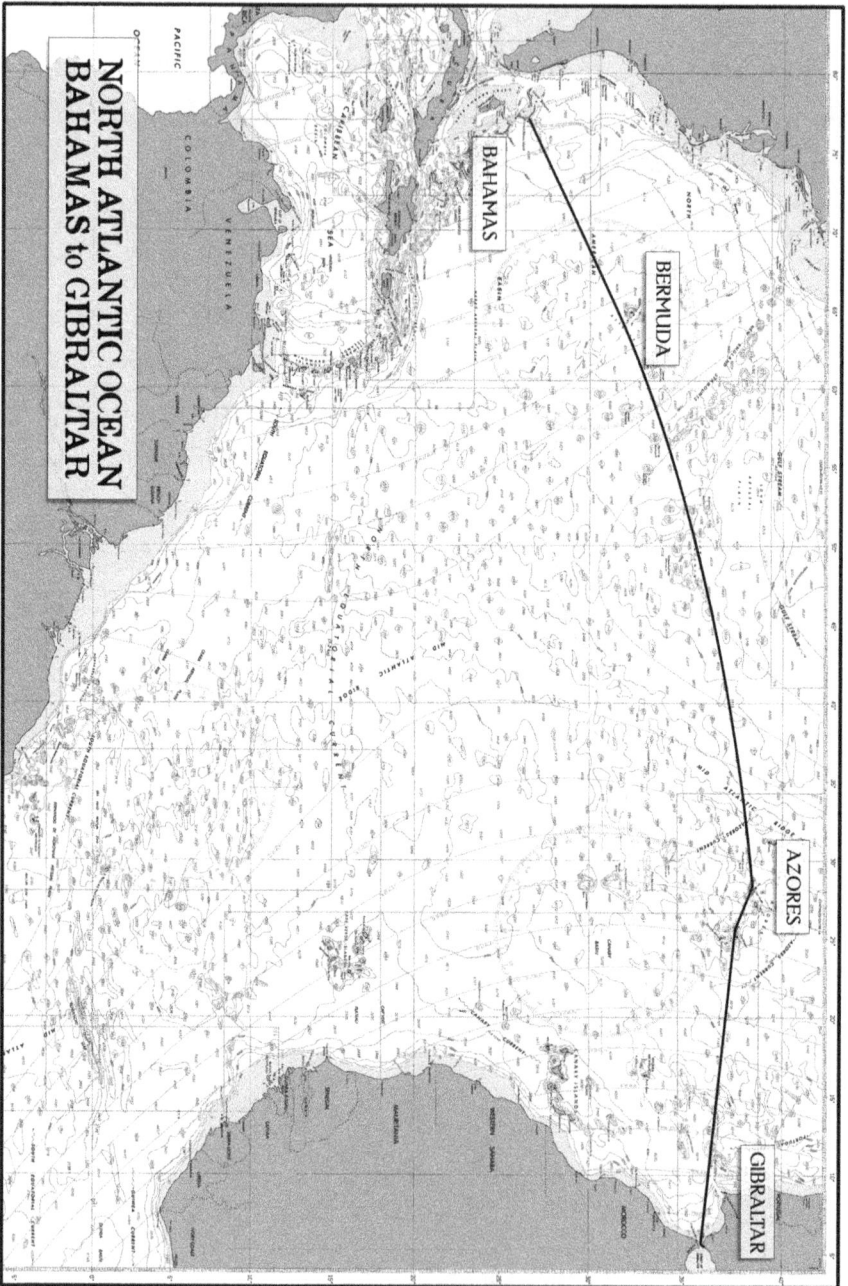

NORTH ATLANTIC OCEAN
BAHAMAS to GIBRALTAR

environment. The *mal de mer* having run its course, I resume eating and am comfortable for the rest of the voyage.

The wind dies, but the seas remain sloppy. These waves are generated, we assume, by some distant storm. Sails flap and rattle as we roll through the swells. The gaff[80] swings noisily from side to side. We start the diesel and furl our canvas.

The main halyard slips out of Gerhard's hand and runs to the top of the mast. I rig a safety line and climb the ratlines to retrieve it. Tossed about as I cling to the rigging, I make a slow ascent, timing my steps between waves, clipping my line to the rungs, and hanging on tight as I'm flung about. Halyard in hand, I consider whether jumping into the sea would be safer than climbing down the way I came, but a bad leap could have worse consequences out here hundreds of miles from the nearest doctor. Careful work returns me to the deck with a few bruises on my arms to show for my efforts.

Day eight.

The wind is calm.

We press on under power.

Cold, dense rain falls. We enjoy an invigorating shower on deck. Bermuda, our planned first stop, is visible in the distance against a gray afternoon sky but we elect to continue on. Exorbitant port charges are one motivator, but mostly we've found a traveling rhythm we can find no compelling reason to break.

---

80 *Gaff* - A gaff-rigged sail has one boom at the bottom and another (the gaff) at the top, usually set at an angle to the mast.

Later that evening the rain abates. The lights of Bermuda sink into the sea. At this latitude, the Gulf Stream swings east toward Europe. We turn, riding the current to pick up what extra speed we can.

Days drift by. The autopilot with its electronic compass diligently manages the chore of steering. We mind the wind, keeping the right sails aloft at the right times, some days roaring along, some days motor-sailing in light air, other days traveling under diesel power across calm seas.

What day of the week is today?

Is it August yet?

Time stops.

We creep forward, moving a half-inch each day across a paper chart.

From rail to horizon roll endless undulating waves—gray at dawn and dusk, deep blue in daylight, sparkling black and silver under the stars.

At night, we sleep, keeping informal watches while the autopilot steers. Neither of us has ever been at sea for more than a day or two; Gerhard and I don't completely trust each other to wake up and scan the horizon. From my bunk in the forward cabin, I poke my head through the fo'c'sle[81] hatch every twenty minutes or so, looking out without quite waking up. Occasionally, distant lights bid me rise to stand by the wheel until a passing ship moves on to be swallowed by

---

81 *Fo'c'sle* (pronounced folk-sole) - nautical speak for the "forecastle"—the forward cabin.

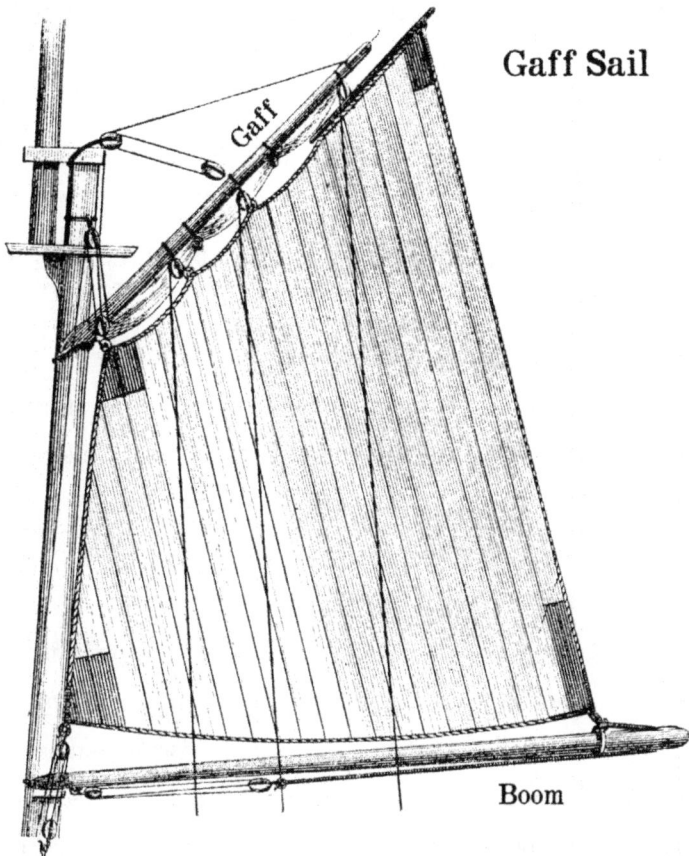

Gaff Sail

Gaff

Boom

the darkness. When we are alone once more amidst the stars and swells, a glance at the sails clears me to resume my slumber.

In mid-ocean, a freighter sets its garbage adrift on a cardboard raft. Sadly, we watch the refuse sink as we pass.

A floating barrel passes within a foot of our hull.

Most days, the trade winds are light but sufficient to keep us moving.

There is no hurry.

There is no destination.

There is no time.

We sit atop a shimmering dome of darkest blue beneath a canopy of radiant light.

We drag a fishing lure behind us but catch nothing.

Matina succumbs to seasickness. She becomes queasy, throws up, immediately recovers, eats, and then repeats the cycle. In three days, she ingests and regurgitates at least a half-dozen foods she once enjoyed but now wishes never to consume again because they remind her of the taste of vomit.

On the foredeck one morning, I'm struck by a flying fish. I reach down to toss her back into the sea but God put flying fish in Earth's oceans to be eaten. Stranded on deck, the fish senses its end has come, trembles and expires. A "mercy reflex" doesn't quite contradict evolutionary science, but it suggests the influence of other mechanisms. Genetic programming that causes an animal to spontaneously die just before being eaten doesn't strike me as a trait that could have much to do with *survival* of a species, but the wayward aviator does make a delicious breakfast.

The rain is back, this time accompanied by wind.

The sky grays over a choppy and colorless sea.

A dark, low squall line approaches.

The clouds boil.

A strange black loop of sinister sky descends before us.

"That thing's going to hit us! Let's get some sails down, *now!*" I shout to Gerhard.

We wrestle with the big mainsail, lowering the gaff, lashing canvas to the boom. On the bow, we hank a small storm jib to the inner forestay.

"Here she comes!"

With a cold blast of air, the writhing cloud loop springs upon us.

Raindrop machine gun fire strafes the deck.

"The wind is switching. Tack! Tack!"

With a push from the engine, we steer *Journeyman* across the wind, but the jib sheet on the port side of the sail was never roven through its turning block—an unfortunate oversight. The heavy canvas flogs itself to shreds in the screeching wind.

The mizzen sail[82] and the engine keep our bow to the waves.

With all sails furled; we sail under hull alone—not fast, but still forward.

The snaky cloud ascends into the gray turbulence above.

The wind diminishes to a forceful but manageable velocity.

We bend a new jib and continue eastward.

The next day is calm.

---

82 *Mizzen* – the mizzen sail is a small sail at the aft end of a ketch or yawl.

We furl our canvas once more, continuing on under power.

In the evenings before the sun sets, we gather in the cockpit for dinner. I read the day's chapter from Herman Melville's *Typee*, the story of a sailor who jumps ship in the South Pacific on an island inhabited by cannibals. Apart from meals at twilight, these readings are one of only a few temporal regularities remaining in our lives.

Day thirteen—or is it fourteen? The SatNav says we're halfway across the North Atlantic, closer to Newfoundland than anywhere else. My sextant loosely concurs. Gerhard bakes a celebratory cake.

I worry about an infected Bahamian mosquito bite that's turned into a nickel-sized crater on Gerhard's shin. Matina treats the wound with various antiseptic creams but it shows no improvement. I decide unilaterally to take over the nursing duties; I have zero desire to perform an amputation at sea. After sterilizing seawater in a cooking pot, I apply wet compresses to the affected area. The infection isn't too deep; the warm saltwater draws out the inflammation. The wound calms from an angry red to a more optimistic pink.

Seven hundred miles from land, tropicbirds accompany us. Fanciful white creatures with long tail feathers, they spend most of their lives in the air, only leaving the sky to mate, lay eggs, or scoop fish from the sea.

A tiny finch lands on the boom gallows,[83] exhausted and hungry, blown far off course and far out to sea. We leave out breadcrumbs,

---

83 The *boom gallows* arches over the cockpit. It holds up the end of the mainsail boom when the sail is furled.

sunflower seeds, and a dish of fresh water, but our guest shows no interest. She rests for a few minutes and flies off.

Still no fish on the line—though we have lost a lure or two.

Gerhard hails a passing Russian freighter on the VHF radio. Mostly, he's just making small talk, looking for news of the world, seeking the comfort of another human voice in this vast blue desert. The crewman who answers speaks some English. Gerhard asks how Mister Gorbachev is doing; the Russian leader was sick in the hospital when we left. The freighter's radioman seems uncomfortable with the potentially political question. He offers a vague reply and politely signs off. Ships move fast. Twenty minutes later, we own the Atlantic again from horizon to horizon.

I draw mermaids, wooden ships, a sea monster, and a floating "Pedro's South of the Border" billboard on our crossing chart. A few times each day, we consult the SatNav oracle and plot another fix.

Each day, we average a hundred miles.

Each day, we connect the dots that mark our path across the endless sea.

The infection in Gerhard's leg is healing well.

Still no fish on the line but more flying fish land on deck. I understand why the big fish like them; they're tasty.

The wind is often lighter at night. We fly a big spinnaker from the topmast; the sail balloons out in front of us like a huge kite.

Before dawn, a crunch of wood and a flapping of canvas awaken me. *Journeyman* feels different. I slide open the hatch over my bunk.

The Blue Monk

Suspended before my face is the top two-thirds of the topmast and shreds of colorful spinnaker cloth. Over time, the tugging of the big sail on the unsupported spar weakened it until it broke.

We have two more forestays on which to fly jibs. The topmast was only an extension added to the undamaged main mast; its failure presents no big dilemma for us, but Gerhard berates himself for having built the spar from kiln-dried lumber. "I should have known better. *Dammit!*" No matter that the rest of the boat is a monument to craftsmanship and woodworking skill, he has offended the wrathful god of shipwrights and now must suffer a horrible death for his sins.

We haul in the damaged sail, retrieve the stay, bend a big jib, and continue eastward.

Days go by.

Gerhard gets over his carpenter's shame.

A few more days go by.

And a few more.

I pull out our Azores charts and go over them with Gerhard. The town of Horta on the island of Faial looks like as good a place as any to make our landing.

We draw closer.

Birds appear.

Tomorrow, we make port.

At two in the morning, lights from small fishing boats surround us. We see no visible signs of either Faial or the 8000-foot high island of Pico behind it, but unmistakable, terrestrial smells of cows and grass mark our transition.

At 5:00 am, dim lights to port reveal our destination. High on a mountainside; they're all we can see of an island shrouded in fog and darkness.

As the sun rises, so does Faial's mist. Her gray skirt ascends slowly, climbing the coast toward the middle of the island. Hues of silver and gray soak up color from the new day, revealing verdant, terraced farms. Pastures latticed with lava rock walls rise in a tapestry of green. Church spires punctuate white, red-roofed villages along the coast. The shore is steep, strewn with dark, volcanic rocks. Headlights move on a coastal road. We expected to find only an inhospitable rock out here a thousand miles from the nearest land, but this is *beautiful*—timeless, provincial, and charming.

At the eastern end of Faial, we pass a tiny lagoon—the submerged remains of an ancient volcanic crater. We straighten up *Journeyman*, neatly furl and cover the sails, disengage the autopilot and turn to port into the *Canal do Faial,* the natural channel between the island and its neighbor Pico four miles to the east.

A yellow quarantine flag climbs the mainmast to the spreader.

To starboard, the top of Pico glows with the light of the new day—a perfect volcanic cone, towering like Hokusai's Fuji.

84 *Hokusai's Fuji* - Readers will be familiar with the Japanese woodblock prints by sight if not by name. Katsushika Hokusai created *Thirty-six Views of Mount Fuji* between 1826–1833.

Rounding one seawall and then another, we tie to the Customs dock in Horta.

Gerhard steps ashore with our passports and the ship's papers in hand.

Will port charges be expensive? Will they search our vessel? Clearing Customs in tiny countries is often a hassle. Cynics both, Gerhard and I expect our first contact with humanity to involve a good fleecing.

Minutes later, Gerhard walks out of the office smiling. "The marina is cheap. We can stay as long as we like. Port charges are nearly nothing. The Customs officer was friendly; he spoke perfect English."

We motor over to the seawall inside the marina to tie up. Above us loom the mountains of Faial. Old, charming buildings overlook the port. Pico stands majestic on the far side of the channel.

I take a breath and step onto the dock. I expect to be off-balance after twenty-six days at sea but I am not. I spin slowly, taking in the vista around me.

"Let's walk," I suggest to Gerhard and Matina.

We haven't walked for a month.

We stroll along the waterfront for almost a mile. The streets are gray cobblestone, the sidewalks inlaid with fanciful patterns and designs.

Neglected leg muscles drag us up a hill into a small park.

I pluck a ripe fig from a tree. I don't usually care for figs but this one's delicious.

We climb higher.

How delightful to soar on the park swings.

We lie in the grass in a shady spot.

Good to be ashore again.

Originally, our goal was to hasten across the Atlantic to Europe, but the voyage is no longer an obstacle. The destination is no longer a challenge. When our journey is complete, we must rejoin the gridded world of schedules and commerce.

Why hurry? Having lost all sense of time, we are in no rush to recover it.

I look at Gerhard to ask if we might stay here a while, but there's no need.

He lies on the soft grass, eyes closed, smiling, breathing deeply. Vines grow up from the soil, encircle him gently and pull him into the warm earth.

I gaze for a moment across the channel at Pico, feel the breeze on my face and the land at my back.

Wherever else *Journeyman* may carry us, our destination is here and now.

AZORES
OR
WESTERN ISLES
(Portuguese)

ISLANDS
IN THE
ATLANTIC OCEAN

SCALE OF MILES

The Azores are all Volcanic. The last eruption was at St Jorge in 1811. St Michael is famous for its Oranges; Pico for its excellent Wines. The islands form a Colonial Government with Angra for their Capital.

Sabrina, volcanic island which, in 1811 rose rose from the Sea in 181 ft. depth to 300 ft. above water, and in 4 months again disappeared.

Longitude W. from Greenwich

Longitude E. from Washington

CORVO
N.S.de Rosario
FLORES
P.do Albernas
S.Pedro
Pta.Cruz
P.Delgada
P.do de Loma
P.dos Illecs
Lagens

FAYAL
P.da Nova
Pta.de Roseira
Ilsl.Caprinas
Ial.Grande
P.do Ultimo
Castêl Branco
C.Spartel
P.Sto.Maubeu
The Peak 6,900 f.
(perpetual snow)
Lagens
Ponta C.Cria
Horta

S. JOR JO
Pta.de S.Jorge
Ca.Negro
Ribeira Bay
Quieira Pta.Gorda
Mte.de Brasi
P.do Toyo

GRACIOSA
Pta.da Pico Negro
Sta.Cruz
Prays
Tha.Branca

TERCEIRA
Pta.Negrito
Run-Juias Ente
Pta.da Caneiro
Villanova
das Lahuras
Angra
Porto Novo
Lus Fradas
P.Malaverenda

SANTO MIGUEL
Baha de Val
Lagoa Grande
Ribeira Grande
Ponta da Ponte
Afra de Pa
Pr.celas
Ponta Delgada
Villa Franca
Porto de Iheas
Ribeira
Mosteiros
Maya
Nordeste

STA.MARIA
Ilhado Fradas
Ba de Sto.
Fornique
Semen Rock
Pta.do Castêlo
St.Marie
Ial.de Arraeira Bra
Ial de Melichorca
Tullock Rocks

Faial

THE AZORES IS HEAVEN. So inspiring is this remote place a thousand miles from the nearest mainland that we stay three weeks.

We arrive in Faial in time for the annual *Mar Semana*—Sea Week. Cruising boats fill the marina, flying strings of nautical and international flags in celebration of the festival. Many come especially for the event. Other visitors fly in to attend from Spain, Portugal, and other parts of Europe.

Free concerts every night offer music for every taste—traditional Portuguese, popular dance music, new wave, heavy metal, and a collection of local brass bands—performed on a stage set up in a park between the marina and the main street of Horta. I listen from among the crowd or from a comfortable perch atop a sail bag on *Journeyman's* foredeck.

After one concert, I attend a local dance but soon take my rightful place at the side of the floor. The Azoreans are superb dancers. Children, teenagers, adults, and seniors cavort like professionals. I feel foolish stumbling about among these spirited, graceful people.

There is no crime to speak of in Horta. Such relief from man's darker nature is not uncommon in an anchorage but marinas are rarely so secure; we never bother to lock up or even close our hatches when we leave *Journeyman*.

Horta marina is covered with paintings left by the hundreds of boaters who have visited the island. Many of these frescoes display the craftsmanship and attention to detail valued by this community of nomads whose lives depend on keeping their vessels sturdy and safe. On the concrete pier, in celebration of the island's whaling history (though I'm glad whales are no longer hunted here), I paint a scrimshawed whale's tooth with our names and a rendering of *Journeyman* on it—the first painting I've ever done.

All here are true sailors. A thousand miles of blue water separate these yachtsmen from the dreamers and talkers on the closest continent. Berthed in Horta marina are people who *do*.

Neal Petersen arrives from South Africa. He docks on the other side of the marina on a small red sloop named *Save Our Sealife*. He built her himself and sailed here solo after being told he wasn't allowed in the yacht club of his home country because of the color of his skin. After losing his rudder on the way up from Capetown, he steered the last half of the journey with his sails and a pair of buckets dragged behind the boat. Though he spends much of his time making repairs, he becomes a friend, poking around Faial with me as he finds time.

Moored behind us on a steel sloop named *Godspeed* is an odd collection of friendly characters from England. Edward hears spirit voices; he often interrupts conversations to tell us what Harriet or Jonathan has to say about whatever is being discussed. He's intelligent and congenial if a bit difficult for his wife to understand. At least he and his spirit friends are good-natured. What's a little undiagnosed schizophrenia between sailors?

A week after we arrive, a big American ketch from Maryland bearing two married doctors and a small brood of children ties to the seawall behind *Godspeed*. *Orchid's* crossing was not so peaceful as ours; the edge of a tropical storm raised seas sufficiently threatening to force the cutting loose of her expensive, inflatable dinghy from its davits.[85] All aboard are grateful to stand on *terra firma* again. With them is Cecilia—crew, nanny, and part-time cook—who has just spent three weeks cooped up on a boat with someone else's children and her two employers. Slender and lightly built with cropped blond hair, she's a few years older than I am—and in need of some good company. Whenever she can find time off from tending to the kids in her charge, we explore Faial together.

Tied in front of us is *Ketchup*, a large, red, steel ketch from Germany. An inside steering station shelters her helmsman from the weather.

---

85 *Davits* – suspend a dinghy (usually) over a vessel's transom where it can be easily launched and retrieved, and stored where marine growth can't foul her hull. Though convenient for coastal cruising, a dinghy on davits can be dangerous offshore when large waves from astern threaten to fill her with heavy seawater.

Gunter and Hilda come to the Azores every summer. They stay late in the season, then ride the southwesterly gales back to Europe. "It gets rough sometimes," they explain, "but our ship is dry and warm inside and the wind is behind us all the way."

Andrew, a sailor with a wooden twenty-four-foot sloop back home in Gibraltar, flies in for the *Mar Semana.* "She's small but she's a real sea boat," he assures me, "a pocket cruiser with a full keel." A few beers put him in a somber mood one night. He confesses he's not having much fun spending the easy money he made running a speedboat full of Moroccan hashish across the Strait of Gibraltar to Cadiz. "I don't feel right flying 'round on vacation, spending my ill-gotten gains; I know I'm better than that." He takes another sip of beer and a hit of hash. "Want some, mate?"

"No thanks. I'm good."

A graying, retired MIT physics professor and his wife sail between the two seawalls that embrace the marina on *Turtle,* their home-built, self-designed trimaran. I doubt he used any other boats as references for his oddly-contoured and strangely-rounded craft, but he made it here from Boston. Maybe he knows something I don't?

The mayor of Horta personally visits each boat, distributing bottles of champagne and inviting the sailors to participate in the annual Cruising Boat Regatta. The township arranges a special party to which all the racers are invited.

A race and a banquet sound like an unbeatable combination to me but sailing *Journeyman* is out of the question; stripping her awnings and sail covers for the sake of an afternoon race is too much work. I could crew aboard any of the boats planning to participate but I conceive a more adventurous possibility, one with a mischievously appealing aspect to it.

I visit the yacht club to ask what the requirements are for a boat to be allowed in the race.

As a non-member, I'm technically not supposed to go into the yacht club but I hold a secret key. Back in Marsh Harbour, I met a kindred spirit, a guitar player and balladeer who hailed from Bermuda with his wife, Susan, and young son, Sean. Taken aback by a stuffy yachtsman who went on about his "yacht club back home," David Rhind founded an informal anti-fraternity—the International Association of Disreputable Boat Bums. One of the first sailors to have a computer and printer aboard, he inducted me into the IADBB, issuing me a membership card complete with skull-and-bones logo. As is common practice, the Faial Yacht Club offers reciprocal privileges to members of other yacht clubs. I flash my IADBB card and am welcomed in.

According to the rules, to qualify as a 'cruising boat,' a vessel must be equipped with a stove, a toilet, a cabin, and a water tank. On the day of the race, Cecilia and I show up at the starting line in Gerhard's eleven-foot dinghy upon which, with a lot of last minute help from Gerhard, I hastily rigged a borrowed windsurfer sail. We equip our vessel with a small camping stove and a bucket with a toilet seat for a head. We tie a corner of the *Journeyman's* blown out spinnaker over the bow to serve as the roof of a tiny cabin. A plastic jug of water completes our complement of cruising gear.

We enjoy a pleasant afternoon sailing in light winds from Horta to Pico and back over a twelve-mile course. The larger boats complete two laps of the course to our one, but we are invited to attend the party and banquet that evening.

Horta is perched on the eastern coast of Faial, facing the island of Pico. This commercial center suffers a degree of traffic and crowding like all urban areas. The town retains, however, an old country charm in its Mediterranean architecture. To explore the surrounding villages and countryside is to visit 16th century Portugal. Many people still wear traditional peasant garb. Stone houses and terraced pasturelands could hardly be different today than centuries ago.

But the most striking features of the Azores are geological. Still-active volcanoes rising from the depths of the North Atlantic continue to form these islands.

Transportation is no problem; friendly locals are happy to stop for hitchhikers. Proud of their beautiful country, some drive out of their way to show us their favorite views.

Cecilia and I thumb a ride to Caphelinos. In 1957, a volcanic eruption began off the west coast of Faial. Over the next year, a mound of rock, lava, and ash rose from the sea. This new land mass eventually connected to Faial, adding several square miles to the island. Today, it's a brown wasteland of rocks and hardy scrub. Ruins of houses destroyed by earthquakes lie partially buried in sand and ash. An old lighthouse stands coldly above the coast, its top gone, much of the building at its base covered with volcanic sand.

The north coast of Faial is the *Costa Brava.* Tall cliffs plunge from lush highlands hundreds of feet to beaches of black volcanic sand. At the edge, I gaze over a vine-covered ravine. Behind me, the top of the island is lost in clouds.

The most remarkable volcano in the archipelago is Pico. Its symmetrical cone rises over 8000 feet.

I resolve to climb it.

Cecilia and I prepare backpacks and then hop the ferry from Horta to Madalena, Pico's port town. We land on a Friday afternoon and can find no place to stay. We ask around but find that aside from an expensive hotel, everything is booked due to the *Mar Semana.* Eventually, a kind Portuguese gentleman who speaks some English drives us to the traditional home of Joaquin and Leonilda who rent a room to travelers at a rate equivalent to US$13.00 per night. Though they speak no English, I am able to communicate with them well enough in Spanish. We sleep that night in a double bed under the watchful eyes of a big-eyed painting of Jesus.

The following morning after breakfast, we put our thumbs out by the road. Cecilia is pretty; we catch a ride quickly but our driver doesn't understand us. He drops us at the wrong spot. We hike for five hours up a steep grade toward the base of Pico's cone.

Walking along, I reach over a rock wall to pluck a bunch of ripe grapes from a vine. From these heights, Faial can be seen in its entirety across the channel. Ironically, the same truck driver who drove us to the wrong place picks us up miles away to deliver us to where we can begin climbing the mountain proper, but we've enjoyed spectacular views of the Pico countryside in the meanwhile. Level with the clouds here, we watch them skitter over the rocky landscape.

We begin our assault on Pico, stopping for a break a half-mile up the volcano's cone at the *furnas*—vents in the side from which gasses and lava once flowed. These small caves are carpeted inside with soft, velvety grass and offer some shelter from the elements. Already exhausted from the day's hike, we consider camping in one, but we haven't brought supplies to sustain us an extra day.

We press onward and upward.

The ascent follows no set path but stakes in the ground every 200 feet mark a general route. A steep climb carries us up lava floes that solidified as they rolled down the mountainside eons before. The terrain varies from sandy to gravelly to rocky. Some wild plant grows on the slope, giving off a strong smell of oregano; it may *be* oregano.

By the time we reach the top, we are hungry.

We descend into the crater to set up camp.

The sun melts into the ocean behind Faial.

I baked a loaf of raisin bread and a loaf of sesame seed bread for our trip. These, in combination with tinned sardines, constitute dinner—hardly a fitting reward for our exertions.

It's Saturday night and we share the crater with twenty young Azoreans who passed us like mountain goats on the way up. They celebrate loudly.

Here at 8000 feet, the air is bitter cold. Their campfire is divine.

When strong Pico wine is passed around, we accept the bottle.

We share a small cave with six other people, resting uncomfortably in sleeping bags on the rocky ground.

One group of Azoreans yells and cheers—*all night long.*

At 5:30 AM, everyone who has been in the caves feigning sleep crawls out to scramble up Little Pico—the summit's summit—a small 200-foot high cone on the crater rim. There, they wait for the sun to rise—*at 7:30.*

Cecilia and I are smarter than that.

On the least uncomfortable part of the rocky floor of our now significantly depopulated bedroom, we grab a few winks of semi-sleep before arising at 7:20 AM to observe the same phenomenon from the crater rim.

The morning sky streaks with orange. A red sun climbs above the horizon. We stare down on the farmlands and the lakes region of Pico. Faial and the distant islands of São Jorge and Terceira reveal themselves through the clouds below us.

Immediately after sunrise, the Azoreans descend the mountain *en masse.*

By 8:00 AM, we have the mountaintop to ourselves. Not to waste an opportunity, we find ourselves a more comfortable cave with a sandy floor and sleep for three more hours.

After breakfast, we climb Little Pico. The slope is particularly steep. After our previous day's hike, my legs feel as if they've been run over by a train.

The top is much like you'd imagine the perfect mountain summit to be. I stand on a big rock to assure myself I've reached the very highest point. Steam escapes from fissures warm to the touch; the monster still breathes if only in the tiniest of wheezes.

Our tortured legs carry us back to the base of the volcano where, providentially, we quickly find a ride to Madalena without having to hike for miles.

The ferry delivers us safely and comfortably back to Horta.

I sleep once more in my comfortable bunk beneath the sturdy deck of *Journeyman.*

Neal Petersen visits the next morning. "I'm heading to England from here," he says. "What's your plan? It's getting late. The seasons are changing."

I'd love to stay here but I'm out of money. I've been playing guitar for change in the marina bar. We have plenty of food on board but that isn't inexhaustible, either.

Neal is right; the seasons are changing.

"Gerhard and I have been discussing our options," I reply. "We'll move from here to São Miguel and then cross to Gibraltar."

"Better get moving," he says.

The Blue Monk

Wind or No Wind

THE SEASONS are changing.

The winter gales are coming.

Wind or no wind, we must continue our journey.

We strip sail covers and awnings.

I bid Cecilia farewell. She smiles a sly smile and confesses she's actually *thirteen* years older than me. I'll miss her footsteps stealing lightly onto the deck late at night when she visits my cabin. This was never a relationship meant to last—and we both knew it from day one—but for the first time in all my sea travels, I've enjoyed sharing my life's adventures. We sailed across Faial Channel together in an eleven-foot dinghy, hitchhiked all over Faial, summited an 8000-foot volcano and even indulged in the mischievous irreverence of sharing a bed beneath a big-eyed painting of Jesus. Though predestined to move on, we have, for each other, been islands worth visiting and remembering.

Neal Petersen embraces me. "Safe travels, my friend. I'm right behind you."

It will be seventeen years before I see him again.

Journeyman puts to sea for São Miguel, the Azores' largest and easternmost island.

Not a breath of wind disturbs the water's surface.

We motor through the night over a dull, leaden sea, making port at Ponta Delgada in the morning.

The marina is full but free moorings accommodate additional yachts in the harbour; all are welcome here.

We stay ten days, waiting for the unseasonable calm to dissipate. In the evenings, I play guitar. Spontaneous parties occur regularly on the dock, attended by yachtsmen from America, Spain, Africa, Portugal, England, Austria, Germany, Holland, and France. To the delight of the other sailors, I accompany a young Dutch jazz singer who works as a teacher in town. Music and laughter are our common language.

Ponta Delgada offers, among its amenities, a modern supermarket with a large and varied selection of goods. We stock up on supplies for the remainder of our journey.

Gerhard, Matina, and I take a bus from Ponta Delgada to Furnas Valley along an inland route that provides a marvelous view of São Miguel's hills and pasturelands. The valley lies within a huge volcanic crater. Sheer walls, dramatic rocks, and an abundance of white, pink, and blue flowers form a stunning backdrop to a geological wonderland, a cross between Yellowstone Park and a Japanese garden. Clouds of steam veil bubbling mud pits and boiling springs. Yellow sulphur deposits and acidic corrosion consume concrete paths and stairways meandering through the site. A woman in black peasant garb retrieves a bag of corn from one of nature's cooking pots.

We hitch a ride home, following a majestic coastal road twenty-two miles to Ponta Delgada. High above the Atlantic, each curve reveals new and inspiring scenery. The back of an empty cattle truck provides an ideal viewing platform. Gerhard is warm, humorous, and congenial at heart but often reserved and serious; there is always work to be done. But along with my recollections of the magnificent coast, I will never forget the expression of boyish delight on his face as the wind blows his hair. He is fifteen again. Work can wait.

The following day, we catch a bus to Mosteiros, a small town on the northwest tip of the island, adjacent to Sete Cidades, a huge volcanic crater in which are hidden two beautiful lakes. We hike through a village lost in time where peasants carry milk jugs on horseback and donkeys pull wagons in the streets.

Our trek continues, climbing for miles through pastures and fields, down roads lined with blue, white, and pink hortensias, across tall forests of Japanese cedar trees. At the top, we peek over a crater rim into a lush valley. Two lakes—Green and Blue according to local folklore—lie before us, divided by a narrow bridge of land. Walking between fields of corn, we descend into an immense circle of green under a painted sky.

After our long walk, we enjoy a simple lunch by one of the lakes—a banquet.

We fall asleep together on the grassy shore.

Hitchhiking home, we stop where a cyclist lies unconscious next to his fallen motorcycle. I urge bystanders not to touch him; his back might be broken.

The man begins to stir. He sits up groggily, rises shakily to his feet and checks himself. He's suffered a scare and a twisted ankle but escaped serious injury.

His motorcycle is less fortunate: the signal lights are broken on one side; part of the plastic cowling is torn off; the front wheel is badly bent.

Our driver offers to put the motorcycle in his truck.

The man's lip begins to quiver. He puts his wrist to his forehead, tilts his head back dramatically and wails.

We wait. The cyclist is despondent—inconsolable.

We leave him at the roadside, weeping with his broken machine.

That night, we go adrift from our mooring—a shackle pin has come undone—but we hardly move; the air is still. I am awakened by the sound of the mooring ball banging against the hull. The float is easily retrieved with a boathook and reconnected. We are lucky; that shackle could have failed in windier conditions, or when nobody was aboard.

The next morning, with Gerhard at the helm, *Journeyman* exits between the protecting arms of the two seawalls that insulate Ponta Delgada's harbor from the North Atlantic.

The ocean is flat.

Journeyman is a flash of color in a gray world. We proceed under power, resuming our eastward voyage. Our bow ploughs a dark groove across the metallic reflection of a pewter sky.

Before São Miguel's peaks drop beneath the horizon, the weather turns cool and rainy.

Land recedes into the mist.

A boundless mirror consumes the world.

The seasons are changing.

The winter gales are coming.

Wind or no wind, we must continue our journey.

The Blue Monk

This is What We Do

S EPTEMBER—late in the season: Though tempted to linger in the enchanting Azores, we must finish our crossing to Europe. Our passage, projected to take ten or eleven days, will be easy compared to the first twenty-six day leg of our voyage. After a summer spent in the company of yachtsmen who made passages of at least a thousand miles to share our dock, this journey is not preceded by the nervous excitement that attended its beginning.

We are sailors. This is what we do.

Each of us understands reaching the far shore represents the terminus of a grand adventure and a transition into a less predictable realm. On the ocean, all men are equal. The sea recognizes no social classes, economic divisions, hard bosses, landowners or toll collectors. The Atlantic may test us or terrify us or even take our lives, but to its depths we ascribe no dark motive or intent to beguile. In the realm of Poseidon, teamwork, perseverance, and clarity are coin; here, we have sufficient accounts to make our journey. Ashore, cash and influence are currency. Soon, we must rebuild our resources where men trade in different measures of labor and value.

We're broke, and Gerhard's original offer to pay me as crew (and thus the promised fare for my return trip and the rent for *Blue Monk's* mooring in the Bahamas) trades on future earnings. After adjusting to life at sea and enjoying an unanticipated vacation in the Azores, rejoining the civilized world will be our challenge.

Open water.

The wind increases excrementally.

The seas grow rough. We run downwind in huge rolling swells.

I vomit.

Matina vomits.

Gerhard vomits.

The autopilot dies.

For the next nine days, we hand-steer around the clock, seasick or not.

How big are these swells? Twenty feet? Thirty feet? More? We ride over the crests, roll over the troughs, and surf into deep valleys of black water under a colorless sky. The cockpit floods and drains. Rivers run up and down the deck, streaming out the scuppers as sea and spray climb aboard. *Journeyman* buries her bow, shudders, and rises from waves that try to swallow her.

On the VHF radio, we hail friends from São Miguel who left in a much smaller boat than ours. We can't see them but they're within range and they answer. Like us, they're uncomfortable and wet, but bashing their way eastward. Chitchatting under these circumstances is absurd, but we find futile comfort in knowing we're not entirely alone out here.

Through the steering wheel in my hands, I sense enormous pressure against the rudder as it resists the seas trying to roll *Journeyman* on her beam-ends.[86] Nine rotations of the wheel are required to turn from one side of the steering range to the other, but even with this tremendous mechanical advantage, keeping our course requires strength and concentration. I understand why the autopilot gave up.

Standing in knee-deep water, I steer until the queasiness comes on, then heave and recover sufficiently to continue steering again. I recall hearing of a seasickness remedy that employs elastic wristbands to push plastic beads against pressure points on the wrists. The next marine store lies nine hundred miles ahead so I improvise with duct tape and two pinto beans. Forty-five minutes later, I am singing in the cockpit, eating and drinking to keep my energy and enthusiasm up, and enjoying the scenery.

By sunset, we are wet, cold, and tired. We heave our vessel to, effectively parking for the night. With an assist from the engine, we round up into the wind, haul up the mizzen sail, and tack back across the gale without bringing the jib to the other side. The mizzen keeps *Journeyman* headed up while the backwinded jib tries to push the bow off the wind. The sails balance; we drift in relative comfort. Down below, all is soaked and in disarray but we're too exhausted to care.

86 *"On her beam-ends"* means heeled over on her side so the deck is almost vertical.

I sleep in my wet foul weather gear on a pile of soggy sail bags shifted onto my bunk. Hundreds of miles from land, we have plenty of sea room; we can drift without worrying about shoals and shores.

Morning light awakens me. My first conscious thought is surprise over having slept at all. Maybe the storm has blown out? It feels surprisingly calm from inside the cabin. My joints ache from the dampness. I open the companionway doors and creakily ascend the steps to the cockpit.

Hove to, *Journeyman* rides comfortably among enormous swells, but contrary to first impressions, the wind has *increased*. From horizon to horizon, the surface of the ocean is a field of churning white foam. The tops of giant rollers are blasted into flying spray by the wind. I am adrift at the center of an exploding world.

Why am I not afraid?

There is no point in being afraid. There is nobody to ask for help, nobody to pay, nobody to seek advice from, no dream to wake from, no port to run to. Three mice cling to a leaf in a tempest; what good would it do to be afraid? Nature prepares us to flee or fight but we are programmed as much to master our destinies and face our fates with cold reserve and hard resolve. There is nowhere to flee, no foe to fight. We have done all we can to ensure our safety. Survival means keeping our heads, minding the wind and seas, and pressing on.

Alone in the cockpit, I sit on the helmsman's seat, watching the shattered face of the North Atlantic.

No, I am not afraid. I am blessed to bear witness to nature's secret rage on this remote part of Planet Earth. Scenes like this don't exist on the terrestrial plane.

A calm slick lingers on the water in the lee of our hull in the path of our slow drift. I see fish schooling around our keel. Perhaps they're seeking shelter behind us? I manage a smile at the irony.

I call our friends on the radio.

No answer.

I assume they're out of range.

I *hope* they're out of range.

A chainplate parts on the mizzenmast. The spar[87] rattles and vibrates, trying to jump out of its step. The restorative comfort of heaving to and the necessary hiatus it delivers from manning the wheel in boiling seas will not be possible if we lose the mizzenmast. I start the engine, which wakes Gerhard, then manage the helm while he wrestles down the sail. Up and over the swells we go and down into the troughs again.

But the gale blows from behind us.

Gibraltar lies ahead.

We are wet and tired, hungry and uncomfortable, but the wind favors our course and Gerhard has built a sturdy ship.

The day wears on.

The storm blows out, fading slowly, almost unnoticeably, spending

---

87 *Spars* are masts, booms, gaffs and similar poles used on a sailing vessel

its power like the mainspring of a great clock until it is time to haul aloft the big gaff mainsail and bend a jib to the forestay.

A pot of stew bubbles on the stove. The decks dry in the sun. Wet sail bags and sea-soaked clothing air out on the cabin top.

The storm is past.

We say little about it.

We survived.

Many miles of ocean lie before us.

We adopt a new rhythm. I retire after dinner at eight o'clock while Gerhard stands watch until midnight, at which time I ascend to the cockpit with my tape player and a selection of cassettes to sing to me through the night.[88] Every night, I stare at the compass, listen to my cassettes one side at a time, and sail into a starry void. *Journeyman's* bowsprit points not across night-shrouded waves, but out into an endless beyond.

We are not floating.

We are flying through space.

I choose a star to keep in a certain place in the rigging. Every so often, I change stars or change my reference point, allowing my guiding light to shift relative to where it hovers over the mast spreader or the lightbox mounted on the shrouds. After a few nights, I learn to slowly compensate for the gradual spin of my guide stars around

---

88 My music library included the original and second Glenn Gould recordings of Bach's *Goldberg Variations, Standards Volume I* by Keith Jarrett, Leo Kottke's *Six and Twelve-String Guitars*, a Frank Zappa tape and others. I can still play those tapes in my head, note for note, as clearly and vividly as if they were playing aloud.

Polaris so they don't pull me off course. How the Polynesians navigated for thousands of miles is no great mystery. They grew up sailing under the stars, developed a sense of heaven's rhythm, and turned slowly, steadily one way as the sky turned the other; they knew intuitively what stars were over what destinations at what times. I check my course against the compass less frequently, steering more and more accurately as the nights go by. The helm demands less concentration. Alone in the cockpit under the Milky Way, I experiment with controlling the speed of time, extending my four-hour watches by two or three hours to allow Gerhard more sleep. As the constellations glide across the celestial dome in a single endless moment, what is another hour or two or three? What is an hour at all?

When I am too tired to keep a straight course any longer and I've listened to my box of tapes and dawn streaks the sky before me, I wake Gerhard and give him the helm. Grateful for the extra sleep, he thanks me before I climb forward into my bunk.

During the days, we keep short, informal watches. Matina practices keeping a straight compass course as we plot tiny eastward-moving crosses on our chart.

The sun marches over our heads through a field of blue, burns the horizon beyond our wake, yields to the stars, purples the east, and rises before us again.

We are aground in a river of time.

We eat.

We sleep.

With the wheel, we turn the ocean round our boat.

Days pass like silken threads on hidden currents of wind.

Hours hover like dust revealed by a sunbeam.

Forever collapses into a moment.

There can be no other side, no destination.

There is only here, only now.

The wind falls light again.

We motor over calm, shimmering seas.

Two fishing vessels appear before us, rising slowly, steadily above the edge of the mirrored plane of the sea. We wave at the men working the boats and steer around the floats that mark the perimeters of their nets.

Gibraltar is close.

With proximity, with the idea of *here* and *there* and distance between, time returns.

No electric excitement, no air of celebration arises with the prospect of completing our Atlantic crossing. In truth, we share a subtle melancholy as more boats and birds and signs of land appear.

Suppressing thoughts of the terrestrial unknowns that lie ahead, we mind the compass, adjust the wheel, trim the sails, mark the chart, check that the bilges are dry, make a pot of coffee, stand our watches, study the waves, discuss what weather the clouds portend, and listen to the sound of the ocean moving past our hull, reveling in our journey's final moments of timelessness before land's inevitable arrival.

We are sailors. This is what we do.

GIBRALTAR BAY

Landfall

TONIGHT is our final night at sea.

Less than a hundred miles lie between our ship and Gibraltar.

Sailing on, we sense the certain presence of land that will mark our passage from a special, quiet, solitary universe so huge it can only exist in a single moment. A different world awaits, driven by great iron gears of clocks and industry. A boundary demarcating the realm of the infinite *now* from the ticking, honking, smoking, grinding realm of time approaches like an invisible line of longitude.

From the broad Atlantic, we approach the Strait of Gibraltar, the narrow entrance to the Mediterranean between Cadiz and Tangier. At the perimeters of fishing nets, blinking red lights flash mutely against the lights of the heavens. All too soon, the incandescent loom of civilization will obscure these stars.

Do not forget this place when they have faded.

With few other vessels in sight, we switch off our navigation lights to conserve battery power.

An aircraft flies over at low altitude—a big four-engine propeller plane. The airmen point a bright searchlight at the water and continue on, droning atop a cone of light above a brilliant circle that skims the sea.

I see men inside the open cargo door. I wonder what they're searching for.

At the helm, I drive eastward, hardly needing the compass, sensing my way toward shore.

The plane makes another pass. I can't distinguish any markings on it through the bright light.

An object falls from the aircraft—a flare of some sort, a sea marker. It lands a hundred feet behind us, burning brightly, hissing and spitting, shooting sparks across the water, spattering the waves with brilliant, fiery orange.

This is no rogue wave or blast of wind from a dark cloud; this is an act of calculated human malice.

For the first time on our voyage, I am afraid—*terrified.*

I flip on navigation lights, deck lights, cockpit lights, shine a spotlight on the sails—everything I can do to make *Journeyman* look like a Christmas display. I don't want to appear to be running or hiding or to bear any resemblance to whatever they're seeking.

"Low-flying aircraft, low-flying aircraft"—(just how *do* you hail an aerial bomber on the VHF radio, anyway? Do airplanes even *have* VHF radios?)—"this is sailing vessel *Journeyman*. We are a pleasure vessel under weigh and do not understand your intentions. Please advise. *Somos el barco Journeyman y vamos al Gibraltar. ¿Cual quieres? ¿Cual quieres?"* My Spanish needs work and for all I know, the plane is from Portugal or Morocco, but short of setting myself on fire and doing jumping jacks on the foredeck, I'm out of communication options.

Are they tracking drug boats? Maybe they think we're a contact waiting for them to drop a load of contraband? That's all I need—five hundred kilos of Moroccan hashish to explain to the Customs officer or whoever else wants it back first. In any case, the possibility of falling asleep on watch is no longer among my concerns.

The pilot does not respond. The plane flies off.

I bet they had a good laugh up there.

I didn't.

Damn the batteries. I switch off the floodlights but leave our running lights on to broadcast our heading and position. People get touchy in this part of the ocean when someone crosses the international stupidity line without proper illumination.

By morning the wind falls calm.

Before long, it fills in from ahead of us. For the first time in our thirty-seven day voyage, we sail hard to windward. By noon, a full gale blasts straight over the bowsprit. Fifty-knot winds and steep waves explode through the Strait. Gerhard pushes the engine as hard as he dares. We motor-sail, bashing into big, uncomfortable seas, making slow headway toward shore.

Down below in the cabin, no obvious signs of leakage are apparent—no drips or rivulets of seawater run down the bulkheads—but the ocean osmotically penetrates our lives and souls. Everything aboard becomes damp and soggy, rough and wretched.

My improvised seasickness bands are a godsend; I won't think of taking them off until I'm in a calm anchorage again.

The helm demands tremendous concentration. Each mountainous wave attempts to turn us from our course. We run through disorganized swells, battling our way toward Gibraltar, standing short watches and then resting to stay focused and alert. The day wears slowly on. Near nightfall, in the lee of the cliffs of Tarifa on the coast of Portugal, the sea subsides and the wind slackens.

Lights dot the shore. Brightly lit ships move through the middle of the Strait in both directions. Beyond them, North Africa sparkles; electric stars flicker on a continent laced with dark tragedy and unimaginable wonder.

The wind peters out. Matina takes the helm. Gerhard and I attempt a cursory tidying of the boat in preparation for arrival.

This coast is surprisingly dark and unpopulated. We motor through the night toward the bright loom of civilization.

Just after two o'clock in the morning, we round the point of Getares into a cacophony of light. To port, dozens of ships, buildings, immense refineries, and urban lights coalesce into a green-tinged fire made all the more dramatic by the incongruity of its soundlessness. As our eyes are assailed by the violence of darkness's defeat, our ears perceive only the clattering of *Journeyman's* diesel and the gentle sound of our hull moving through water.

Gibraltar rises ahead of us. The Rock. Unmistakable. Oddly different from the surrounding landscape. Vessels of all sizes sleep at
its feet.

We hail the port on the radio and receive a reply from a Customs
officer who directs us to a dock. Gerhard steps ashore with our
passports. A few minutes later, he emerges with stamped paperwork
from a small building with a simple yellow lightbulb over the door.
"There's a free anchorage they call 'The Graveyard' over on the other
side of the marina," he explains.

We cast off and motor slowly around a long spit of land to where
we find the promised Graveyard—two or three rows of boats tied
side-by-side about a dozen deep. We tie up to our neighbors and,
without a note of celebration or fanfare, collapse exhausted into
our wet bunks.

At first light the deafening roar of some all-pervasive, ominous
force turns me instantly out of my bunk. My world shakes to a
deep bass rumble unlike anything I've heard before. Charged with
adrenaline, I rush to the closest porthole, curious for a glimpse of
what will surely be our demise. The apocalypse is upon us. How
strange that we should perish after so recently completing our trial
at sea.

On the high seas, natural forces determine one's fate. Here in the
lee of Gibraltar, I have no such faith. The killing machines a mere
hundred yards from *Journeyman* are real, but we are not their target
today. The strip of land we are moored behind is a runway. Two

Royal Air Force F-16 fighter jets scream off into the sky, blue flame pouring from their afterburners.

My heart slowly descends to its natural place within my chest as the aircraft blast out of sight and out of earshot. Sadly, the two most terrifying moments of my life—the bombing at sea and the intrusion of this most unholy noise—occurred within twenty-four hours of making port. Neither had anything whatsoever to do with the natural dangers of offshore sailing.

After the shock of waking, a return to sleep is impossible. Called by some insidious societal clock, we prepare breakfast, retrieve empty water jugs from a locker, gather sacks of laundry, collect a bag of trash, launch the dinghy, and ready ourselves to live productively in this strange realm, putting aside burdensome thoughts of how little sense it makes to us any more. In this new world, the natural course is to get up and get to work.

Today we are unemployed and out of money.

Yesterday, we just *were*.

We row around the end of the runway to shore, tie the dinghy inside the marina and hike up the road into town. Cars, motorcycles, buildings, Arabs, Jews, Spaniards, Englishmen, cobblestones, restaurants, bars, and shops blend into a mix of noise, culture, history, and technology. We buy groceries, fill water jugs, and make half-hearted inquiries about work. I place a collect phone call to let my family know I'm still alive.

Enough of urban life for one day. By lunchtime, we return to the boat to prepare a meal.

Journeyman is oddly motionless. We clean up, adjust the lines that secure us to the vessel next to us and the inflatable fenders that keep us from banging against her. We neatly fold and bag the sails, and coil the sheetlines. We haul up the mainsail, then lower it slowly, flaking it accordion-style on the boom before snapping on and zipping up its canvas cover. We have much to do ashore but the call to tend to our ship asserts priority.

Night falls.

We eat.

We make small talk.

We shuffle restlessly in a world of overwhelming stasis.

No waves hiss.

No wooden groans issue from the no-longer-swinging gaff.

No flapping canvas calls to be trimmed.

The wheel stands idle in the cockpit.

A metal sun cover hides the compass.

Distant auto horns, tires on pavement, the groan of a truck transmission downshifting, occasional aircraft on the nearby runway, and a strange symphony of other unidentifiable sounds accompany an artificial daylight that obscures all but the brightest stars.

But I remember them well.

The Blue Monk

The Rock

"It was the Law of the Sea, they said.
Civilization ends at the waterline.
Beyond that, we all enter the food chain,
and not always right at the top."

—*Hunter S. Thompson*

THE SMALL CITY OF GIBRALTAR intertwines with a British military base—the two embrace the rock like a pair of gigantic octopi. To prevent the commingling of its disparate interests, a labyrinth of tunnels, walls, fences, and bridges provides isolated conduits for traffic. Having landed in Gibraltar without a shilling in my pocket, I try playing guitar in the pedestrian tunnels that pass beneath its tentacles. My performance scores me a few coins, but mostly passers-by toss cigarettes in my guitar case.

I despise smoking.

By afternoon's end, I accumulate sufficient funds to buy postage stamps, peanut butter, and a few other items. I toss a handful of cigarettes into the guitar case of the busker at the other end of the tunnel on my way home.

A better gig must surely be available in one of Gibraltar's hundreds of bars.

Pubs are required to have a special license to offer live music, but my search turns up two places willing to pay an American musician under the table. One is El Paso, a new American-themed bar and restaurant. The pay is minimal—mostly food—but it's something. I also score one night a week at The Canon Bar where I accompany silent soccer games—"football" over here—on British satellite television.

My explorations take me past a furniture shop. I inquire and yes, they can use some carpentry help, but Gerhard has already accepted a backbreaking, low-paying job with a Dutch construction company. Each morning at 5:00 AM, we rise, make him lunch, and row him ashore. Each morning, he complains bitterly. For reasons I cannot fathom, he refuses to abandon the construction job to work in the furniture shop. "I've already committed to this," he says. "I'm not a quitter."

Matina enrolls in school.

I continue to look for work.

A small advertising agency—CAMS: Creative Advertising & Marketing Services—has recently purchased a new Macintosh computer and Aldus Pagemaker software. They understand the machine's potential but don't know how to use it. Tony, the agency's proprietor, an Englishman with a wonderful, dry sense of humor, hires me for £200 a week. The wage isn't much, but living aboard *Journeyman* in the Graveyard, my only practical expense is food.

My work at CAMS is creative and rewarding. Carlos, the other designer, hails from just over the border in La Linea, Spain. We laugh and enjoy ourselves, designing ads and brochures, writing radio commercials, and working at a comfortable pace, each of us practicing our respective second languages.

I continue to perform a few nights a week. I find it ironic to have sailed forty-two hundred miles across the Atlantic to play American music in a Tex-Mex restaurant. The place is packed with home-grown American rednecks training to do steelwork in Algeciras on the opposite side of Gibraltar Bay. I wear my cowboy hat and speak with a drawl; they howl for more. I spend weekends learning Lynyrd Skynyrd and Hank Williams tunes.

On tour, the British Army Drum and Bugle Corps marches into the El Paso Bar one Saturday night. I accompany the commander and the sergeant on a selection of old Western songs. The two sing "Red River Valley" with a strong Scottish accent. And these Brits are not going to be shown up by some Yank guitar picker; out come the drums and bugles and uniforms and even the black lights and glow-in-the-dark drumsticks. They put on their own concert before drinking themselves unconscious.

I bid them all goodnight and head home before the body count gets too high.

The Blue Monk

In October, I treat myself to a birthday present, a week off work in Gibraltar to spend five days in Sevilla, Spain attending a guitar festival. The concerts are part of a prelude to the 1992 World's Fair being held next year. Among the musicians are some of the most famous guitarists in the world[89] performing a range of musical styles. I am privileged to see the older players; some are legends rarely seen in small auditoriums.

A block of seats in the front and center of the concert hall is reserved for guests and affiliates of the concert promoter; this section always has empty seats. I arrive early every night, speak English, and walk nonchalantly past the security people to sit in the first three rows.

I hike through Sevilla's ancient, cobblestoned streets, connecting with the history beneath my feet. I visit the Cathedral that supposedly houses the tomb of Christopher Columbus (apparently, he has another tomb in the Dominican Republic). The women of Sevilla are beautiful. An atmosphere of romance hovers over the city. Lovers kiss in the parks and hold hands in the streets.

How do I get inside? I need a guide, someone who lives here and knows this place. I speak the world's only true universal language; I never travel without a guitar. I hike over to the University of Sevilla,

---

89 The narrative would stumble over the long list of performers but the names provide historical context, so they are included here as a footnote: Albert Collins, B.B. King, Bo Diddley, Brian May, Dave Edmunds, George Benson, Jack Bruce, Joe Walsh, Joe Satriani, John McLaughlin, Keith Richards, Larry Coryell, Les Paul, Nuno Bettencourt, Paco De Lucia, Phil Manzanera, Richard Thompson, Robbie Robertson, Robert Cray, Roger Waters, Roger McGuinn, Stanley Clarke, Steve Cropper, Steve Vai, Vicente Amigo and others.

hoping to find a music school. I don't find one, but Antonio, Raul, and Carmen have posted advertisements on a bulletin board seeking partners with whom to practice speaking English.

Carmen somehow sounds intuitively more interesting than Antonio and Raul.

I give her a call.

Soon, I'm in her apartment, explaining in broken Spanish how I came to be here and expressing my wish to exchange some English-Spanish conversation for an inside view of Sevilla. "It's okay," she tells me. "You can practice Spanish another time; you have only a few days here. Tomorrow night, you are invited to join me for a night in town."

After Friday's concert, I make my way through the narrow streets to meet Carmen and her friends at the Pianilla, a folk and flamenco club. Revelers pass guitars around. Young women dance traditional flamenco dances as others clap *compás* in a circle around them. Delightfully informal, the atmosphere is more like a private party than a club.

We leave at 3:00 AM when the Pianilla Bar closes.

I'm tired, and my nagging sniffle is turning into a cold.

But the night is young. We move on to a disco—way too noisy for me.

I stay outside, practicing my Spanish with Carmen's friend, the beautiful Maria José, while the others dance.

I wish I didn't feel so lousy.

We breakfast at a tiny restaurant until 5:00 AM, at which point I make my way back to my room.

Maria José follows me back to my hostel.

I'm surprised. She's sweet and pretty, but shy.

I feel terrible. My head is stuffy. I'm sneezing. My eyes are watering and swollen. I'm sure I have a fever.

I thank Maria José for an excellent evening and leave her at the door. Forty-two hundred miles of sailing: one regret.

Upon returning to Gibraltar, I look for a way home. *Blue Monk* is calling me.

I run into Andrew, the hashish smuggler I met in the Horta marina. He shows me the twenty-four foot sloop he spoke of; she really is a sea boat. She has a small cockpit and a high bridgedeck to keep the ocean out of her cabin, a deep keel, and a self-steering vane.

Could I do this? Sail back solo on a wooden boat? I could follow the trade winds and currents south, stop at the Canary Islands and then cross the Atlantic to the Caribbean.[90] If I can get a good enough bargain on the boat to buy her with the money I've saved from working at CAMS, I can sell her at the classic wooden boat regatta in Antigua, then hitchhike north to the Bahamas. It would be a challenge and an adventure worth writing about.

---

90 The trade winds and currents make a large clockwise circle around the North Atlantic Ocean. Sailing south, across the Atlantic and back north to the United States is a faster and easier trip than sailing west against the wind and current.

Andrew is willing to sell but his price is too high. He doesn't really need the money. Away from the verdant mountains of the Azores, he's hardened, focused on making a "good deal."

I decline a hit of hash and move on.

One of Gerhard's coworkers comes by *Journeyman* one evening to offer a business proposition. A film crew is in need of a ride across the Strait of Gibraltar to Tangier. Committed to be on the job site, he can't take them on his own boat. Gerhard has to work, too but can I pilot *Journeyman* across? The pay, after he takes his finder's fee, will be £450, not bad for a day of sailing.

I tell Tony I need a day off from my work at CAMS. He's happy to accommodate me.

In the morning, I tie up to the marina, take on fuel, and help the film crew aboard with their gear. I set off across Gibraltar Bay with Matina and Billy, Gerhard's friend's ten-year-old son, as "crew." Billy is sandy-haired and gangly with adult teeth crowding the front of his young mouth; his shirt and jeans fit about as well. Perpetually in the way, he drifts about the cockpit, slumping here and then there, displaying profound obliviousness to *Journeyman's* operations.

My passengers are filming an interesting project. Seven catamarans are to be sailed across seven of the world's major straits.[91] Each has a mainsail painted by pop artist Raphael Gray.

---

91 *Strait or straits* - a narrow channel of water connecting two larger, navigable bodies of water. It most commonly refers to a channel of water that lies between two land masses.

The crew sets up its cameras on the bow. In light air, the catamaran sails ahead of us out of Gibraltar Bay while we motor behind.

A long, low, gentle swell rolls in the straight.

The wind dies.

The swell flattens.

The sea is glass.

We circle around a few times to get some shots, then tow the catamaran toward the mountains of North Africa.

Despite the dead calm conditions, Billy is somehow seasick at the rail.

In the afternoon, I pull into the marina in Tangier, tying alongside two boats already moored to the Customs dock.

Billy neglected to bring his passport. I order him not to show his face on deck. "Go hide in the forward bunk with the bulkhead door closed behind you." Still green from the crossing, he's happy to oblige.

I omit his name from the passenger list, submit our papers and passports, and tell the Customs man Matina and I won't be leaving the marina.

Fortunately, he doesn't come aboard.

I'm hugely disappointed. It's not as if I get to set foot on African soil every day. Mosques and hints of Moorish architecture peek over the marina walls. It would be so wonderful to walk around for an hour before heading back, if only to be able to say, "I have been to Africa."

My passengers delivered safely to Tangier, I disconnect the dock-lines and push gently off the lifelines of the boat *Journeyman* is tied to.

An arrogant American voice assaults me. "You're not supposed to push off those lifelines, son. Don't you know they're for safety?"

I roll my eyes, inhale deeply and look at Matina. Smiling, I grab the shrouds of the world's most well-constructed wooden boat and step onto the top lifeline.

Don't let me down, Gerhard.

Journeyman idles, adrift in the harbour.

I jump up and down on the cable. "I don't know what kind of shit they built your boat out of, asshole, but I suggest you upgrade to something seaworthy!"

Around the small harbour basin, yachtsmen from around the world laugh aloud in their cockpits. This American jerk had it coming, and the fact that *it* came from an American kid with a boat that makes his look like a giant bleach bottle makes the putting-in-his-place even better.

I know how to drive this ship; after all these miles, she's part of me. With confident turns of the wheel and vigorous working of the throttle and shift levers, I pirouette *Journeyman* around perfectly in place.

When my bowsprit points north to Europe, I wave and exit the harbour with a smile and a final push on the throttle.

The Blue Monk

Lights of ships skim over their reflections in the flat-calm strait.

The loom of Gibraltar and the oil refineries on the other side of Gibraltar Bay cast a greenish glow in the sky.

The diesel clatters steadily away, pushing us home to The Rock.

Billy staggers up the companionway ladder and vomits over the rail.

Farewell, Gibraltar

MY VOYAGE TO TANGIER complete, I return *Journeyman* to Gibraltar's Graveyard Anchorage and call Gerhard on the VHF radio.

He rows home from his friend's boat where he's awaited our return and puts £450 on the table. Money is tight; the profit from our day charter is a welcome windfall.

"How would you like to divide this up?" Gerhard asks.

"This is free cash. I just sailed around and had fun for a day. I don't want any of it; forget my share. All I need is what you offered me—a plane ticket and money to cover *Blue Monk's* mooring in the Bahamas. The rest, you can pay me some day after you find your fortune."

"The rest?" Gerhard's eyes flash; suddenly he's offended I expect to be paid for crewing.

Wasn't that our agreement?

"I'm sorry things worked out this way," he says. "I think it's time you make your plans and move on."

Gerhard has been stern, grouchy, and cynical ever since he started working on the construction site. I'm confused and hurt, but philosophical; the universe is telling me it's time to pull my anchors. The disagreement is disappointing but not a disaster; I've saved enough money working at CAMS to get back to the Bahamas and pay for *Blue Monk's* mooring on my own if I must. I don't understand what's eating Gerhard, but he'll have to figure it out for himself. For me, this voyage has been nothing but a grand adventure; I'm not about to allow a petty conflict to sully it. I exhale deeply, turn, and leave the cash on the table.

Geoff and Julie are anchorage neighbors from England who live with their two young daughters aboard their catamaran, *Teela*. Though they work unpleasant jobs for low pay in Gibraltar, *Teela's* cabin is always full of laughter and warmth. They kindly offer me a bunk.

Johnny Borges, a local bass player and schoolteacher, hears me play at the El Paso Bar and strikes up a conversation. He's never been off The Rock. We talk about music and Gibraltar and the world beyond the Iberian Peninsula. He carries me to the top of The Rock on the back of his motorcycle to see the resident apes and the old fortifications. We continue around the southern point where we hike into a cave once inhabited by Neanderthals.[92] Johnny muses over what led to the extinction of these early humans, but I assure him I encountered a *bona fide* living specimen only yesterday in the Tangier Marina.

---

92 Evidence of Neanderthal inhabitation was actually discovered at Gorham's Cave, a quarter-mile away from the cave we hiked into. It's logical to assume this excellent shelter was used by that same community of early humans.

We sit at the edge of a cliff, watching speedboats smuggle cigarettes around the point. Apparently, a disparity exists between duties imposed on tobacco imports by the adjacent Spanish and British authorities. This presents an irresistible opportunity for "entrepreneurs" inclined to pursue careers in "importing and exporting."

Upon learning of my circumstances, Johnny and his mother practically beg me to stay with them.

Tony, my boss, offers a small, furnished apartment in town.

I thank everyone and choose the apartment.

I can't figure out what went wrong with Gerhard. Matina and I puzzle over his change of heart. It's awkward; she's caught between our friendship and her loyalty to her father.

She tells Gerhard where I'm staying.

He shows up at my apartment with a wad of cash.

"Gerhard, you don't understand. I only wanted to take my expenses out of the charter. The money you offered me for crewing can wait; pay me some day when you've got money to burn—or never. I'm just trying to make things easier."

Perhaps his backbreaking job has soured him? Or the disappointment of moving from the Bahamas and the Azores to a construction job in this industrial place? He doesn't seem to get what I'm saying. He looks at me sternly. "Here's your money." He extends a handful of crumpled bills. "It's all here—the plane ticket money, wages for your services as crew, your mooring expenses, and half the profit from the run to Tangier."

"Gerhard, the last thing I want is to clean you out. This isn't..."

Gerhard dumps the cash into a plant on the porch, turns, and leaves. I'm disappointed. This isn't the Gerhard I know. I pray we'll reconnect some day when he weathers his storm and finds his way to his home port.

I offer to crew on *Mariah,* a 41-foot sloop. Bob's plan is to return to the U.S. via the Canary Islands and the Caribbean. I move my gear aboard and arrange to leave Friday night after my final day of work.

I thank Tony, say goodbye to Johnny and Geoff and Julie, play my last gig at the El Paso, and show up on the dock ready to go.

Bob greets me coldly. "Where the hell have you been? We've been waitin' on you all day."

"I told you Friday would be my last work day. I just finished. I'm ready, but the weather report calls for a gale tomorrow. I honestly didn't think we'd leave today, anyway."

"What part of 'leavin' on Friday' do you not understand?"

I have doubts about Bob's seamanship.

As we stand on the dock, Bob and Richard, his second crewmember finish their cigarettes and light new ones.

I look him in the eye. "It's one thing to catch weather at sea—it's going to happen—but to knowingly sail into a storm? The wind's going to blow forty-plus knots out there and Richard's never sailed before. That's one hell of a way to break in a green crewmember. If you think he's green now, wait until tomorrow night!"

Bob takes a drag on his cigarette and taps the ashes onto the ground. "You ready to go or not?"

"Just give me a few minutes to put my stuff on the dock. I won't hold you up any longer."

I pull my gear from the boat.

I try to imagine what it would be like hove to in a gale, trapped down below with two chain smokers.

I'm much better off standing on the dock with my bags, my guitar, and my sextant.

I stash my gear under an old dinghy and wait nearly an hour before I can hitch a ride to the Graveyard. Knocking on the hull of *Journeyman* after midnight is awkward, but I've given Tony my apartment key and I have no other place to go.

To his credit, Gerhard silently offers me a bunk.

In the morning, to Tony's surprise, I show up for work at CAMS. Gib Airlines is one of his clients. He makes a few phone calls.

The next day, I'm off to Miami via England, flying first class. As we speed down the runway and take to the air, Geoff and Julie and their daughters wave at my plane from The Graveyard.

How quickly the miles pass beneath a jetliner! But at forty thousand feet—even at five hundred miles per hour—with no land in sight, the Atlantic betrays no sign of our progress. We hover motionless over a cobalt plain. Through the window, I study the infinite expanse of blue below me as if I might encounter a familiar landmark, as if experience and memory could impress some tangible track upon the water, as if *Journeyman's* bow had carved some great furrow upon the face of the sea. But beyond the gridded world of human industry, time and place are imaginary constructs; the sea knows only here and now.

Return to The Tropics

December, 1991

FIVE MONTHS have passed since I left the Bahamas bound for Europe. *Blue Monk* waits safely at Man-O-War Cay on a mooring in front of the boatyard in town. I step off the ferry into her cockpit, slide open her main hatch and remove the dropboards from her companionway. How strange to hop from Gibraltar to Miami to Man-O-War in a matter of days. All is as if I never left—like waking from a vivid dream to find myself safe in a familiar bed.

I pay Mr. Albury for *Blue Monk's* mooring, stock up with groceries, and purchase a brand-new Yamaha outboard motor to replace the aging Evinrude mounted on her transom.

I've sailed many miles since *Blue Monk* left Miami over a year ago. My plan is to slowly make my way home to work, connect with friends, and make improvements to the boat. These objectives admittedly sound contrived; I have no sound rationale for leaving paradise. *Blue Monk* is well provisioned and, by my usual standards, my wallet is full to bursting. The voice of empirical reason says, *"Onward!"* But perhaps the ongoing narrative of existence is best consumed in chapters? My life's moon is full; my soul's tide is at flood; I am pulled not to the sea but to the source. This episode demands not continuance but conclusion—the setting of anchors in the familiar mud of my home port to share stories of a voyage complete.

I remove the mainsail from storage in the forward berth and bend the canvas to the boom. The jib—still in its bag—is hanked to the forestay. Mostly, *Blue Monk* needs a good airing out but for that, Abaco's cool December breezes are ideal.

Rowing up the harbour to make a mail run to the Man-O-War post office, I pass Bill on *Voyager* reading a Bible in his cockpit.

"Mornin', Dave," he calls and waves. "Welcome back. Did you have a good crossing?"

"Thanks," I reply, pulling alongside. "Magic! The Azores were straight out of a fairy tale and with the exception of a few rough days, we had light, comfortable weather."

Bill, retired on his twenty-eight foot sloop, lives like a king off a fishing spear and a Social Security check. He keeps to the shade of his cockpit awning. As the morning's low sun paints a bright triangle of light across his cockpit, he adjusts a towel over his bare legs. We chat about my Atlantic crossing for a few minutes before I change the subject on him. "I hope you don't mind me asking, but what's with the Bible? You're the last person I figured...."

"Oh, this?" Bill laughs through his beard. "I'm no holy roller; I'm not even religious. Much of it sounds far-fetched, I admit. A few passages seem to go on forever but the Bible is loaded with stories of struggle, romance, and adventure. People have fought over it for thousands of years; it has a rich history. If nothing else, the Good Book is a pivotal piece of who we are as a society."

"I tried to read it a few times," I confess, "but I never got past Genesis."

Bill smiles. "It's a long crossing. I've been chipping away at it for years, but like life, it has lessons and surprises to offer if you don't take it too seriously...or experience some powerful epiphany and run around telling the rest of the world what it 'really' means." He winks at me, grins, and raises a silver eyebrow.

After a few days of preparation, I bid farewell to Man-O-War Cay, exit through the narrow coral cut, and enjoy the short jaunt across the Sea of Abaco to Marsh Harbour. In these islands, sailing is comfortable and familiar. I know where the rocks are and what part of the tree line to aim for on Great Abaco. After an hour's reach, I round the point at Fanny Bay and anchor off the Government dock in Marsh Harbour.

Karen flies in from New Mexico to join me for the journey back to Florida, taking time off between jobs after finally burning out at her art museum director position. A stint on a sailboat in the Bahamas is just what she needs. I pick her up at the Marsh Harbour airport terminal in the 'truckster,' a battered Jeep pickup borrowed from my teacher friends at the St. Frances de Sales mission. Driving on the left side of the road feels wrong, but the trip is short; I manage okay. Karen arrives as she did the first time I met her—with a duffel bag, a floppy sun hat, a sketchpad, and an array of chalks, charcoals, and colored pencils.

After a conch sandwich at the Tiki Hut to celebrate her return to the islands, we row out to *Blue Monk* and prepare to head south. From Little Harbour, where the out-islands converge with the mainland of Great Abaco, we plan to run southwest to the Berry Islands, transit the Great Bahama Bank to Bimini, and then wait for fair weather to cross the Gulf Stream to Miami.

In the morning, we depart Marsh Harbour for a day's sail along the coast of Great Abaco. The guidebook suggests compass headings and landmarks to steer us around shoal waters and rocks, but I've made this trip plenty of times; the book is more for Karen's benefit. In the afternoon, we bump on the shallow bar at the entrance to Little Harbour's protected cove and get stuck. Karen looks concerned. "No problem," I assure her. "The tide's coming in; we'll float free soon enough." I furl the sails and tidy up the sheet lines on deck. By the time I'm finished, we're already bouncing lightly on the bottom. A push from the outboard motor sends us over the shoal into the lagoon where we anchor in front of dramatic limestone cliffs.

Randolph Johnston, an art professor fed up with academic and cultural politics, settled in this cove in the 1950's. He lived in the caves on the north side of the harbour with his family, ultimately building a home, a studio with a bronze foundry, and an art gallery across the lagoon.

Little Harbour is protected by cliffs on one side and by a beach and hilly bluffs on the other. Keyhole shaped, it offers an excellent storm refuge. Coral reefs and grass beds lie just offshore, loaded with conch and fish. And because of the Johnstons' efforts to protect sea turtles and their nests, Little Harbour abounds with them; it is not uncommon to see a half-dozen at a time. A white owl lives above the mouth of a cave that extends far back into the limestone bluff. We explore with flashlights as bats squeak and flutter around us.

We climb the winding path up the hill past the gallery, through the sentry plants, prickly pear cacti, and scrub grass on the east side of the harbour, to visit the old lighthouse on the bluff. The abandoned structure's roof is in poor condition, and the original beacon has been replaced with an ugly electric light tower erected at the edge of the cliff. Ignoring the "Keep Off" signs, we're careful on the rickety stairs. From the upstairs window, the view of the surf on the North Atlantic is spectacular, especially during this northeast wind. Ocean swells collide with the cliffs below us. The hissing and thundering of the ocean and the vibration beneath our feet are as dramatic as the scenery.

Karen and I see in the New Year—January 1, 1992. John Nation arrives on *Zebra Dun*. We play banjo and guitar at Pete Johnston's pub before returning to our boats to celebrate with a simple dinner.

We retire not long after dark; waking up rested before dawn will enable us to navigate farther on these short winter days.

In the morning, the wind direction is favorable but gusting to 30 knots; the ocean will be rough, especially for Karen who has no blue water sailing experience. And exiting the Bahama Banks at Little Harbour requires navigating between two reefs—a passage best made in conditions of good visibility. We elect to make our way back north up the Abaco chain to explore the little-used passage around the back side of Great Abaco. *Blue Monk* has shallow-enough draft at high tide, and the guidebook recommends the trip. Also, I'm familiar with the out-islands between here and Foxtown. I'll be a better tour guide for Karen if we stay in the Abacos a while longer.

Departing Little Harbour, we head northwest up the island chain, dropping anchor in the channel between Tilloo Cay and Lubber's Quarters in the afternoon. Tilloo has no formal settlement but scattered houses stand in various stages of construction on the southwest side. On the ocean side is Junk Beach, located at the end of a footpath through a hardwood hammock. I point out the black, oily sap and orange bark of poisonwood trees along the way and how, interestingly, the bark of the gumelemi tree that grows alongside it provides an antidote and palliative for painful poisonwood rash.

The hike is short; a gateway of sunlight beckons beyond the trees. Winds and currents make this beach a natural repository for wood, plastic, bottles, and other detritus from around the world.

A beachcomber's paradise, Junk Beach is decorated with totems—collections of found objects affixed to sticks, planted in the earth by visitors. Styrofoam fishing floats make ready foundations for dozens of improvised totem pole heads. Old sandals, long-separated from their mates, lie scattered among piles of seaweed, driftwood, and sun-faded fragments of plastic in this bizarre landscape where man's forgotten trash mingles with nature's beauty. We walk alone on the sand, examining unusual artifacts from faraway places—a hairless doll, a faded toy football. Maybe we'll find a glass Japanese fishing float? The root system from a stand of bamboo chopped off at the stalks and washed clean of soil by the sea stands like a work of abstract sculpture among the collection of crude heads on sticks. Here's a child's diving fin and a frayed piece of green ship's hawser snaking in and out of the weed line. This is the dimension of lost things; your other sock and your missing earring are here—somewhere. Above the beach, windswept hills are carpeted with succulent vines, sea oats, and a few hardy seagrape trees. Low and barren, desolate and forgotten, cold and windy, Junk Beach is the beach at the end of the world.

In the afternoon, we sail around the inside of Elbow Cay where the Abaco chain makes a sharp bend to the northwest. After skimming over sand and seagrass beneath the clear waters, we anchor for the night in Hopetown Harbour. Hopetown's protected lagoon and proximity to the reef made this island a pirate's den and a wrecker's paradise until the British government erected the lighthouse in 1864. The red and white candy-striped tower—built with walls over three feet thick to withstand hurricane winds and the ravages of salt air— employs a floating kerosene lantern that rotates in a pool of mercury. The ingenious light can be spun with a single finger in spite of its enormous weight. The old glass Fresnel lens and the ancient mechanism still work; the tall beacon throws its powerful beam across these islands each night. An iron staircase winds like a nautilus shell through a pink-painted interior to the light chamber and balcony at the top—the apex of the Abacos.

We bypass familiar Man-O-War Cay, taking advantage of the northeast wind to make northwesterly progress, leave the Fowl Cays to starboard, and continue along the coasts of Scotland Cay and Great Guana Cay.

To port lies Foote's Cay where I worked varnishing the house and fell overboard rescuing my outboard motor during the October gale of 1989. To starboard lies Guana Cay Harbour, the place Karen and I anchored after our first sail together. We pass Shell Island where John Nation and I celebrated our saturnalia one starry night. Around the tip of Guana Cay, we reach out into Whale Cay passage, the deep cut through which I departed the Abacos bound for Europe the previous July.

Featureless and barren, Whale Cay would be a novel place to visit at low tide after a few days of calm weather. A wide shoal connects this island to the Abaco mainland. Small boats can navigate through the shallows via a poorly marked route on the inside, but it makes better sense to exit the deep channel, pass into the Atlantic between the island and the offshore reefs, and then return to the Sea of Abaco on the other side of the shoal.

Accustomed to the light chop of Abaco's protected bay, I'm surprised at how small *Blue Monk* is in the big ocean rollers. Up and over the swells we ride, leaving the waveswept face of Whale Cay to port and the exposed rocky teeth of the barrier reef well to starboard. The journey is pleasant and uneventful; the brief passage through ocean waves reminds me that, though small, *Blue Monk* was designed to handle these very conditions. Karen, emboldened by my confidence, is more impressed than concerned by the big seas.

As we angle south around Whale Cay and into the north cut, the seas diminish quickly.

We enjoy a calm anchorage and the pleasure of a hot meal in the lee of Green Turtle Cay.

Karen beams. In a few days, we've traveled from Marsh Harbour to Little Harbour to Junk Beach, through Whale Cay Passage to Green Turtle Cay, passing places like Man-O-War and Guana Cay that are already part of her collection of cherished memories. "You know," she says. "This world is impossible to describe to someone who hasn't seen it in person."

I smile back at her. "Much of it sounds far-fetched. A few passages seem to go on forever, but life here is loaded with stories of struggle, romance, and adventure. If nothing else, once you experience these islands, they become a pivotal piece of who you are."

Gulf Stream Crossing IV

Proceeding up the abaco chain, Karen and I spend a night
anchored at Alans-Pensacola Cay before sailing seven miles north
to Moraine Cay. Few boaters call here; this island is off the beaten
path, but the reef—an extension of the island itself—is easily accessible. Though the main reef is oddly lacking in fish, the small heads
and ledges inshore of it abound with hogfish and grouper. Conch
hobble across the bottom. A white beach stretches out before an
array of coconut palms, spaced perfectly for hanging a hammock.

The Fish Cays are our next stop. Karen and I stay here a few days,
awaiting fair winds. Beautiful but desolate, these tiny islands remind
me of the Exuma Cays farther south.

Beaches littered with thousands of sun-blackened conch shells
testify to a tragic detachment of man from his environment. Easily
picked off the bottom by the boatload, populations of these tasty sea
snails are quickly being reduced. In Nassau, it is illegal to dump the
empty shells. With the meat of well over five million conch exported
through that port each year, the harbour would soon fill up. Old
timers in the islands talk about days when conch were numerous

everywhere. Today, they're harder to find, but every so often, you look down and there they are—large, weed-covered mollusks humping through the seagrass.

Two or three conch provide plenty of meat for a meal—as long as you know the proper technique for getting them out of their shells. With a hammer and screwdriver, punch a slot the width of your thumb two inches down the small, conical part of the shell. Then, insert a blade to detach the snail. As this arrangement is disagreeable to the conch, the animal should be dispatched quickly—out of sympathy and also to stop the secretion of copious amounts of clear, sticky, disgusting slime. The meat is quite tough but after you slice a crosshatch pattern in it with a sharp knife and pound it vigorously with a mallet, the mild white flesh is ready for cooking—like chicken—in just about any way one cares to imagine.

We arrive at the Fish Cays in a perfect calm. Before sundown, we enjoy a rowing tour around one of the islets, gliding on the smooth, clear water over a coral garden resplendent with tropical fish and other colorful creatures.

As the calm sea and high cirrus clouds portended, a cold front arrives.

The wind fills in from the northwest, making our now-exposed anchorage bouncy.

Blue Monk swings with the breeze.

Ten feet behind our rudder, a coral head reaches for the surface.

Blue Monk follows the wind around to the north. We have better protection now from the windblown swells, but another large coral head appears behind us—too close. Usually, the big heads are found on the ocean side of the islands—not here in the protected Sea of Abaco. Unknowingly, I anchored inside a cluster of them.

I adjust my anchor lines to distance myself from the rocks, but the water in our anchorage is churned up by the weather. I can't tell how many corals heads lie around us or where they are.

Time to get out of here—carefully.

In the early morning at high tide, we cross the rocky bar at the west end of Little Abaco to enter the Bight of Abaco on the south side of the mainland, a shallow place few cruisers go. But the water is clear; the shoals are easily discernible. We proceed through Spence Rock Passage, flying across sand and grass beds and soft coral gardens barely deep enough to accommodate us; our keel occasionally kisses the sandy bottom. I sheet the sails in tight, keeping *Blue Monk* heeled over to reduce her draft, praying we don't run aground in the middle of this untraveled wilderness.

The wind is *perfect.*

Blue Monk flies along at hull speed.

On a beam reach with the dinghy planing along behind, we fly across the banks for hours. The tall BATELCO tower on Mores Island is visible for almost twenty miles. We sail right in on it. After sundown, the wind begins to die again. Making landfall after dark is inadvisable in these shallow islands. On arrival, I approach the shore slowly, but, unable to see the bottom or judge the water's depth, I stay a few hundred yards off the coast. We drop anchor in the island's lee at 10:00 PM to sleep on a flat calm sea.

Mores Island has two small fishing villages on it, the largest of which is named Hard Bargain. Morning reveals wooden houses of sky blue, conch shell pink, sand shoal beige and other cheerful pastels spattered like paint on green hills, but we have no time to visit; another cold front is coming. I hope to keep its slowly clocking winds on our beam as we sail south to the Berry Islands and then west across the Great Bahama Banks to Florida.

Channel Cay marks a southern point where vessels enter and leave the Little Bahama Bank. Beyond lies Northwest Providence Channel, a canyon of deep water thirty miles wide and a mile deep that divides the Little Bahama Bank from the Great Bahama Bank. With binoculars, we search for the marker. It turns out to be a stick cemented into a rock the size of a grapefruit. How this insignificant toilet plunger ever attained the status of "lighthouse" on my charts is a mystery, but in this wild place, any guidepost is a comfort.

The hoped-for wind fills in. A rocket sled ride conveys us across Northwest Providence Channel to Great Stirrup Cay in the Berry Islands. Offshore, we encounter eight-foot seas as we approach the Great Bahama Banks, but *Blue Monk* enjoys the romp. Tearing along behind us, the dinghy laughs at the waves.

After sailing most of the day, we pass onto the shallow banks under the shadows of two enormous ocean liners anchored off Great Stirrup Cay in the Berry Islands. On the cruise ships' private beach, passengers listen to calypso music and drink at a bamboo bar with a thatched roof. We're here at the same time and place, having a staggeringly different experience.

The Great Bahama Banks are the Sahara of the islands— 80 nautical miles of clear water and featureless white sand, bordered on the western edge by the island oases of the Bimini chain. The breeze carries us through the night across the banks. As hoped, the shifting wind stays on our beam as we curve westward toward the Gulf Stream.

The air chills as the next cold front fills in.

Karen stays up late with me at the helm and then finally falls asleep, warm and comfortable in the bunk below.

I imagine myself back on *Journeyman*, alone in the cockpit in the middle of the Atlantic, sailing through the night using the stars as a compass.

We make excellent time, picking up the high hills of Ocean Cay shortly after sunrise. I don't bother to compensate for the tide; in approximately twelve hours of sailing, the shifting current will set us an equal distance one way and then the other.

The breeze fades and ultimately falls calm.

We motor the last ten miles beneath a perfect, cloudless blue sky.

After a twenty-eight hour non-stop run from Mores Island, we anchor on the east side of Gun Cay, a mile-long island that shields us from the surf crashing in from the Gulf Stream. Our anchorage is rolly during the first day, but the wind soon clocks around to the west, making conditions calmer.

We remain here a few days, exploring the island, waiting for the front to pass before starting our Gulf Stream crossing. A military installation on the north end—not much more than a fenced-in compound—encloses a postcard lighthouse. We row ashore to watch the Gulf Stream surf explode on the rocky coast. Small waterfalls on the east side of Gun Cay drain windblown waves from the west side.

Forty-five miles of deep, fast-moving water lie between *Blue Monk* and Biscayne Bay.

Listening to the weather radio, we plan a strategy for crossing. *Blue Monk* has no navigation instruments save for a compass and a primitive radio direction finder, but we should be able to finish the last quarter of the passage with the lights of downtown Miami in sight.

The easterly trade winds show no sign of returning; the weather radio says a gale is headed our way. This anchorage will soon become a rough and uncomfortable place. We don't want to get sandwiched between the rocky coast of Gun Cay and a strong northeaster. We consider paying $40 a night for a sheltered slip at nearby Cat Cay Marina but these northeasterly winds are light and predicted to remain so overnight; conditions in the Gulf Stream shouldn't be too bad. If we reach southwest, we'll have the wind on our beam while the current pulls us north to Miami. If the wind clocks around to the east, so much the better—as long as it doesn't blow like hell with the wind opposing the current.

Before sunset, we sail past Gun Cay Lighthouse into the Gulf Stream with sails shortened as a precaution. Under reefed mainsail and a small jib, we fly along as we did across Northwest Providence Channel.

For eight hours, we enjoy an exhilarating sail through six-foot seas. *Blue Monk* shows her North Sea Folk Boat heritage. With her heavy, full keel, she is balanced and comfortable.

Night falls.

The wind increases.

The temperature drops.

I take down the mainsail.

The wind increases.

The temperature drops.

We continue under jib alone, flying along with gusty winds of 30 knots and disorganized twelve-foot seas.

I look behind us. The dinghy is fifteen feet in the air.

It must be 40° Fahrenheit out here.

Repeatedly, I'm blasted with cold air, then drenched by warm Gulf Stream waves crashing over my ship.

I tie a rope around my waist and secure the other end to a winch pad, lashing myself into the cockpit.

Karen is cold and uncomfortable in her light foul weather gear. Even under shortened sail, managing the helm in these waves requires force, concentration, and experience. "Put the bunk cushions on the cabinsole where you can't get tossed out of bed," I suggest. "Lie down on the floor. Stay warm and dry. I'll stay at the tiller and keep us on course."

The batteries are failing. My running lights are dim, hardly visible.

I dodge two enormous freighters and a brilliantly lit cruise ship converging on our position. Behind the windows of the ocean liner, colored lights illuminate the bodies of dancing tourists. *Is my tiny boat even visible to their radar in these big seas?*

Blue Monk flies off a wave top, falls and crashes sideways into the trough.

Karen calls out to me. "Did we hit something?"

"Nah, just a big wave. Everything's fine."

I'm not so sure.

Lights at the tops of radio towers appear on the horizon.

I think I see the sweeping beam of a lighthouse.

There it is again.

What lighthouse is this? The flashing pattern is wrong; it doesn't match anything on my chart.

The Gulf Stream should have pushed us north, but perhaps these northerly winds have pushed us south? *Where in hell are we?* Somewhere in the northern Florida Keys, I guess. Maybe Key Largo? *How could that be?* It's as if the northbound current had no effect on our course at all.

The sky purples behind us—slowly.

If this is the Florida Keys, I know we must avoid the dangerous reefs offshore. I watch carefully for breakers.

I struggle to hold a steady course while studying the flashing patterns of various Florida lighthouses indicated on the chart. *Could this be Carysfort Light? Could we be this far south?*

The lighthouse flashes red.[93]

The keel bumps hard on the bottom.

Blue Monk is lifted by the swell and continues forward.

"What was *that?*" Karen looks up at me through the companionway.

Another bump.

The lighthouse beacon glows red and then turns white again.

We're past the shallows, inside the barrier reef.

I threaded a needle in the dark. A more experienced sailor would have hove to and waited for daylight. Cold, young, wet, tired, and scared, I guessed at *Blue Monk's* position relative to a lighthouse I wasn't certain I'd identified correctly. The sea will forgive ignorance—at times, even drunkenness and stupidity—but the sea will not suffer apathy. Poseidon waved me through, leaving me alive to

---

93 Some lighthouses have *red sectors*, portions of the lens colored red to indicate the general direction of reefs, rocks, and shoals. The rest of the lens is clear (white). When passing across the reef line, the light will change from white (deep water) to red (watch out for rocks and shoals) and then back to white (safely inside the reef).

ponder why. Never again will I tow a dinghy offshore. Never again will I make landfall in the dark without being certain of my course. I know better now. I would never survive another such indiscretion.

The waves are already calmer here in the lee of whatever land this is. The coast presents no tall buildings or signs of industrial civilization, only an endless line of mangroves. We must be south of Biscayne Bay. Ah, there's the "robot radio tower." We're in Key Largo.

My hands are too numb from the cold to adjust the jib sheet. Karen comes up to the cockpit to help round up into the wind so we can anchor.

Our passage took fourteen hours. We passed over the shallows into Florida a few miles north of Carysfort Reef Light. *Blue Monk* was pushed twenty-five miles south of her destination.

Exhausted and hypothermic, I shiver uncontrollably. Karen wraps me in blankets and makes me hot tea.

A warm meal and a few hours of sleep restore me. This beats the Gulf Stream for comfort but we're exposed here, anchored in an uncomfortable chop. I crave a night in a calm anchorage.

We motorsail through the day up Hawk's Channel, along the coasts of the Florida Keys, against the wind and waves. Before sundown, we round the north end of Key Largo into Caesar's Creek to enter the protected waters of Biscayne Bay.

"Elliot Key, Biscayne National Park—the first place I ever spent a night on a boat," I tell Karen.

The tops of buildings in downtown Miami are faintly visible on the northern horizon.

"Are we really that close to Miami?" Karen asks. "It feels so far away."

I gesture across the clear waters of our anchorage at the nearby mangrove island, the tops of its trees tinted orange by the sun setting on the other side of the bay. "Take all this home with you," I suggest. "Flip it around. When you're back in the land of clocks and calendars, you'll always know it's *this* that isn't as far away as it seems."

I'm talking as much to myself as to her.

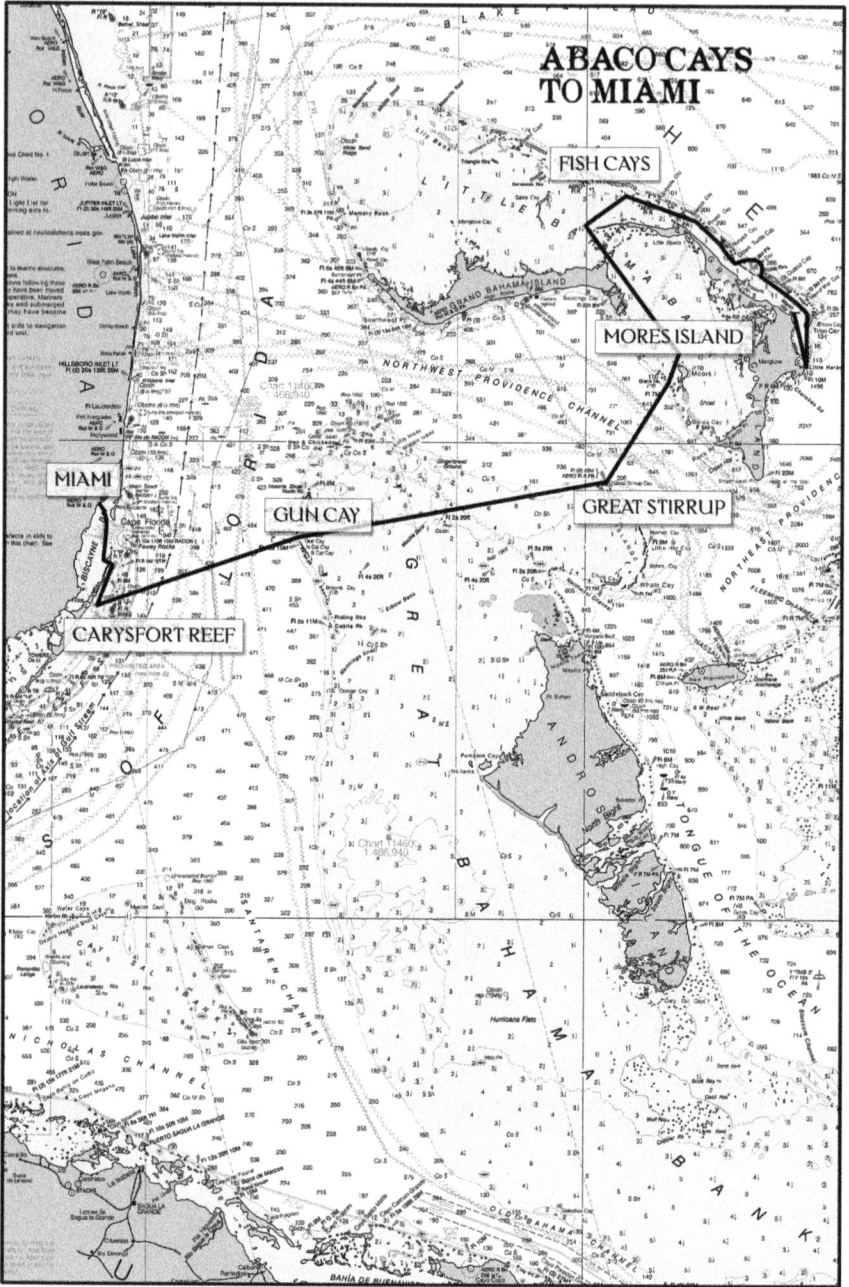

ABACO CAYS
TO MIAMI

FISH CAYS

MORES ISLAND

MIAMI

GUN CAY

GREAT STIRRUP

CARYSFORT REEF

Miami

Charity begins at home, and justice begins next door.
—Charles Dickens

M Y MOTHER picks us up at the marina.

A hot homemade meal and a long hot shower are unimaginable luxuries.

Instead of driving us to the dock, my stepfather offers the use of his car.

I park at Dinner Key.

We walk to the dinghy dock.

Karen and I row out to *Blue Monk*.

In the morning, less than twenty-four hours after arriving, the car is gone—stolen.

Ah, Miami.

Thank God for Dinner Key Anchorage and my secret world beyond the spoil islands.

The Blue Monk

Darkness Before the Dawn

Karen flies home to New Mexico to begin her new job. I dig my anchors into the Dinner Key seagrass and look for work.

Life afloat in Dinner Key Anchorage is much as it was before I left.

At 5:00 AM, the shrimp boats return from the dark bay, rumbling in through the anchorage with trawls lashed tight to the sides of their cabins, their live catch bound for Florida's bait shops. The shrimpers pass through the sleeping community of anchored boats with a certain lightness, courtesy, and respect. Aboard our boats, we rarely awaken, subconsciously dismissing the passing boats as friendly sounds of the night, as a terrestrial sleeper might dismiss a passing train. To the extent we are aware of them at all, the engines are comforting. The diesels assure us there is yet time to rest in the embrace of the sea; the approaching sun is still far beyond the Gulf Stream. Behind each shrimp boat, long, solitary waves spread across the cool, black tranquility of Biscayne Bay. A gentle rocking accompanies the sounds of the wakes crossing my hull.

Even with the shrimp boats' passage, morning is a quiet time. The misty solitude absorbs the intrusion of the working boats with profound dignity. The tired fishermen honor the dawn with hushed voices and a deliberate but slower pace as they converge from the sea to the dock.

This morning is different.

So was yesterday and the day before.

Sounds of screeching guitars, drums, rattling gear, and roaring engines shatter the stillness.

Someone doesn't get it.

I scrape the sleep from my eyes, throw open my forward hatch, and stand on my bunk, poking my head through the foredeck to confront this violator of the sanctity of the hour. He ties his shrimp boat alongside a nearby sailboat, leaving his big diesels idling and his stereo blasting while he transfers gear from one boat to the other.

I shout at him over the din. "Hey buddy, we're all trying to sleep out here. Could you maybe have a little courtesy?"

The shrimper looks at me and scowls. "Fuck you," he responds tersely before turning away to focus on his business.

"No. Fuck you!" I return. "What's your problem?"

This is a stupid move on his part. The man who owns that shrimp boat lives out here in the anchorage on a grand old wooden Sparkman and Stephens sloop. Munshaw won't suffer having one of his captains practice that kind of seamanship.

"Fuck you," the shrimper responds, summoning up the pinnacle of his wit.

I consider what alternatives I have—short of firing a flare gun—to engaging in a long exchange of childish insults at five in the morning, but my thoughts are interrupted.

Wolfgang's forward hatch pops open next door on *Sailmaker*. "No. Fuck you!"

A similar epithet issues from Ray Montana as his head emerges through his deck.

Like prairie dogs popping from their burrows, anchorites fling open hatches and leap to the defense of the morning, repeating the singular insult with a note of challenge and seriousness.

"No. Fuck you!"

"Fuck you!"

"Fuck you!"

The shrimper looks around uncomfortably at the serious eyes and clenched jaws of the angry boaters. Surrounded, outnumbered, and without much of a case to plead, he reconsiders his Old Milwaukee standoff, silences the stereo, unties the shrimp boat, and retreats to the shrimp docks.

We sailors are disgruntled but feel some sense of victory won through solidarity. After exchanging a few greetings and smiles over the absurdity of the exchange, we retreat through open hatches into warm bunks.

⧢ The Blue Monk

Today is a work day. After a few more hours of not very restful sleep, my oars carry me toward shore. As I pass the shrimp dock, I lock eyes with the inconsiderate shrimper but say nothing. I stare until his eyes burn and he's forced to turn away.

At day's end, I row out through the channel to where *Blue Monk* awaits on her mooring. After dinner, I sit on the foredeck watching the stars, the lights of the city, and the reflections of the anchored boats in the still water. I read in my bunk for a half hour and fall asleep.

In the early morning, the shrimp boats return as always. I don't awaken. The tired fishermen honor the dawn with hushed voices and a deliberate but slower pace as they converge from the sea to the dock.

Summer

AUGUST IN MIAMI—a final, desperate campaign before October calls in the year's first cold front to break the back of its brutal occupation. The afternoon air is hot, muggy, penetrating, still. Heat waves dance wildly over black asphalt and gridlocked traffic. West of Miami, a vast wilderness of black water, cypress, and sawgrass stews in the summer heat. The water's surface is nearly 100°F. Evaporating moisture rises invisibly at first, cooling slowly as it gains altitude. Every thousand feet, the temperature falls 3.5°F. Water vapor condenses into tiny droplets. A cloud forms, spreading outward and climbing upward.

The cloud soon holds more cool, condensed water than it can carry. Rain streams beneath it. Cumulonimbus—a classic mushroom cloud—looms like Hiroshima's ghost over the land. Driven by high altitude winds, the thunderhead marches slowly toward open water. At fifty thousand feet, a stream of ice crystals blows off the top of the cloud bloom. Falling water collides with the still-rising heat, ascending into the sky again before ever hitting the ground.

Man, is it hot!

On Biscayne Bay in the anchorage, the air is heavy, thick, stifling. With no wind to blow them back on their mooring lines, the boats float at odd angles to one another. A tiny wake from a dinghy rowing in the channel spreads slowly, a thin black snake sidewinding across a flat desert of bright, reflected sky. Amplified by the silence, sonic wakes carried by still air are as perceptible as their liquid counterparts. A clunking of oars in oar locks, a distant conversation, a cough— sounds normally too faint to be heard—skim across the hot glass bay.

Slack low tide. Inside the spoil islands in the dredged marina, the bottom is dark, grassless, and murky. Languid water bakes in the sun. Sheets of algae rise from the mud beneath the boats like fragments of old, rotten blanket. Lines hang loose. Boats sit motionless in their slips. Dock residents walk quickly along the white concrete edges of the piers, avoiding the wooden planks in the center. Heat rises from the boards as from a bed of coals. The scent of baking lumber hovers in the salt air.

The storm advances. Distant thunder rumbles from somewhere inland. In the shadow of the storm, the rising heat can no longer drive the rain back up into the sky. A gray curtain descends to earth.

Jerry St. Jacques and Ray Montana stand on their foredecks talking about the weather, their boats hanging in no particular directions. "Looks like we're gonna get another one," says Ray.

"Yep," says Jerry, "and I hope that sonofabitch over there with his piece-of-crap boats and twisted-up anchor lines doesn't drift down on anyone when the wind comes up."

Jerry's referring to the collection of quasi-abandoned boats in the middle of the anchorage—salvaged, stolen, or otherwise unofficially owned by Crazy Jim—tied together and covered with broken dinghies, old masts and rigging, faded fenders, broken outboards, and a thick layer of cormorant scat. Nobody's quite sure how his horrible collection of jetsam is fastened to the bottom, but a coil of frayed and twisted lines as thick as a man's leg extends from the bow of the central hulk down into the water.

"I swear I'm gonna cut all that junk loose some dark night when there's a west wind blowing," says Ray.

Jerry laughs. It's something we all threaten to do under our breath, especially when the most innocent exchange with Crazy Jim provokes a screaming, cursing rage about his "rights." But though we'd love to see him and his trash collection go, as sailors, we don't have it in us to cut anyone's lines, however poorly tended they might be.

The thunderhead obscures the sun.

The air turns green. The light is vivid, unusually clear, as if frequencies not normally visible can be perceived. An electric presence charges the atmosphere, an excitement. We're at the edge of something not quite identifiable that inspires vigilance, alertness, a note of fear. Summer squalls don't last long but they can blow with hurricane force.

A bright crackle-flash of lightning accompanies an enormous boom of thunder.

That one must have hit the marina.

꩜ The Blue Monk

A single halyard clangs nervously against a mast somewhere.

A second one joins it.

The tinkling sound spreads slowly, subtly across the marina and through the anchorage—a mad chorus of warning bells.

The temperature plummets.

The ringing halyards are joined by a low humming of lines and rigging.

A cold blast of air jerks our boats back on their anchors. A few, caught broadside by the gust, heel awkwardly and sail forward until, arrested by their mooring lines, they fall back with the others.

I insert all but the top dropboard into my companionway, then pull the main hatch closed over my head as the first fat raindrops spatter against my wooden cockpit locker top.

Another blast of wind rips through the anchorage. My neighbor's wind generator spins up with a hissy growl.

More rain.

Lines and rigging hum, vibrating like the strings of an instrument resonating through the air-filled hulls to which they are affixed. When the wind reaches a certain speed, when the vibrations are just so, the rigging harmonizes awkwardly, producing what violin makers call a 'wolf tone.' *Blue Monk* pumps as if played by a gigantic bow.

Lightning strikes again somewhere close, close enough to hear it sizzle as it flashes and explodes. I comfort myself thinking about how many other boats in the anchorage have taller masts than mine.

The edge of the cloud is above us now.

Cold air falls and collides with the earth, spreading across the water as jets of wet wind. I watch through the top companionway board slot. The curtain of rain advances from shore, obscuring the buildings in Coconut Grove, then the tops of the masts of boats in the marina behind the spoil islands. The island behind me disappears.

I'm in it now.

Charged by fast-moving air, the bay whips into an angry chop. Anchored boats hobbyhorse wildly, straining at their lines. Salt spray and rain obscure my view through the ports on the cabin sides; *Blue Monk* has no forward-facing windows. If a boat blows down on me, I won't see it coming. I'm dry, but in my foul weather jacket and pants, I sweat in my stuffy cabin, straining to see the boats around me, looking for changes in their relative positions and angles to the wind that might indicate dragging anchors—theirs or mine.

A blast sounds from a horn somewhere. There's nothing I can do to help; I have only my rowing dinghy. I hope nobody drags down on me but I won't venture out unless I must.

After a few minutes, the wind blows itself out. Water spirals down the cockpit drains. The rain falls steadily but gently now, calming the sea. The torrent fades to a drizzle, then a sprinkle before finally moving on across the bay.

The air remains humid but the temperature is cooler now. I open my hatch, remove the dropboards, and climb out to the cockpit, stripping off my rain gear. A small sailboat has blown up on the island.

A shirtless man stands next to it in ankle-deep water, his hands on his hips. He's lucky; the tide is low and his boat has a shallow draft. He'll set some anchors and tow her off at high water no worse for the wear.

Crazy Jim's collection of junk still floats here in all its glory.

A breath of light, easterly breeze fills in. Anchorites open hatches and raise wind scoops. The easy chop we're accustomed to returns. With it comes the gentle, soothing, hypnotic slapping of waves against our bows.

Jerry comes out on deck and hollers over to Ray Montana, "I clocked sixty-three knots on my wind indicator."

"I'm not surprised," Ray returns, "but at least it cooled things down."

"Amen," says Jerry. "Amen to that."

"Hey Dave," Ray calls over to me, "I've got a cooler full of ice here. Come on over."

I smile back, shoot him a thumbs-up, bail out my half-sunk dinghy, and row over to join him.

Ray gestures toward the tall buildings in Coconut Grove. "I wonder what it's like to be in a storm high up in one of those big condo towers over there?" He descends into his cabin and then follows two cold glasses up through the companionway to join me in the cockpit.

"They probably don't even notice," I conjecture.

"That's too bad," he says. "That's too bad."

The Blue Monk

Tropical Disturbance

August, 1992

E VERY DAY, I listen to the automated NOAA weather radio broad-
caster's robotic voice for news of the tropics.

A tropical wave drifts off the distant Sahara.

Something is not right about this one.

Over the next week, the wave becomes a tropical depression.

"Keep your eye on this one, buckaroo," admonishes John Nation.
He senses something, too.

The depression becomes a tropical storm.

Hurricane Andrew is born.

Here in Dinner Key Anchorage, we've prepared for hurricanes
before. The drill involves hauling anchors, moving our boats to some
sheltered inland spot, and securing them with every anchor and every
line aboard to the bottom and the shore.

The task takes a full day of hard work to accomplish.

And another full day to un-accomplish.

But the hurricane gods often accept these labors as sacrifice. Maybe
it's their idea of a joke? We've storm-prepped our boats many times

before. Every approaching cyclone veers away from Miami, leaving us to wrestle up muddy anchors and heavy chain, untie lines from mangroves, bend sails to spars and return to Dinner Key, mostly relieved, but—as foolish as it sounds—slightly disappointed that our efforts were wasted.

We listen to the radio frequently, monitoring the storm.

Geoff and Julie, friends from Gibraltar's "Graveyard" anchorage, arrive at Dinner Key on their catamaran, *Teela*. I'd much rather catch up with them than move my boat to some infernal inland waterway. "So glad you could make it. You got here just in time."

Saturday afternoon.

Andrew picks up strength. The hurricane is predicted to hit Florida's east coast late tomorrow.

That's *us*.

Time to move.

I ready *Blue Monk* to sail and drag extra anchors to the foredeck. Joel leaves, too, on his ketch, *Phyllis Louise*. Phinheas is aboard as his crew. They follow me to a waterway six miles south of the anchorage in Coral Gables, just north of Matheson Hammock. Joel tows his motor skiff behind him. It slows us down, but we'll need his workboat to ferry us back to the anchorage.

Ray Montana is out of town, visiting relatives in New Hampshire. Phinheas answers Joel's cell phone when Ray calls to ask about the storm.

"No, Ray. That's okay. We have everything covered here."

"Phinheas? Why would you say that? Tell him to get his ass on the next plane!"

Phinheas, pathologically helpful, looks at me innocently. "Ray's a thousand miles away. I didn't want him to worry."

I try calling back but I can't raise Ray on the phone.

Late afternoon. The wind opposes us. The sky fades from blue to orange to purple to black. We putter around Biscayne Bay, trying to pick out one blinking channel marker from the others against the lights on shore. I have my hands full sailing my ship by myself, but Phinheas is aboard to assist Joel. I come alongside *Phyllis Louise* to loan him my bright spotlight.

Just before midnight, we finally locate the channel. Phinheas illuminates the markers with the light. We pass between the red and green triangles and squares, round the sand bar, and motor up a canal to a small, tree-lined basin in Coral Gables.

Several boats have already tied to the mangroves and casaurina trees. Joel finds a spot for *Phyllis Louise* along the shore.

Why is everyone tying their boats to the land? Do they know something I don't?

I go with my gut.

A boat should be able to swing with the wind. I don't want her blowing against the shore.

I anchor *Blue Monk* in the center of the basin.

Joel's motor skiff proves useful for setting anchors quickly. When we've finished securing the boats, we head off in her, motoring through the dark back to Dinner Key. The breeze is up. The water is choppy. Phinheas has no foul weather gear. At 2:30 in the morning, we splash into the Anchorage.

Starving, we three tired and ragged sailors jump in Joel's truck and head to Denny's; it's the only place open at that hour.

At 4:30 in the morning, we return to Dinner Key. Plenty of work remains to be done. The hurricane continues to move toward us.

At seven o'clock, after a brief, hardly restful sleep, we tow Joel's houseboat behind the north island at Dinner Key. Phinheas helps me retrieve a large anchor I left behind—a 45-pound Danforth buried deep in the Dinner Key bottom. He keeps Joel's skiff close by while I dive down to dig the hook out of the mud. My excavations stir up the bottom; I can't see an inch in front of my dive mask, but I manage to peel away enough clay to get my fingers under an anchor fluke. Eventually, the anchor releases its grip on the seabed. Phinheas hauls it up into the skiff.

After we recover the anchor, we pick up Joel; he's finished securing his houseboat and packing his possessions into a half-dozen black garbage bags.

We cram his belongings in the bed of the truck under a stack of dinghies. The dinghies get distributed to various friend's garages ashore. Moving them costs me half the big toenail on my right foot, but I don't have the luxury of time to acknowledge the pain. The wind is already gusting hard; we need every remaining second. After stowing the dinghies, we drive off down Old Cutler Road to finish preparing our sailboats for the storm.

John Nation finds a spot for *Zebra Dun* near our boats along the shore of the basin.

A small sailboat, secured only by four small anchors on very short lines, has already dragged and tangled itself up with *Blue Monk;* the rising tide lifted its moorings clear of the bottom. This anchoring job suggests either profound ignorance or an insurance fraud strategy that disregards the safety of every boat here. I tow the offending vessel to a place farther down the waterway where it can blow up on the rocks without taking anyone else's boat with it.

We continue stripping sails and securing hatches as Hurricane Andrew's spiral bands spin across the sky.

Joel, Phinheas, and I make a last dash back to the anchorage in Joel's truck to try to secure Ray Montana's boat, *Tava.*

We pass John Nation hiking six miles from the Coral Gables Waterway to a friend's house near Dinner Key, carrying his cat in a box. We regret not stopping but we have no room; we have no time.

Clouds race overhead.

The wind gusts to 30 knots.

Rain bands move briskly across the anchorage.

We're too late to move *Tava* to our safe harbor in Coral Gables. Some well-intentioned neighbor tossed Ray's anchors in; they're a tangled heap of line, chain, and steel; we can't budge any of them from the bottom with this wind blowing. We abandon the ground tackle, motor *Tava* behind the southernmost Dinner Key spoil island, strip her sails, and tie her to three of the Coconut Grove Sailing Club's moorings—it's the best we can do.

The sky reddens in the west.

We toss Ray's dinghy and outboard motor in the back of Joel's truck and race off through the deserted Miami streets.

Joel drops me off at a friend's house at 10:30 PM.

The wind howls through the banyan trees.

I collapse in bed, literally hallucinating from fatigue.

In her tiny lagoon, *Blue Monk* strains at her anchor lines, struggling to keep her bow into the growing tempest.

Hurricane Andrew

A N INTENSE JET OF POWER blasts the walls of the house. The screaming wind is surreal.

3:00 AM: I drag myself out of bed to join Shauna and her roommates in the hall closet of their Coral Gables house. We lost our electricity hours ago. The air is stuffy and hot.

5:00 AM: The wind liquefies; a sideways Niagara Falls of air uproots trees and rips roofs from houses. We cower together in the dark. The air is thick and humid. Time is slow, gelatinous, dense.

Window glass breaks.

Outside, branches, coconuts, lawn chairs, and shingles hurtle through the air.

8:00 AM: The worst of the storm is over.

We poke our heads tentatively out the front door to survey a strange new landscape. Branches litter the ground, along with roof tiles and other debris, but our sturdy old Coral Gables house withstood the blow. Freed from the confines of the hall closet, we react to our transformed surroundings not with horror, but with childlike levity. The destruction is too much to process. We find comic relief in the haphazard rearrangement of neighborhood objects. "Didn't this come from the house a few streets over?" Huge banyan trees lie uprooted on their sides; their exposed root systems inspire curiosity and fascination.

Like my closetmates, I take comfort in finding humor amidst the chaos. Soon enough, I'll know the answer to my one nagging question. Did *Blue Monk* survive the storm?

11:00 AM: Joel, Phineas, and John Nation manage to get within two blocks of me, relying on the truck's four-wheel drive to crawl over the rugged terrain. They hike in to collect me and we motor off through the wreckage to check on our boats.

Many roads are blocked.

Power lines and poles lie on the ground.

Most of the traffic lights are down. One displays both red and green signals. "Reminds me of women I've dated," observes Phinheas.

We backtrack when we must, borrowing circular driveways and lawns to circumvent obstacles in the streets.

I catch glimpses of masts of boats moored in the canals as we approach the Coral Gables waterways; few stand upright.

We prepare for the worst.

Behind John's schooner, a forty-foot ketch has blown ashore. *Zebra Dun's* mainmast is broken. Her bowsprit is damaged and her rail is chewed up, but she's afloat. Joel's *Phyllis Louise* is hardly visible behind two other vessels that dragged into her, but she's floating. Her main mast is torn off. Her bowsprit and her motor bracket are gone. But Joel is the world's fastest carpenter; all is repairable.

The idiot boat moored with four tiny anchors lies on her side well up on shore. She's not badly damaged, but more importantly, she didn't hit anyone else.

In the center of the carnage, bobbing peacefully at anchor with nothing more than a light patina of green plant dust to attest to her having been through a cyclone, is *Blue Monk*. Atop her mast, the wind indicator arrow is bent backward—the extent of the damage.

The Blue Monk

Aftermath and Transition

W E DISENTANGLE John's and Joel's vessels from the trees. John fires up *Zebra Dun's* faithful diesel and sets off for Dinner Key Anchorage with *Phyllis Louise* in tow. I leave *Blue Monk* where she is and drive Joel's truck home to Dinner Key.

What I find there is unimaginable.

Boats are stacked on, under, and through the piers like toys. Hundreds of masts lean in hundreds of different directions. Vessels rode up on the storm surge only to be impaled on dock pilings when the sea receded. Bows and sterns and stumps of masts jut from the water. Tattered sails hang like defeated flags of war. Almost every boat is damaged. Boards from the piers are strewn haphazardly about. Many sections are missing altogether.

The lack of seamanship evident at Dinner Key Marina is heartbreaking. These boats could have been anchored in a sheltered harbor; many would have survived. All were abandoned to face the wind and rising water. Few boat owners even bothered to strip sails, double docklines, or stow gear below deck—all these beautiful ships were passively surrendered to the storm.

Across the street from the marina at Coconut Grove Bank, a boat squats in the drive-through teller tunnel.

Shrimper Dave's nineteen-foot sailboat stands in perfect condition, leaning upright against a light pole a hundred feet inshore of the marina as if placed there with a crane by a team of Swiss engineers.

The dinghy dock lies on shore next to the boat ramp.

I step over the waterlogged keyboard from Diana's piano.

Out beyond the marina, wrecks litter the spoil islands. The casaurina pines are shredded.

Joel's houseboat survived with minimal damage. In fact, some desperate mariner tied another boat to her stern at the last minute; both vessels made it through.

Crazy Jim's collection of derelicts and junk squats in the middle of the anchorage, hanging from its frayed and twisted mooring lines as it has for years.

I search for *Tava;* I can't find her anywhere.

I locate Ray Montana's ship on shore just south of the Coconut Grove Sailing Club. She's scratched up, but sitting upright, tangled with a boat that dragged down and broke her away from her mooring.

Hopeful, I tie up the dinghy and walk over.

Everything below the waterline is missing, as if her bottom half had been cut away with an immense chain saw. Standing on wet grass where her floorboards once were, I go through Ray's lockers, retrieving soggy photo albums and other items I know will have to be dried quickly to be salvaged.

Daniel owns a big Morgan Out-Island 41 ketch. A scan of Biscayne Bay with binoculars reveals she's floating a mile out. She dragged a long, tangled string of anchors and chain across the bottom, but she's undamaged.

Swordfish, a 1930s Tancook Schooner, was abandoned to weather the storm in the anchorage. She was blown over the middle island and now lies sunk inside the marina. Only her transom and faded nameplate are visible above the water.

The Music Man is missing. She's found high up in the mangroves near Matheson Hammock a few miles south of Dinner Key, not far from where I secured *Blue Monk.* Broken up entirely, she's a pile of rubble; nothing is salvageable.

On the beach of the north Dinner Key spoil island lies a six-foot section from the bow of a sailboat. It looks oddly familiar. I study it, trying to understand why it catches my eye.

An eternity ago, I lay in my bunk gazing past my feet at this same series of hollow triangular forms. This section of bow is all that's left of Trimaran John's *Chanson de Mer.*

The marina is closed. Fuel covers the water. The piers are missing their boards. Most of the marina boats are sunk or smashed against the pilings or the docks. Owners of the few vessels that survived the storm are directed by the city to move to the anchorage.

The dock office was flooded. All public records pertaining to the marina were stored there. All were conveniently destroyed. A sign written on City of Miami stationery is placed on the door near the wrecked washers and dryers:

No Anchorage People Allowed in Showers.

The showers under City Hall—the ones granted to us by Cesar Odious—are closed. We are told they were destroyed by floodwaters (though ten years later, they are offered as an available asset during a waterfront planning process). But the city's plastic shower and dock keys are easily copied with a leather punch and a piece of vinyl cut to size. The loss of a restroom facility affects us little, but costs the city a revenue stream.

Up at the City NET office, the bureaucrats establish an aid station. Some of the now-homeless Dog Patch folks show up looking for food and other assistance. "We're glad you people were blown away," city employees tell them. "You freeloaders won't get any assistance from us."

But the National Guard provides help to those who need it. Diana lost her houseboat. Though she's homeless, she's here to help others. She gives the Guardsmen a list of names of people who should be allowed to come and go.

A team of anchorites, equipped with muscles and mainsheet tackles, wrestles the dinghy dock back into the water before the city can have it hauled away as junk.

The Federal Emergency Management Agency goes on a check-writing spree, compensating those who lost their homes. Even Crazy Jim gets a big payout from Saint FEMA—though he's lost nothing and what he owns was worthless before the storm.

Weeks pass.

The soldiers leave.

Utility people repair the power lines and clear debris from the streets. Enormous cranes stand some of the banyan trees back up. Others are cut up and cleared away.

Months pass.

The marina remains dark.

The Dinner Key Marina parking lot becomes a homeless encampment, abandoned and ignored by law enforcement in spite of its proximity to City Hall.

The spoil islands, channels, and piers remain covered with wrecks.

By and by, it becomes clear that neither boat owners nor insurance companies care about submerged and deteriorating sails, engines, and other gear. Covert salvage operations begin. Lines and rigging, furling systems, spars, diesel engines, steering systems—anything that can be used or repaired—are removed by "looters" from the wrecks.

Years pass before a barge and crane show up to remove the broken boats. Salvors drag up the wrecks, dump them unceremoniously on a rusty barge, and cart them away to the landfill.

Soldier Key was scoured clean by the storm. No signs remain of anyone having ever lived there. The treehouse and the lookout tower and the main house were carried off by the sea and wind.

Montana Ray buys *Eryngo* from Brad. She's mastless and beat up but Ray is a capable carpenter and he has Patty with him now; they need a bigger vessel with room for two to replace *Tava*.

Months go by before we hear about Bud Maddock on *Antigone*. Anchored off Elliot Key, he was lifted from his cockpit by a Coast Guard helicopter hours before the storm. When he returned, his ship was intact, but blown far into the trees on the island—picked up by a tornado, apparently, and set gently down a hundred yards from the shore. The Park Service wants to fine him for destroying protected mangroves. They want to cut his boat up and haul her away. Bud stays aboard, fighting off raccoons, mosquitoes, incompetent rescuers, and petty bureaucrats for a year-and-a-half before a change in park management brings a constructive solution.

The Dinner Key Boatyard, managed with typical City of Miami idiocy, bustles after the storm. An army of drunks shows up to grind fiberglass and sand teak for beer money. Would-be marine contractors hawk contrived painting and shipbuilding skills, lining up to feast on FEMA handouts and fat insurance checks.

For those with more skill than cash, the storm brings afford-able "project boats." Forest and Suzy buy a big ketch with a six-foot hole in her hull. Forest makes a mold from her port side, transfers the lines to her starboard side, and takes his family cruis-ing in the Caribbean. Months after the storm, Junemarie shows up at the boatyard with another salvage boat, a holed 36-foot sloop that's been sunk at a dock. The boat smells like rotting barnacles for a few weeks, but she's soon patched and made shipshape again.

Topaz is an old 38-foot Pearson Invicta I've always admired, a 1963 classic yawl built of inch-thick fiberglass. Her rudder is gone. Her stern rail is a twisted mess. Her rails are smashed. Her topsides are hopelessly scratched up. She sits in the Dinner Key boatyard on jackstands.

Gypsy Jan, one of the teachers I became close with at the Abaco Mission, loans me the money to buy her.

After four months of hard work, financial hemorrhage, and nego-tiation with poseurs and charlatans, I launch my new boat. Dinner Key has no lift; I hire a crane to move *Topaz* to the water. Because of some "safety" requirement, I am not allowed aboard until the jackstands are moved and her 21,500 pounds of weight have been completely transferred to the crane. Deferring to the interests of safety, I shinny twenty feet up a rope above hard concrete to get into her cockpit.

Immediately after launch, a piece of sunken canvas wreckage in the staging area wraps around my propeller, stopping the engine. After a quick dive to clear the obstruction, I motor *Topaz* out the channel, through the secret gap between the middle island and Idiot Shoal, and out to Dinner Key Anchorage.

One of the boatyard boozers buys *Blue Monk*. Jack often drinks too much to find his way home—he occasionally falls asleep on the wrong boat—but like many at Dinner Key, he's a good soul. He works hard in the boatyard and pays me like clockwork, usually giving me more than the agreed-upon monthly payment.

After six months, he gives her back to me and tells me to think of the payments he's made as rent money. Then he moves on.

A longtime anchorage neighbor buys *Blue Monk* from me for the amount left unpaid by Jack. Kim lives with her husband aboard *Camelot,* a big ketch, but she wants a room of her own. Her husband is less than pleased with her purchase. Kim eventually sells her.

Five years and five thousand miles after I first looked at a little blue project boat languishing in a marina, *Blue Monk's* new owner sails her away to New Orleans.

Onword

*T*OPAZ is gone now, too—sold to a collector in New York. I lived aboard her for seven years and sailed her to the Abacos once. But in spite of her potential to go 'round the world, I mostly sailed her up and down Biscayne Bay, living aboard in the style I loved, taking comfort in knowing the horizon was at my beck and call.

Captain Midnight's green '59 Cadillac limousine, left parked on the circle in front of Miami City Hall, was destroyed by Hurricane Andrew. Midnight and his dogs were rumored to have been aboard when their boat blew ashore in Coral Gables. He moved away from the anchorage after the storm but for many years afterward, he could be seen driving around town in a nondescript 1980s model Chevrolet with his junk stacked haphazardly on the roof. Though nothing was tied down, it strangely refused to fall off.

Light Blue, along with the spruce oars I built behind the rigging shop where Ray Montana worked, was stolen from the dinghy dock on my birthday in October, 1992.

Sadly, Wilbur was killed by a passing car in 2004 while crossing South Bayshore Drive. The fate of his vintage postcard collection is unknown.

Ray Newgarden climbed on and off the wagon until his family rescued him and took him home to Tennessee. Years later, he escaped to become a professional poker player in Las Vegas.

Drew, who I rowed with to Man-O-War reef, survived cancer, sold his boat, and became an avid tennis player. He lives in North Carolina or South Florida depending on the suitability of the season for playing his sport.

Ray Montana brought *Eryngo* to Maine, eventually sold her, and then built his family an off-grid house.

Bud Maddock's *Antigone* was wrecked in South America. He lives in Germany with his two sons and their mother, Heike. I reconnected with Bud while researching this book; he became a friend and a valuable contributor during the editing stages. His own book, *Waiting on God*, about his adventures stranded on Elliot Key after Hurricane Andrew is forthcoming.

John Nation parked *Zebra Dun* in a boat yard in Marshalburg, North Carolina. He completed most of a ¾-scale, flying replica of a British Spitfire before setting off to backpack through Europe and the Canary Islands.

Seventeen years after the voyages of *Blue Monk*, social networking and the Internet make it easier to track down lost friends. I resumed my friendship with Neal Petersen who I'd met in the Azores. A Russian freighter struck his boat after we left São Miguel for Gibraltar. He hand-pumped seawater out of his hull for ten days—twenty minutes each hour, around the clock—until making landfall in Ireland. Neal patched her up and went on to become the first black sailor to race alone around the world; he ultimately became a successful inspirational speaker.

I reconnected with Gerhard and received a gracious hand-written letter expressing his regret over how we parted company. Gerhard remains a friend. *Journeyman* is docked in a wooden boat museum in Kapeln, Germany near the Dutch border when he's not sailing her.

Matina lives in Jacksonville, Florida with her husband and children.

David Rhind hit a shipping container on his way from the Bahamas to Bermuda with his wife Susan and toddler son Sean. As they prepared to abandon *Mystic Lady*, a freighter heard their distress call and came to their rescue.

Years later, around Christmastime, I visited them in Nova Scotia just before Susan succumbed to cancer. She was not uncomfort-able—or didn't show it—and accepted what was to come with a humble, dignified grace.

Because of a late bus, I hitchhiked ninety miles north to catch the last ferry across the Bay of Fundy to the mainland before the holidays. A group of kind people picked me up somewhere in the Canadian wilderness. I played guitar at their Christmas party in a little Norman Rockwell house with a woodstove until morning when they drove me to the ferry dock.

⑤ The Blue Monk

In 1995, I crossed from Miami to the Abacos with David Rhind and Sean aboard their new wooden ketch to scatter Susan's ashes at Little Harbour.

Along the way, I taught myself HTML from a book. I started a web design studio when I got back—even though most people still thought "Internet" was a hair product at the time. A few years later, when I found myself at odds with my business partner, I set up shop on a houseboat in Dinner Key Marina and enjoyed the pleasure of rowing to work every day.

Dinner Key Anchorage is still here. Many see only a sparsely filled mooring field, rows of buoys extending from the spoil islands out into Biscayne Bay—another of the City of Miami's failed attempts to make 'those people' go away—but I suppose every good story needs its wicked witch. Along the fringes, tucked in the cove behind the sandbar or anchored near the spoil islands, are shanty boats, well-kept sailing yachts, and a wide spectrum between. A few old-timers still anchor out here along with newcomers and transients. In ways that matter, Dinner Key is unchanged—a secret floating village lying just beyond the world as you know it.

Afterword

I KNOW LITTLE of my grandparents. Though I met them all, I can recount only a few fragments of their lives. Edmund Dersofi, my mother's father, played the violin, taught music, and liked fishing. He was born in Hungary. My mother's mother, Eva, was born in Boston. She dropped out of college to help with the war effort during the 1940s. When she returned to school to finish a degree in the 1990's, she had to fight to get her original Boston University credits honored. My father's parents were born in Denver, Colorado. Eli Bricker ran a corset shop called Charis before the Great Depression put him out of business. He moved on to real estate and did well. My grandmother Rose Quiat was a talented landscape painter. Beyond that, I'd have a difficult time filling the rest of this page with what I know of them.

I imagine they had their adventures, struggles, successes, failures, romances, and perspectives forged by experience, but by the time they settled down into parenting and nest-building and setting in motion the mitosis that would become my parents and ultimately me, many of their best stories were already relegated to memories attached to nameless people who now smile without context from yellowed photos in faded albums.

I'm no better than they were and no different, save for the times I live in. Like my predecessors, I've moved on from the carefree explorations and adventurous experimentation of youth into a 'normal' existence. I'm married. I have a daughter. I have a house and a car and a job teaching graphic design at a university.

That stuff is all good and satisfying, but years ago, I set aside time in my life to purposefully and intentionally venture out to accumulate stories, not so much as a journalist but as a *protagonist,* as a *participant.* After I finished dragging myself through the process of earning a college degree, I took off in a small sailboat with a few twenty-dollar bills and an acoustic guitar to experience life on my own terms for my own reasons. Echoes of those experiences inform everything I do in my contemporary life, but a story, by nature, is a thing that must be shared; I wish to honor the people and places I encountered, and to indulge a romantic notion that my own progeny might be amused someday to think of my history as their own.

I grew up in Miami, Florida, a comparatively young American city sprung from tropical hardwood hammocks and sawgrass swamps, inhabited by Seminole Indians up through the beginning of the twentieth century. Until the Flagler Railroad pushed its way south through Miami to the Florida Keys, the principal means of conveyance from points north to the pineapple plantations on the Miami

River and early settlements like Cocoanut Grove on Biscayne Bay was *the sailboat.*

That history is well documented. Numerous photographs show tall ships anchored off Miami; old postcards show private yachts at anchor. 'Commodore' Bill Monroe, a friend and contemporary of the famous naval architect Nathanael Herschoff, designed and built his own shallow-draft "Presto Boats" specifically for Biscayne Bay's shoal waters.

Road graders, internal combustion engines, rails, and real estate agents put an end to Miami's dependence on sailboats and trade winds. Dinner Key became a U.S. Navy air base, and then a terminal for Pan-American Airline's Havana Clippers—great flying boats that shuttled tourists to and from Havana, Cuba—and later, a U.S. Coast Guard station. The old seaplane channel and hangars are still there. Miami City Hall is located in the original Pan-Am terminal building. The immense rotating globe that once occupied its lobby spins in the entrance hall of Miami's Museum of Science—at least until the new museum opens downtown.

What's less known is the history of Dinner Key Anchorage. The State of Florida deeded[94] the Dinner Key Bottomlands to the City of Miami "for public use, not excluding municipal use" in 1949. The only reasonable use I can conceive of for submerged lands adjacent to a fast-growing city is for an anchoring area, but based on

94 Deed #19488

photographs and old postcards, I believe Miami's anchorage community appeared in the late 1960s, around the time of the closing of the Dinner Key Coast Guard base in 1965. Though Dinner Key has been a traditional sailboat anchorage since Miami's pioneer days, the anchorage liveaboard community blossomed at a time when Vietnam veterans were returning home and hippies were exploring alternative lifestyles. Dreamers of limited means built plywood trimarans from mail-order plans and sailed off to Tahiti.

Fiberglass boats were manufactured *en masse* during the 1960s. Neglected wooden boats rotted and sank quickly but fiberglass hulls, especially those heavily built from pre-1973 oil embargo resins were far more resilient. Aluminum masts likewise outlived their spruce complements. Oil economics pushed cheap yachts onto the market during the 1970s. Fiberglass sailboats were easily had, and plenty of young people wanted to explore a new dream. Sailing, once thought of as a rich man's sport, became accessible to anyone with the mettle to "escape the grid."

By the time I encountered Dinner Key Anchorage, the locale already celebrated its share of stories and traditions, old-timers, and colorful characters. I wandered into a magic community of charismatic people and a world of possibilities I could never have imagined.

Part of my purpose in writing, then, is to document a unique fragment of Miami's history. Special, powerful, meaningful, valuable, rare, and important things happened out beyond those spoil islands. To some extent, they're still happening, but to the casual observer, Dinner Key Anchorage is nothing more than a collection of deteriorating shanty-boats anchored on the outskirts of an empty mooring field. But the exclusion of Dinner Key Anchorage from the historical record based on the perceptions of casual observers would be an unfortunate loss; the Dinner Key Anchorage is as much a part of Miami's history as Virginia Key or Overtown or Key Biscayne.

But my story journeys thousands of miles beyond Dinner Key to the Bahamas, the Azores, and Gibraltar. Inspired and emboldened by my experiences in Miami's anchorage, I endeavored to make each day remarkable—a day worth writing about. Those intentions got me into and out of some outrageous trouble and some fantastic places, and ultimately landed me here, with you, on this page.

Memoir has an admittedly selfish aspect to it. Galavanting around in a small sailboat accumulating stories is a solitary business. Putting those stories in a format that can be shared may be a noble exercise, but it's one fueled entirely by things meaningful to *me*—an endeavor every bit as self-indulgent as quitting my job, throwing my keys into Biscayne Bay, hauling my anchors, raising my sails, and hightailing it for the horizon. But having done that and returned to civilization loaded down with the treasure I set out to discover, I find myself burdened with its curse—a story without a listener is valueless.

Tag.

You're it.

I was once told I was crazy to even consider such a journey among my options.

I wasn't.

I'm not.

Imagine limitations and they become real.

Imagine possibilities and the world is yours.

That sounds like great philosophical fluff, but stripped of its aphoristic, wind-chimey pleasantness, I maintain it holds true for those willing to work for their stories.

Beyond offering this unsolicited contribution to the historical record, beyond offering a humble homage to the Dinner Key Anchorage and the remarkable people I met there, beyond unburdening myself of the experiences that affected me so profoundly, beyond sharing my personal encounters with hell and paradise, I delight in the tiny possibility that I might provoke a reader or two to find a personal, metaphorical, or literal anchorage—a home port where the water is clear and the seas are calm—and then voyage beyond it in search of richer stories and a life worth writing about.

As literature, my book has a classic theme—a story of a young person in search of self. But "self" is nothing more than a convenient conceptual carrying handle for a thing far too heavy to lift. "Self" is endless, eternal, boundless, abstract, yet eminently *findable*. Ah, but I hear wind chimes again.

This is my message in a bottle. I wish it safe passage through the oceans of time.

These are my stories—a portrait of my self and my world.
Thank you for sharing them with me.

The Blue Monk

About This Book

The Blue Monk was sailed, written, designed, typeset, and published by its author to meet or exceed the highest standards of the publishing industry.

Prior to being professionally edited by the insightful and perceptive Steven Bauer of Hollow Tree Literary Services, the manuscript underwent a group editing process whereby Anne Warner, Bud Maddock, Kimberly Wharin Aden, Richard Geller, James Hesketh, and Michael Dunn reviewed one chapter each week. This more granular approach helped polish the book in a way that might have been overlooked by a traditional "whole book" editing process. To all who participated, I offer my heartfelt thanks.

The Blue Monk was conceived in two forms: a paper version typeset in a fashion reminiscent of Victorian sea novels from the 1880s, and an eBook version that combines a printed aesthetic with a new eBook format devised for the book.

With the advent of mass-marketed books, book design—especially with respect to typography—declined. The business risks associated with enormous print runs demanded the use of smaller type packed tightly inside narrow margins. But today's production technology allows single books to be manufactured to order. Why not return to an aesthetic characterized by the glorious days of hot metal type-setting? The printed edition of *The Blue Monk* is cloth-bound, foil stamped, printed on creme stock, wrapped in an attractive dust jacket, and priced affordably. The additional pages required to accommodate its classic margins and legible type add negligibly to its cost.

The electronic book is an evolving form that has, until recently, regarded a book as a mere container for text data. Book designers saw much of their work dispensed with in the interest of making text flowable and independent of numbered pages. Fortunately, new eBook formats allow for much greater control of typography and layout. Additionally, eBooks are empowered to display photographs and video and to include interactive and audio content.

How, then, to combine these media in a way that preserves the "bookness" of the piece? Skeptics make compelling arguments against the new functionality. "*Moby-Dick* would hardly have been improved by the inclusion of video," they say. Certainly, a torrent of unimaginative "click to make the cow moo" children's books is likely to bolster the cause of the naysayers.

My answer is to start with the prose. First and foremost, *The Blue Monk* is a book. As the author, my piece is stated entirely in writing. The layout and typography are specifically adapted from classic book designs to the electronic format. Over 300 clips gathered from video interviews, 200 photographs, 100 photo footnotes, and 80 interactive maps are included, but positioned to be supportive of and subordinate to the text. What is an electronic book? How does it differ from a website, a mobile application, or a game? How should new media be tastefully integrated into eBook form?

The Blue Monk is my answer.

If you would be kind enough to post an honest review of your on-or-off-screen reading experience in the online bookstore or readers' forum of your choice, I would be most grateful.

—Dave Bricker, January, 2014

The Blue Monk

About the Author

DAVE BRICKER, MFA lives in Miami, Florida with his wife and daughter where he teaches graphic design, operates a marketing and design studio, and plays guitar in an acoustic swing band. He has published three novels: *The Dance, Waves,* and *Currents,* and is also the author of *The One-Hour Guide to Self-Publishing: Straight Talk for Fiction and Nonfiction Writers About Producing and Marketing Your Own Books.* His forthcoming book is entitled *The Writer's Guide to Powerful Prose.*

The Blue Monk

Colophon

THE TEXT OF *THE BLUE MONK* is set in Centaur, a refinement of Roman inscriptional capitals designed by Bruce Rogers as a titling design for signage in the Metropolitan Museum. Rogers later designed a lowercase based on Nicolas Jenson's work from the mid-1460s, turning the titling into a full typeface.

The book's title and section headers are set in Old Standard, a digital revival by Alexey Kryukov of a serif typeface commonly used in the late 19TH and early 20TH century, but almost completely abandoned later.

The corner ornament was selected from Lanston Typeface Corporation's Keystone Ornaments, a set of glyphs based on "running border" ornaments from the Keystone Type foundry of Philadelphia, circa 1903.

The titles on the chart illustrations and the Essential Absurdities Logotype are set in Behrens Antiqua, designed by Peter Behrens in 1902 as a corporate typeface to emulate hand-rendered display lettering while maintaining consistency across artists and applications.

The book's margins are based on the Van de Graaf canon.

The Blue Monk

Home

2009

MY FRIEND MILLER has been paying dock rent in Hollywood, Florida. His fortunes have changed; such luxuries are no longer affordable. On my suggestion, we motor his small sloop down the Intracoastal Waterway to the free anchorage in Miami. We make hasty preparations to leave after dark on a windless Friday night. The running lights don't work. The VHF radio would if the battery wasn't dead.

Proceeding south down the waterway past tall buildings, luxury homes, marinas and mangroves, we alert drawbridges to our presence with a horn affixed to a can of compressed air.

3:30 AM—A chill penetrates the air. We pass the Miami *Herald* Building, a sleeping downtown Miami, the port of Miami, the open mouth of the Miami River, and tall buildings on Brickell Avenue—all bathed in stark yellow light, exuding an inaudible yet powerful electric hum, the snoring of a gigantic urban rhinoceros masked by the drone of the outboard motor. Off to port, Virginia Key is pitch dark save for a few lights along the shore of the Miami Marine Stadium—an abandoned edifice perhaps better likened to a white elephant than a sleeping rhinoceros—but this is Miami; such travesties are not uncommon here. Ahead of us rises Rickenbacker Causeway Bridge, an arch of light, gateway to the open waters of Biscayne Bay. A field of electric stars on the shoreline moves slowly behind the flashing channel markers. We strain our eyes to find them.

"I see a red flasher at one o'clock. Aim a few points to starboard."

A moment later, Miller sees the marker, too. We alter course to align ourselves with the channel and the approaching bridge.

Even at this very late, very early hour, tires swoosh across the concrete leviathan above us. To either side of us, wooden catwalks girdle massive pylons supporting the span.

We're through.

Darkness.

The moon has long since set.

The sky is overcast.

Biscayne Bay is not only dark, it's foggy—unusual weather. Some indeterminable distance ahead, channel markers throw vapor-refracted halos of red and green. Hazy lights of buildings shimmer to starboard but mostly, our path leads into a black abyss; we might as well be headed straight down. Miller is not so much nervous as reality-stricken. He trusts me. He knows I've done some sailing. He doesn't know I find it scary, too—still. I've just learned to press on. We're navigating a small boat in the middle of a black, windless night, motoring with a diminishing fuel supply into open water away from the familiar gridlines of civilization. *It's okay,* I quietly assure myself. *Not too far to go.* Perhaps I'm selfishly curious to know if I can still find my old home port after all this time, flying with the visor down.

Dead calm.

I consider dropping anchor in the lee of Rickenbacker Causeway to wait for daylight before completing the final few miles of our journey but I still the impulse. If a barge is moving across this darkness, I'd rather be awake and ready to take evasive action. If we get lost or run aground, morning will arrive soon enough. The fog will lift. The tide will rise. We'll finish our journey.

Logic wins. Fear and doubt retreat.

We continue into the black.

"Off to starboard, over by Vizcaya, there's a shoal we want to avoid." I gesture into the foggy darkness. "Let's continue south for another twenty minutes and then alter course gradually toward shore. Hopefully, as we get closer, we'll pick out some recognizable buildings in Coconut Grove and the masts of the boats at Dinner Key." Miller nods and smiles. He's enjoying the lunacy of this, the sheer incongruity between daily life and this crazy stab into nothing's eye.

We stare across glistening black, fog-shrouded water through the haze of four-in-the-morning eyes into the distant glow ashore. Familiar reference points elude me, hiding in nebulous shapes and clusters of light. "Turn a bit more to starboard," I suggest. "I think we're past the shoal now. Let's get closer; maybe I can make out something familiar."

We alter course and carry on.

Time harmonizes with the oddly musical hum of the outboard—the unending meditative chant of a mechanical Zen monk, a repeated mantra I can't quite make out. We don't bother to check how much fuel remains. No wind blows to offer an alternative mode of loco-motion. If we run out of fuel, we'll anchor and wait. The wind will blow again eventually; it always does.

"This must be Dinner Key Channel. See the marker lights? Our boat has shallow-enough draft to sail across the channel way out here, but the water gets shallow on the south side closer to shore—'Idiot Shoal,' they call it." We cross the channel and make our turn.

A form appears out of the gloom ahead, a sleeping sailboat. The white hull and darkened ports approach like a ghost in the mist.

Another appears.

We throttle back to slow our progress.

A battered powerboat covered with old dinghies and marine junk squats on the black water, listing precariously beneath the veil of fog. Boats appear around us now—abandoned hulks, a beautiful ketch, a high-tech trimaran hovering like a gigantic water-bug, trash, treasure, jetsam, flotsam, wood, fiberglass, and canvas, a menagerie of old and new, rich and poor, promise and betrayal, dreams forgotten, realized and clung to, tragedy, comedy, desperation, and hope.

"Welcome to Dinner Key Anchorage," I say. "The world as you know it ends here."

Ethereal boats pass in and out of the gloom as we continue toward shore.

As if tiptoeing stealthily past a ring of sleeping fairies in an ancient forest, we glide between the scattered boats. Miller is awake now. Certainly, slipping from a black abyss into a secret anchorage is surprising and surreal but that's not really *it*. There are people here—unusual people, people who choose to be in this otherworldly place, people who must therefore be *different*. Within a half-mile of the urban sprawl of Miami, hidden behind a few low islands littered with storm-tossed mangroves and gnarled casuarina pines and broken hulls, lies a secret floating village.

Miller can't know yet. He can only sense something's different, but that's good enough for now. All will make itself apparent. It wasn't me who brought him here. He's another one, caught like the ocean by the gravity of a prankster moon and pulled like the tide to Dinner Key.

We leave the slumbering hulks and hulls behind to pass through an empty field of small, white buoys closer to shore. "This all used to be anchorage," I explain. "Now, it's a mooring field; floating parking meters for 'respectable' boaters. Most of the original anchorage boats have left or moved farther out or off to the sides of the field. They don't want to pay to anchor and the City still hasn't officially opened the moorings. This area's been sitting empty for months."

I know exactly where we are now.

I sense the shadows of the souls of boats and people like me who sailed on but never left this place.

The channel marker at the entrance to the marina flashes green. We pass into a realm washed in waxy, incandescent light. After turning to starboard between the piers and the islands, we round the point of the northernmost one and head a short way out to a small, shallow cove. We used to call this Trimaran Cove, but only one mastless trimaran anchors here now.

The splash of the anchor and the rattle of running chain signify the end of our journey. Sharp tugs on the line set the flukes securely into the mud beneath the seagrass.

Miller shuts down the engine.

Silence settles over us, enveloping us as surely as the fog.

I am home.

David E. Bricker

www.ingramcontent.com/pod-product-compliance
Lightning Source LLC
Chambersburg PA
CBHW030943150426

42812CB00065B/3149/J